HORNCHURCH EAGLES

The Life Stories of Eight of the Airfield's
Distinguished WWII Fighter Pilots

RICHARD C. SMITH

GRUB STREET · LONDON

Published by
Grub Street
The Basement
10 Chivalry Road
London SW11 1HT

Copyright © 2002 Grub Street, London
Text copyright © Richard C. Smith

British Library Cataloguing in Publication Data
Smith, Richard C.
  Hornchurch Eagles: the complete combat experience as seen through
  the eyes of eight of the airfield's distinguished WWII fighter pilots
  1. Great Britain. Royal Flying Corps 2. RAF Hornchurch
  3. Fighter pilots – Great Britain – Biography
  I. Title
  358.4′00922422

ISBN 1-904010-00-8

Typeset by Pearl Graphics, Hemel Hempstead

Printed and bound in Great Britain by
Biddles Ltd, Guildford and King's Lynn

CONTENTS

ACKNOWLEDGEMENTS

I am again indebted to the following men and women who are listed below, who gave of their time, patience and memories to bring this book to fruition.

Without their help, it would not have been possible. I thank them also for the use of their personal papers, unique photographs, logbooks and historical documents, some of which have not been seen for over fifty years. It has been a privilege to meet, talk and correspond with them over the last 10 years. Sadly, since the beginning of my research covering the three books on Sutton's Farm and RAF Hornchurch, some of these great personalities have passed on. I thank them all on behalf of present and future generations.

Flight Lieutenant William 'Tex' Ash, MBE
Squadron Leader Cyril Bamberger DFC, RAF Retd
Squadron Leader Patrick 'Paddy' Barthropp, DFC, AFC, RAF Retd
Wing Commander Eric Barwell, DFC, RAF Retd
The late Air Chief Marshal Sir Harry Broadhurst, GCB, KCB, KBE, CB, DSO, DFC, AFC
Air Marshal Sir Ivor Broom KCB, CBE, DSO, DFC, AFC, RAF Retd
Squadron Leader Douglas Brown RNZAF
Squadron Leader Peter Brown, AFC, RAF Retd
Flying Officer Max Collett, Secretary of No.485 RNZAF Squadron
Association Lieutenant General Baron Michael Donnet, CVO, DFC, FR, AE, Retd
Wing Commander Frank Dowling, OBE, RAF Retd
The late Group Captain Sir Hugh Dundas, CBE, DSO, DFC
Flight Lieutenant Roy Ford
The late Squadron Leader E.D. 'Dave' Glaser, DFC
Flight Lieutenant L.P. Griffith DFC RNZAF
Squadron Leader Iain Hutchinson TD, RAF Retd
The late Air Vice-Marshal J.E. 'Johnnie' Johnson, CB, CBE, DSO, DFC
Wing Commander A.J. Little
Squadron Leader Leslie Lunn, AFC, RAF Retd
The late Squadron Leader Jeffrey Quill, OBE, AFC
Flight Lieutenant Jack Rae, DFC RNZAF
Wing Commander James Sanders, DFC, RAF Retd
The late Group Captain Wilfred Duncan Smith, DSO, DFC
Wing Commander William Stapleton, CBE, RAF Retd
Squadron Leader Harvey Sweetman, DFC RNZAF
Group Captain Edward Wells, DSO, DFC, RAF Retd
Clifford Broadbent
Clare Broadhurst

The late Lady Jane Broadhurst
Chloe Crawford-Compton
Mrs Andy Glaser
Mr Peter Glaser
Mrs Rodica Glaser
Mrs Diana Lunn (daughter of ACM Sir Harry Broadhurst)
Mr Sam Prince
Mrs Joan Statham
Mrs Angela Stevenson
Mr John Thorpe

Special thanks go out again to the following friends and fellow historians who have helped in this project, or encouraged me over the years:

Jack and Pamela Broad, Squadron Leader Peter Brown AFC, RAF Retd, Steve and Val Butler, David and Alison Campbell (Lashendon Air Warfare Museum), Joy Caldwell, Reg Clark, John Coleman, John and Anne Cox, Joe and Drene Crawshaw (Chairman of No.222 Natal Squadron Association), Dave Davis, Wing Commander Frank Dowling OBE, RAF Retd, Alan and Sue Gosling, Squadron Leader Chris Goss M.A., aviation author and historian, Flight Lieutenant Leslie Harvey, Lawrence J. Hickey, Gary Lilley, Geoff and Lesley Nutkins (aviation artist and founders of the Shoreham Village Aircraft Museum, Kent), Peter 'Onion' Oliver, Emma Palmer, Ricky Richardson, David Ross (author of the *Richard Hillary* biography), Christopher Shores, (author of *Aces High*), Air Marshal Sir Frederick Sowrey KCB, CBE, AFC, RAF Retd, Squadron Leader Gerald 'Stapme' Stapleton, DFC, RAF Retd, Wing Commander John Young, AFC, RAF Retd, Historian of the Battle of Britain Fighter Association. To all who support the work of 'The Hornchurch Wing Collection' at the Purfleet Heritage & Military Centre.

Thanks also to the Public Record Office, Kew, The Imperial War Museum, Sound Archives Department, London. Mr Malcolm Smith, Honorary Secretary of The Battle of Britain Fighter Association. The RAF Historical Branch, the Personnel Management Agency at RAF Innesworth, Mr Clive Denny and staff at the Historic Aircraft Collection, Duxford, No.452 Air Training Corps, Hornchurch, the *Romford Recorder*, the Sanders Draper School, and the *Shropshire Star*.

A special Thank <u>YOU</u> goes out to my publisher John Davies, Anne Dolamore and Amy, also Dominic and Louise at Grub Street – What's next?

Finally, to my wife Kim and two sons, David and Robert, for your help and love during the long days of research and travel and what ever else needed to be dealt with.

FOREWORD

Hornchurch Airfield, situated very close to the Thames estuary on the east side of London, played a vital role in the Battle of Britain in 1940. Leadership quickly came to the fore. Many pilots who were stationed there became natural leaders and led from the front by example.

Each story in this book is very personal. One chapter for example tells of Pilot Officer Eric Lock who joined the Royal Air Force at 19 years of age as an airman under pilot training. In May 1939, he was awarded his pilot's certificate and post 1939 he used his pilot's skill to great advantage. On 5th September 1940 alone he claimed four enemy aircraft destroyed and one probable. In 1941, he attended an Investiture Ceremony at Buckingham Palace and was the first individual to be conferred three honours at the same Investiture by His Majesty The King.

The description of some of the aerial combats especially those of Air Chief Marshal Sir Harry Broadhurst, make you feel you are right there in the cockpit with him.

Broadhurst had a charmed life, always led from the front and was rewarded by rapid promotion. He was both an excellent commander and a pilot who provided outstanding leadership to those under his command. He followed his illustrious career by rising to the rank of Air Chief Marshal commanding Bomber Command. I had the privilege of serving under him in the mid-fifties when commanding a squadron of Canberras and he was admired and respected by all who served under him.

The majority of these men, whose stories are told in this book, flew from Hornchurch during the Battle of Britain or during the early days of 1941. Each pilot tells of his own unique contribution to the war in the air while serving in Fighter Command and of his comrades in arms. If Britain had capitulated at this time it would have been the end of democracy in Europe.

I commend the author Richard Smith on this outstanding work and I hope you enjoy reading this fascinating book as much as I have done.

Air Marshal Sir Ivor Broom KCB, CBE, DSO, DFC & 2 Bars, AFC
June 2002

INTRODUCTION

During the last ten years I have been privileged to meet and talk with many pilots, ground crews and WAAFs who had one thing in common; they all served at RAF Hornchurch during one time or another. Following the publication of my first two books, *Hornchurch Scramble* and *Hornchurch Offensive*, which told the history of this famous fighter airfield over two world wars, I decided to complete this Hornchurch trilogy by approaching the subject from a more personal angle. The book would therefore take the form of eight pilots' life stories, their Royal Air Force careers especially during their time at Hornchurch and afterwards and later during peacetime.

The next decision then was who to choose? Since the end of the Second World War, especially in the last 20 years, many famous Royal Air Force aces have either written their own autobiographies or have had biographies written about them; men like 'Sailor' Malan, Robert Stanford Tuck, Alan Deere, 'Paddy' Finucane and Richard Hillary. They all either started their illustrious careers from Hornchurch or had flown from the station during the Battle of Britain and their stories are well known.

I have therefore chosen a cross-section of Royal Air Force pilots who differed in rank, and came from various walks of life and countries. Some joined the service as pre-war regular servicemen when the biplane was still a mainstay of the Royal Air Force, while others learnt the art of flying with local flying clubs, university air squadrons or the volunteer reserve.

When war was declared against Germany in 1939, these men and many others were ready to take up the challenge that confronted them and see it through to the bitter end. During the next five years of war, they would fight over Dunkirk, during the Battle of Britain, take part in the Dieppe Raid, fly dangerous operations over occupied France escorting the bombers, or carry out patrols on D-Day during the invasion of Normandy. They would serve on many various campaigns in different climates and countries. Others would with their own battle-hardened experience, train the new recruit pilots that the Royal Air Force needed to replace its heavy losses. Some would be shot down, but would carry on the fight as prisoners of war.

The brotherhood between airmen was commonplace and they would make good friends, but also they would see many of their comrades die in battle in the skies over France, Belgium, Holland, North Africa and finally Germany until peace became the final victory. After the war's end, some would continue within the Royal Air Force, while others would try to adapt to a war-torn peacetime existence and take up new civilian careers. But the one thing that shines through is the undoubted spirit of the fighter pilot, his courage, his singular aggressiveness, his passion for flying, and his spirit of fair play and dedication to overcome massive odds.

It is now over sixty years since the men in this book took to the skies as young men, willing to risk everything to fight for the freedom of their country and indeed the rest of Europe. Their calibre in flying and fighting is without question; they did not have today's technology to set up a target many miles away and just press a button to attack.

Air fighting was personal, fast and often without warning. Many young pilots did not survive their first sortie; experience of war in the air could not be taught in the class room, and death was always on hand to punish those who did not learn in time.

And death was not always clean and instantaneous. Young men died trapped in falling burning aircraft unable to release themselves from the flaming pyres, or fell from the sky in parachutes that failed to open. The air war was as cruel as on the ground and a fighter pilot lived and often died on his own.

The story of RAF Hornchurch is the story of these men and others like them, because an airfield without the people who serve there, is just an empty field and buildings without a heart.

It has been a great honour for me to meet six of the eight pilots in this book, and record their contribution to the nation for posterity. I hope you will enjoy each individual story and understand the essence of the fighter pilot. I hope too that future generations will remember them. . . .

Richard C. Smith

CHAPTER 1

RED TWO
Squadron Leader Maurice Peter Brown AFC

Peter Brown joined the Royal Air Force in the late 1930s. He gave up a secure position as a young civil servant because he felt that to be a pilot in the Royal Air Force would give him a more active and fulfilling life, with the opportunity to serve his country. After initial training, he became a commissioned regular officer at a time when the Royal Air Force was being equipped with the latest and fastest eight-gun monoplane fighters. The comparison of flying a Hawker Hart biplane to the new Supermarine Spitfire or Hawker Hurricane was a quantum leap for the young pilots. When war was declared on Germany in September 1939, Peter was eager to get to grips with the new challenge that was at hand. He went into action over Dunkirk, during the Battle of Britain, and had many harrowing escapes against a determined enemy. During his operational flying, he flew many times in the position which was known as 'Red 2' covering his flight commander from attack. This job required concentration, reliability and courage in order to protect the leader's tail at all times once combat with the enemy had been met. And this he did successfully.

Maurice Peter Brown was born in London on 17th June 1919 and was educated at the Holloway School, a day public school in North London. In the 1930s its academic standing was very high and it helped him to matriculate with distinction in the University of London at the age of fifteen. He had planned to continue his education and gain a degree in science, but family problems forced him later to change course. He played for his school at soccer, two years younger than the rest of the team, in the cricket team, and at tennis. He was a school prefect. As well as playing sports at school and with local clubs, he also had other activities:

> My great hobby at this time of my life was being a member of the Boy Scouts. I had great fun with my friends at meetings and at camps. I worked hard for my badges and managed to achieve the high award of King's Scout. As a patrol leader I learnt about responsibility and loyalty to the team. I have no doubt that being a dedicated member of a large scout troop had an important impact on my attitudes to life. Remember that in those formative days at that time we had no television or computers and not much pocket money, and so our lives were what we made of them.

On leaving school, Peter took the civil service examination and passed high enough to choose which department he wanted to work for. He loved aeroplanes and the Royal Air Force and so he naturally chose the Air Ministry in the centre of London. He was posted to the Directorate of Equipment. To be a civil servant in 1937 was to have the best future and security prospects available, but he soon realised that his temperament and need to be an individual would make life in the civil service an impossibility for him. His work close to the activities of the RAF confirmed his hidden ambitions for a short service commission as a pilot. His decision to make his application was also influenced by his belief that war with Hitler was inevitable, and should that happen he wanted to be fighting as a pilot in the Royal Air Force.

In March 1938, he received a letter from the Air Ministry advising him that his application for a short service commission in the RAF had been accepted and he was told there was a place there for him on the Ab Initio Training Course to be held at Hanworth Aerodrome in Middlesex commencing on 4th April 1938. Peter's RAF serial number was 40796. This was a preliminary course lasting about six weeks in which candidates were taught to fly and then given 60 hours of flying training. It was during this period that those that did not have the basic aptitude to fly were eliminated and about 20% of the course did not go through. Peter Brown remembers his first days at Hanworth:

> Hanworth was a flying club as were all the other 20 elementary flying schools used by the RAF. It was the first time we had met and we were still civilians. We were housed in a large building in the middle of the aerodrome where we ate, slept, and had our lectures. At Hanworth I was trained on an aircraft called the Blackburn B2. This was different from most trainers in that the pupil and instructor sat side by side, so that the relationship was total and not only through a piece of voice pipe tubing. I went solo after about ten hours and ten minutes, which was average. To go solo at eight hours was very good but if you hadn't gone solo by about 12 or 13 hours, there would be grave doubts about proceeding any further with flying training. I did a total of 60 hours flying there, by day of course, and I carried out the standard programme of take-offs and landings, turns, climbs, spinning and a cross country. I enjoyed my first solo very much. After ten hours sitting with an instructor by your side you become desperate to get off and fly off on your own. To my surprise I wasn't nervous, I just wanted to get on with it.

Like all pupil pilots Peter was very happy when he had achieved his first solo flight, which he carried out successfully on 14th April 1938 in a Blackburn B2 biplane, Civil Serial No. G-AEBL. It was on this course that he first met Dennis David, who went with him when he later moved up to No. 5 Flying Training School. They became very close friends during the time they were together on the course and they both played for the course football team.

Peter's next move was from Hanworth to RAF Uxbridge in Middlesex on 4th June 1938, which was the main training depot for the Royal Air Force. It was full of parade grounds and the aim was to indoctrinate men into the RAF.

For Peter and the others it was to convert them from civilians into officers on probation. Whilst there Peter along with others was visited by service tailors, including Austin Reed and Moss Brothers, who measured them in order to make their uniforms so that they could be dressed as officers before they left Uxbridge. While here, they practiced saluting, marching and parading, and had lectures on air force procedures, all of which was obviously very necessary. The course members came from the Dominions and all parts of Britain, from all walks of life with different educations and backgrounds. What was crucial was that they learned the code of behaviour and discipline expected in the Royal Air Force. Peter Brown remembers that time very distinctly:

A flight lieutenant addressed us in the camp cinema. He stated to us, that, as you are now about to join the Royal Air Force, you will find that we do things differently here; that is the way we do them and we expect you to observe our code of behaviour. If you find that you cannot, then let us know as soon as possible and we will arrange for your early release. I was quite impressed with that as I thought it was a very fair approach that either you became one of the team, whatever the rules or regulations were, or go on your way. Before we finished at Uxbridge, the uniforms had arrived and our preliminary conversion to Acting Pilot Officers on Probation was complete. We felt very smart young officers. My appointment as an officer of the Royal Air Force is dated 4th June 1938, while I was still 18 years of age.

We were now about to follow a planned process of flying training in the Royal Air Force, which was being carried out at ten training school stations throughout the country. It was an accelerated programme of recruiting and training short service commission pilots. The timing was absolutely right, because by the time war was declared in 1939, they had all gone through their training with another year of flying experience.

From Uxbridge, Peter went to No. 5 Flying Training School at Sealand on 23rd June 1938, which was near Chester and on the Dee estuary not far from the steel works. The course members found the original discipline irksome but soon bonded together and had more fun than was first anticipated. The aircraft that Peter trained on were Hawker Harts and Audaxes. These were both biplanes with open cockpits and flying was at the mercy of the elements.

His first instructor, a newly commissioned pilot officer, was very formal and disciplined and Peter found it hard going. It is absolutely crucial when learning to fly that you should have a rapport with your instructor. The other instructors that Peter flew with were more experienced, and he found their tuition enjoyable and much more helpful. Peter recalls his first solo flight on a Hawker Hart aircraft:

I was sent off on my first solo by the pilot officer instructor and he was absolutely emphatic that under no circumstances should I use the engine in my approach and that I had to do a dead-stick landing.

The result was I'm afraid, that on the first two approaches I
overshot and had to go around again. The third time I came in I
used my engine, as needed, and did a perfect landing.

At the end of the first term he took his wings examinations. He came second
in ground subjects and was rated as average in his flying test. He had to admit
that on the two cross-countries that he had to undertake, he had missed the
target on both occasions. However each time he landed on a nearby aerodrome,
he had a quick word with the duty pilot, and then flew on to the correct airfield.
He didn't force-land or do any damage to his aircraft, but finished up with a
'Navigation Weak' assessment in his logbook after the first term.

Along with the others on the course Peter then qualified for his wings. The
flying badge went up on their uniforms within a short time of being formally
notified of this great event, and suddenly they had become Royal Air Force
pilots. Peter was proud:

The wings on my chest seemed to me to be as bright as the lights
in Piccadilly Circus in London. I think I still felt the same way
about my wings when I left the RAF some seven years later.

At FTS the course was divided into two groups, one training on
single and the other on twin-engine aircraft. My ambition to be a
single-engine fighter pilot was going to be fulfilled linked with
Dennis David, who later became a Battle of Britain ace, and John
Drummond. We became very firm friends as we practiced together
in our Hawker Furies. We did all our formation flying together and
we were a team. Sadly Drummond was killed in the Battle of
Britain having shot down several German aircraft and had been
awarded the DFC. During the second term we were officially
allowed to have motorcars. Dennis David and I counted our
resources and decided we could afford to buy a car, a big Austin
saloon. We soon became the free taxi service for others in our
squad for visits into Chester, to one of the three hotels, which by
service procedure were reserved for use by officers only.

During our time at FTS we were indoctrinated into the ways of
the Service. We dressed for dinner in mess kit four nights a week.
We learned to march in order and to take parades, part of our officer
training.

In September 1938 when we were on half term holiday I
received a telegram at my home recalling me to duty immediately,
as indeed did everyone else on the course. It was the time of the
Munich Crisis and it showed how serious the situation was with a
total recall and a bringing to readiness of every unit in the Royal
Air Force. They had even found it necessary to bring the FTS
pupils back to their stations. However, fortunately we were not
needed and the RAF had gained another 12 months flying time
before we actually were at war with the Germans. Those 12 months
were absolutely crucial for Fighter Command in re-equipping with
Hurricanes and Spitfires.

I think I should mention night flying at FTS. The flight path on the grass airfield was laid out with what were known as "goose neck flares", about eight of them. They were very much like large watering cans but instead of the rose, there was a large wick, which went down the neck into paraffin in the can. When they were lit the paraffin burned with a large flame and that was it. There was just one line of flares except that at the end of the line there was another one off to the side to give a width and to mark the end of the flare path. The landing and take-off were made within the layout of these flares. They worked quite well because the light from them illuminated the can, which helped to give some idea of the height above the ground. For their time, although primitive, they were effective and adequate.

While stationed at Sealand, Peter's sporting abilities were again noticed and he was chosen to play for the station both at football and cricket. He also represented the station in the RAF Group boxing championships. Peter recalls:

I remember that in our cricket team we had a sergeant who represented the RAF at cricket and bowled very fast. We opened our bowling with him and if our opponent's wickets fell too quickly, he was taken off and the Padre was called on for half a dozen overs. This gave them a chance to get some runs and make the match much more even.

At the end of his training at Sealand on 12th January 1939, Peter was then sent off to Penrhos, an armament-training airfield in North Wales to carry out air-fighting exercises, firing at drogues and also targets floating in the sea. Whilst there, he also practiced dog fighting, and with the use of camera guns, the pilots were able to see how well they had done with their deflection shooting. This was a very enjoyable part of fighter training, because they were getting that much closer to being service pilots:

When our final postings came through at the end of January, I was disappointed to find that I had not been posted to a fighter squadron and that Drummond and David had been posted to fighter pools ready for posting fairly quickly into real fighter squadrons. My posting on 29th January was as a staff pilot to No.1 Electrical and Wireless School at Cranwell in Lincolnshire. At the time I was unhappy with the posting, but in the event and over the years it has served me very well.

RAF Cranwell was a very large station and included the RAF College, which was in the west camp and rather superior, and the Electrical and Wireless School, which trained boys and apprentices to be wireless operators; there was also a large unit for the training of instrument fitters. Peter Brown was a member of the Signal Squadron equipped with passenger carrying planes, whose main task was to give live air experience to the boys and apprentices under training. When they had reached a certain level of proficiency with the transmitting and receiving equipment on the ground, they would be flown varied distances from base, to be tested on their ability to send and receive radio messages. Peter takes up the story:

It was a fairly monotonous job, but I enjoyed the flying and it was adding to my air experience. The single-engine flight was equipped with Westland Wapitis and Wallaces both with radial engines. The Wapiti had no brakes, no flaps, the undercarriage certainly didn't retract, there was no hood, only an open cockpit. My flight commander tested me out in the Wapiti, but my next trip when I flew solo was in a Wallace, which was a more modern version by 1939 standards. The Wallace was the first RAF aircraft to fly above Mount Everest at 29,000 feet. The Wallace in fact had brakes and a hood and so it was much more comfortable to fly. I spent some eight months flying Wallaces and Wapitis. But that was only half of the story, because as well as flying I had my administrative duties. I was the officer in charge of the 500 men under training to be instrument fitters and I was responsible for their welfare, accommodation, and discipline and it was very valuable training. I had the duty of dealing with men charged with offences and could award up to seven days loss of pay or confinement to camp. I was only 19 years old at the time and I had no training to do this. However I had a very good warrant officer to assist me and managed to deal with the charges, mainly on a Monday morning when the trainees were arriving back late from the weekend break. During my time at Cranwell I still played football. We had an annual knockout competition of seven-a-side football with some 40 sides playing including some from the College. I played for the Cranwell Officers' Mess team and we got through to the final. I remember that the other finalists playing were one of the 'boys' teams; they were about 16 or 17 years of age and they were all at least 6 feet tall against my 5 feet 7 inches. I didn't mind so much being knocked to the ground, and then being trodden on, but I did feel slightly aggrieved when somebody put their boot in my face and broke my nose. However, glory for the day, we won the final and I still have the cup that was awarded to each of our team on that great occasion at Cranwell.

We didn't often meet with the College staff at Cranwell, because they were at the other end of the camp and also they had their own airfield. It was quite large and there was an extension added to it to be used by people who had planned to cross the Atlantic on an east-to-west flight. With the extension to the airfield it gave a very good take-off run. This airfield was later used for the first trial take-off of the Whittle jet prototype. I enjoyed the administrative side very much, and I was soon able to find my way through the manuals of air force law. I also learned quite a lot about the background to service life when I was dealing with men brought up on charges. By September 1939 of course we all knew that war was imminent and then we were restricted as to how far we were allowed to be from base.

On 1st September 1939, the German Army crossed the border into Poland and launched lightning attacks against the Polish Army and Air Force, which was quickly overwhelmed. Both French and British Governments sent the German leader Adolf Hitler an ultimatum to withdraw from Poland or suffer the consequences of war. The British ambassador Sir William Henderson delivered the British document at 9 am on 3rd September. Hitler did not reply and at 11.15 am Prime Minister Neville Chamberlain relayed to the British people by wireless that Britain was now at war. Peter Brown remembers that day which would change his life forever:

> On Sunday morning, all the officers were sitting in the Mess by the radio waiting to hear a message from the Prime Minister. There was a great feeling of sadness, but also of inspiration as well of course, but we knew that life would never ever again be the same. Strangely, about 15 minutes after the speech, all the air raid sirens on the camp sounded the alarm, and everybody dutifully grabbed their gas masks and went out to their allocated shelters. There were some air raid shelters on the airfield and I went there to meet the men of my instrument fitters unit. When I arrived at the shelters there was a large number of WAAFs waiting outside one and I said 'What are you girls doing out here, you are supposed to be inside.' They said 'We can't get inside the men won't let us in.' So I went to the entrance and ordered all the men out and the girls then went into the shelters. I marched the surplus men off to the football field as I thought we would be as safe there as anywhere else. Half an hour later, the all clear went and everyone marched back to their unit. It was surprising the impact the air raid siren had, sounding 15 minutes after the Prime Minister's speech. For me also, it was a shock to find that the WAAFs had been left outside and had not been given priority of place in the shelters. In 1939 I still believed in chivalry. I stayed on flying duties for two or three weeks and then my posting came to report to a fighter squadron, No. 611 Squadron of the Auxiliary Air Force. I was sent to Speke near Liverpool, where the airfield was their home base. After a cross-country trip by rail, I arrived to find that the squadron wasn't there and hadn't been there for two or three weeks; they were in fact at their initial war station at Duxford. The next day I travelled to Duxford via Crewe and Cambridge. In wartime it seemed that every rail journey necessitated going through Crewe. It is odd that after two weeks of war the Air Ministry didn't know where my fighter squadron was stationed.

On 21st September 1939, Peter joined 611 'West Lancashire' Squadron at RAF Duxford in Cambridgeshire in 12 Group. Once at Duxford, Peter found that the CO was Squadron Leader James McComb, a peacetime solicitor, and that Flight Lieutenant Banham, a regular officer of the RAF, had been transferred to be one of the flight commanders. There were also half a dozen regular officers and NCO pilots.

To Peter Brown's delight the squadron was equipped with Spitfires. He

reported to the CO James McComb, and answered his questions on his
previous flying experience and the work he had been doing. Peter Brown liked
him straight away. McComb was six feet tall and he looked down at Peter
Brown, and said; 'From now on, you are going to be known as "Sneezy"
Brown.' Soon after, Peter had the cartoon picture painted on the fuselage of
his Spitfire and started a squadron fashion. Having reported to the squadron,
the first task Peter had to undertake was to convert to Spitfires. At this time
the RAF had not set up formal operational training units. Basic training and
conversion on to Spitfires and Hurricanes was generally done at the
squadrons. Peter reflects:

> The day after I had arrived my flight commander said to me; 'Right
> you had better fly a Spitfire then'. He gave me a handbook and I
> read that for half-an-hour. Then he said, 'Sit in the cockpit for
> fifteen minutes and find out where everything is'. After the fifteen
> minutes my flight commander said 'We'll start up the engine and
> then off you go, and come back when you are ready. There's only
> one piece of advice, don't push the stick too far forward, otherwise
> you'll smash the propeller.' I had just left a unit where I had been
> flying Wallaces and Wapitis which had a cruising speed of about
> 110 mph, both biplanes with radial engines, no retractable
> undercarriages, no flaps, no variable controls on the engine, and
> totally different take-off and landing speeds. They were a world
> apart. It was like driving an old taxicab and then suddenly being
> faced with a formula one racing car. Like everyone else on their
> first solo in a Spitfire I taxied to take-off with two emotions. One
> was the fear that I might not be able to take off and land safely,
> never having flown a monoplane before. Secondly, there was a
> feeling of exhilaration that I was about to be flying what was
> considered to be the finest and the fastest fighter aircraft in the
> world. I think God was with me that day because I took off and
> landed without incident and walked in to the dispersal hut feeling
> about ten feet tall.
>   Within a week or so the squadron moved north to Digby in
> Lincolnshire, which was to be its new war base and which already
> held No. 46 Hurricane Squadron with Squadron Leader 'Bing'
> Cross as the commanding officer. We shared the work of patrolling
> convoys on alternative days for many months. Local knowledge
> was easy for me because I had just previously spent about eight
> months flying in that area of Lincolnshire. Digby was only about
> four miles away by air from Cranwell and I knew all the landmarks
> out to the coast including North Coates Fittes, which was our
> forward base. Our adjutant was Robin Birley, an auxiliary air force
> officer who in peacetime had been a barrister. He quickly found out
> about my experience of air force law and I was officially appointed
> the assistant adjutant. At that time Fighter Command's
> responsibility was to defend England and Scotland from bomber
> attacks over the North Sea from Germany and perhaps over
> Holland. Most of the flying training we did was to carry out Fighter

Command attacks numbers one to nine. We never seriously considered fighting Me109s, because there would have been no chance that they could have come into action from Germany. I can't remember doing any serious practice of dog fighting or attacking fighters after FTS. It was very much a military approach of getting in the correct formation to attack the bombers. That was it; basic Fighter Command attacks from astern operating generally either as a flight or a section.

During the late months of November/December and the early part of 1940, 611 Squadron was restricted to investigating unidentified raids and patrolling over the North Sea on convoy duties. It was cold and tiring work for the pilots, especially during those winter months. Peter Brown recollects the arduous patrols that had to be undertaken from day to day:

> We were of course permanently at some degree of readiness to be prepared to intercept and attack any Luftwaffe formations that were raiding No.12 Group territory and were picked up on the radar system. Our other duty was to investigate X raids. An X raid was a plot that came up in the Ops Room and nobody knew if it was hostile or not; so two aircraft were generally sent off to investigate. We did our regular escort duty for the convoy patrols on the North Sea, generally in sections of three. This was a miserable business in the winter of 1939/1940, one of the worst winters we had had for many years. We were patrolling some 15 miles out to sea, perhaps with snow and sleet, flying round and round the convoy and trying to keep wide awake, because there would be very little time to spot any attacker which could sneak in under the low cloud. We found that using oxygen was a help. We sometimes patrolled at 500 feet because of low cloud. An engine failure would mean certain death in the freezing water of the North Sea. The thing that enlivened it for us was that at the end of every patrol, with the convoys normally on parallel lines, and having made quite certain that the gunners on the ships knew that we were on their side, we would then fly down the line one at a time at zero feet, the target being lower than the ship's bridges. The sailors would be looking down at us as we flew by and did a lot of waving. Convoy patrols, as far as we were concerned, were best forgotten. We certainly lost one pilot due to atrocious weather.
>
> In November His Majesty King George VI visited Digby to inspect both of the squadrons. We were at readiness when he arrived and were wearing full flying kit, mae wests and helmets when we lined up for his inspection. I have often wondered what would have happened if the scramble bell had sounded. I suspect that the King would have enjoyed the high-speed take-off.

On 10th May, the Germans attacked France and Belgium having already invaded Czechoslovakia, Poland, Norway and Denmark. They moved across Western Europe at very great speed and within two or three weeks they had reached the Channel coast. The British Expeditionary Force, which had been forced back by the Germans, found themselves trapped in the port of Dunkirk, the only harbour left free of the German invasion.

More than 300,000 troops were now locked in there and the problem was how to save them. The Germans had totally overrun Northern France and its Channel coast and to get back to England was the British forces' only hope. How could this be done? As always, the British, at their best with their backs to the wall, rallied around. The Government announced that any man that had a working or pleasure boat that was capable of sailing across to Dunkirk was needed to pick up troops and bring them back. They were to report to Sheerness and there they would be equipped with fuel and food and sometimes a naval rating to help them. Then they set off and together with ferry boats and many other types of small vessels they went across to Dunkirk to face the bombing and save Allied troops.

The Royal Navy of course had destroyers there in the rescue and the Luftwaffe was heavily attacking them. Junkers Ju87 Stuka bombers began bombing the beaches where the men were resting, while the Messerschmitt 109s were sitting high up protecting the Ju87 bombers. No.611 Squadron was now brought in to the action for the first time. Peter Brown hasn't forgotten his first baptism of fire over the beaches:

> Dunkirk gave me my first involvement in real life and death action although I had been a fighter pilot since the end of September 1939. On 2nd June, the squadron took off from Digby at dawn and we flew out to Martlesham Heath, near Ipswich. We refuelled, had the traditional cup of tea and then we flew off with 92 Squadron led by Flight Lieutenant Robert Stanford Tuck to protect the British troops at Dunkirk. We were flying at 15,000 feet over the beaches. Soon after we arrived, and without any warning the sky was full of yellow-nosed Me109s. We hadn't seen them in time and when they bounced us two of our pilots were killed instantly. I was attacked by a Me109 and as I felt the bullets hitting my aircraft I realised for the first time that war was a very serious and killing business. I managed to escape from the 109 attack and climbed up again to 15,000ft. And after 10 minutes flying very unwisely on my own I flew back to England over the North Sea not knowing how much damage had been done to my aircraft. I eventually arrived back at Rochford airport near Southend, which was a Hornchurch satellite airfield, with 30 bullet holes in my aircraft. As I carefully touched down my aircraft lurched dangerously to the left. One of the bullets had burst the port tyre in its wing housing. This was the squadron's first action, and we had received no briefing. It confirmed the adage that a fighter pilot's first five engagements are the most dangerous. We had met an experienced enemy that had been battle honed in Spain, Poland, and France.

Peter Brown's actual combat report for that day states:

> When patrolling at 15,000 feet with A Flight, at 08.05 am, Me109s

suddenly appeared in our formation. I attacked a Me109 using deflection, but saw no apparent hits. I then realised that a Me109 was on my tail and firing. I dived to evade the enemy aircraft fire, but was followed down by the enemy fighter. My engine began missing and I went down towards the beach, where it picked up again. I went over Dunkirk at about 100 feet still followed by the enemy aircraft. When I opened the boost full out, I felt no more shots from the enemy and found I had evaded him. Climbing up to 10,000 feet I saw two squadrons of Ju87Bs, about 24 aircraft in the distance, but I did not approach. I circled around for ten minutes, but could not see any sign of other aircraft. I then returned to England, arriving at Burnham-on-Crouch. I then followed the coast and landed at Southend aerodrome. My aircraft was hit by machine-gun fire on the port mainplane, rudder, fin, fuselage, port tyre and possibly the engine.

Peter continues:

For ten days Fighter Command's Hurricanes and Spitfires fought their first real battle with Me109s. We lost some 120 aircraft and 85 pilots over Dunkirk, killed or made POWs, which was approximately 25% of the Fighter Command force, which had been reserved to defend Britain from attack by the Germans. But 330,000 British and Allied troops were brought back safely to England. Unfortunately, their armour was left behind in France and some arrived back in Britain with only their uniforms and some wearing only blankets. This achievement was Britain at its best and I always refer to it as the miracle of Dunkirk.

The next day was the last day of major patrols by Fighter Command squadrons over the beaches, and the evacuation was ended. We were still stationed in 12 Group at Digby, but we were now expecting an invasion to take place within weeks. The Luftwaffe would soon have time to recover from its losses in the Battle of France, rebuild its squadrons, and build new airfields along the coast. Now they were within 23 miles of the English coast and only a few minutes flying distance. We had been trained for a war in which we were fighting an enemy that had to fly some hundreds of miles in bombers to attack us and now they were only a few minutes away, and could be given fighter protection. This was indeed a great tactical turn around.

The bombers needed protection by fighters, their fighter's range was limited to 11 Group boundaries and that is where the Battle of Britain was basically fought. Soon after, France surrendered and Britain was then alone and the whole world believed that within a few weeks Britain itself would be invaded or would just surrender to the Germans. That would have been the end of Europe, which would have been taken over by the Nazis. There would have been ethnic cleansing on an appalling scale and democracy would have vanished from Europe for at least a century. However, the people of

Britain never believed for one moment that the Germans would
ever arrive, the only force that could save us was Fighter
Command. As Winston Churchill wrote, 'Our fate now depends on
victory in the air.'

On 10th July 1940, the day that is officially recorded as the start of the Battle
of Britain, German Luftwaffe squadrons launched an attack against a Channel
convoy code-named 'Bread,' which was sailing through the Channel off North
Foreland at 10.40 am. The German dive-bomber and fighter formations were
met by RAF fighters and so began the fight in the air to save Britain from
invasion. During this time Peter Brown with 611 Squadron was still stationed
at Digby, and many of the pilots became frustrated at not being able to get into
the fighting with their comrades down in 11 Group.

During July and August, the pilots in 11 Group were heavily engaged
with the Luftwaffe raids and starting to take heavy casualties themselves, with
10 Group providing support for them. The RAF's position was precarious
during this period, although aircraft could be replaced quite quickly, pilots
could not. 611 Squadron finally got into action in late August, as Peter
remembers:

In 611 Squadron we still carried on with our convoy patrols although
always at readiness and expecting the great battle to take place when
the Germans invaded. On 21st August 1940, I was in a section of
three, which was vectored out from Mablethorpe on the coast to
attack three Dornier 17 bombers, which were about ten miles off the
coast. We attacked them in a standard Fighter Command technique
and they immediately set course for home at high speed and in tight
formation; they weren't planning to stay around. We shot down two
out of the three and when we arrived back at our advanced landing
airfield at North Coates, we discovered that we had all been hit by
return fire and my aircraft had been hit in the nose and the wing, one
of the bullets bursting a tyre. I also had some rather unpleasant bullet
holes in the tail. I didn't realise until I touched down on landing that
once again I had a burst tyre.

I managed to keep control and avoided rolling over. The other
section of our flight intercepted another three Dornier 17s and they
shot down two out of the three. I think we can assume that the
Germans realised that if they were losing four out of six aircraft in
one single raid it was unsafe to attempt to bomb England other than
in the southeast where they could have fighter protection. This
encounter with the German bombers impressed me because of their
professionalism. Their formation was so tight that we could only
attack astern with two fighters without risking a collision. All three
of us were damaged and could have finished up in the sea with
them. Attacking German bombers was not an easy option.

In the middle of August, 611 Squadron was equipped with Spitfire Mk IIs,
which was a distinctly improved version of the Spitfire Mk I. Effectively the
fighter squadrons in 11 Group were still battling on with Spitfire Is when they

should have been equipped with the best Spitfires that were available. What was the reason for this tactical organisation? Peter relays his thoughts on how the battle was being fought during this period:

> Towards the end of August, we flew in daily to Duxford, close to the borders of 11 Group to give support. The pilots were all very concerned in 12 Group because we had been sitting at readiness day after day at Digby and Duxford and our squadrons had not been called into the battle, whereas 11 Group were fighting to the death. I personally felt that a brick wall had been put up, and that we were deliberately being kept out of the fight, while 11 Group squadrons were taking such heavy losses, and that view has always stayed with me. We took off at dawn, arrived at Duxford, refuelled or sometimes just went straight on patrol without landing. The patrol could take us over an 11 Group sector base, it could be over London, or we could be patrolling Hornchurch. All the time we did that, we never got into the action and although it might have been a very useful and important function, if you are a fighter pilot you really need to get into the action. As we were not continuously going into battle and therefore not losing any of our pilots except senior ones that were posted away to be flight commanders in other squadrons, we had surplus pilots on the Squadron. So pilots weren't required to fly everyday as they did in 11 Group who were short of pilots. The strained relationship between the commanders of 11 Group and 12 Group and personal ambitions, kept 12 Group squadrons less effective in the real war over the 11 Group sector, which led to higher casualties.

On 30th August 1940, the squadrons in 12 Group waited for the call that would send them into action down south to help their comrades in 11 Group. After discussions between Air Chief Marshal Dowding and his two group commanders, Keith Park and Leigh-Mallory, a decision was made to use the squadrons of 12 Group as support to 11 Group and help in protecting the 11 Group airfields against the Luftwaffe raids that were now launched against them. Peter Brown now records what happened on that day:

> We flew down to the Duxford satellite Fowlmere, where 19 Squadron, also equipped with Spitfires, was based. Squadron Leader Douglas Bader, the legless pilot, with his Hurricane squadron was at Duxford three miles away, when a German bomber raid came in without any Messerschmitt 109 support. No.12 Group Operations sent off only one squadron, 242 Squadron led by Bader who had never led a squadron into action before, although four squadrons were immediately available. Clearly Air Vice-Marshal Leigh-Mallory and 12 Group had no concept of using Wing formations at that date. We just sat at readiness while they went off into action against what was reported to be a formation of 100 enemy aircraft. They did quite well in fact, although their claims were exaggerated by about 3 to 1, and

squadrons from other sectors were also involved in the action. I believe they claimed 12 aircraft shot down which would have been an enormous success compared with anything that 11 Group had reported. Air Vice-Marshal Trafford Leigh-Mallory was so impressed with this, and with Bader who was his protégé, that he agreed to let Bader have two more squadrons because Bader had said *'If I had more squadrons we could have shot down more aircraft'*. Any squadron commander in 11 Group could have said the same thing. However, he got his squadrons and that was the beginning of the Big Wing controversy. The Big Wing philosophy and controversy has always been of major interest to me.

Later on in life I did a great deal of research and presented a number of papers on the subject. There was no planning for the Wing whatsoever and it was just an *ad hoc* operation. The squadrons never rehearsed, the Wing couldn't operate until Bader flew into Duxford from his base in Coltishall 65 miles away. We couldn't take part in it until we flew in from Digby, about 70 miles north; in fact on the great day of 15th September 1940, we joined the Wing in the air, when they were already on their way south for the battle over London.

611 Squadron continued to fly and fight as part of the Duxford Wing throughout the early weeks of September, claiming successes against the Germans. On 3rd September, Peter received notification of promotion in rank to flying officer.

It was on 15th September 1940, now known as Battle of Britain Day, that the Royal Air Force put up the strongest defence of fighter aircraft they could muster, to counter the Luftwaffe's massive raids against London and the southeast. The Luftwaffe pilots were shocked to see not only the usual small fighter units from 11 Group, but also a Wing formation of 60 Hurricanes and Spitfires from 12 Group coming in to attack them. Among that formation flying his Spitfire was Flying Officer Peter Brown, and he reflects on that momentous day:

However on September 15th, I flew with the Wing and was involved in the two battles over London. When we arrived with the Wing we were the last and top squadron of the five-squadron Wing, which had three Hurricane squadrons followed by two Spitfire squadrons. There were so many aircraft in the sky with the Germans being attacked by numerous other British fighters that we had to circle above waiting to get in to the battle. I felt at the time that there was something wrong with the control of our squadrons. In fact later reports show that sometimes there were two or even three British fighters queuing up to shoot down one German aircraft, whereas other formations were not attacked. The problem with the Bader Wing was that there was a heavily committed concentration of force that was not needed at that point. In the afternoon engagement, I attacked a Dornier 215, which had previously been attacked by my CO, Squadron Leader McComb, but my windscreen quickly became covered in oil and I had to break away. I then saw a Heinkel 111 on its own, and after I had opened fire it went into a steep dive with the escape hatch over the cockpit open. I last saw it diving vertically to the ground and claimed this as a probable. Later I learned that two other pilots had also attacked this aircraft, which crashed so the most I can claim is a third!

Peter's combat report for the day clearly states the following engagement with the German bombers:

After evading an enemy fighter, I attacked an enemy formation and fired one burst at a Dornier 215 after Red 1 had put his engine out of action. Oil from the enemy aircraft covered my windscreen and I had to break away.

I then attacked one aircraft, which broke away from the enemy formation and turned. I used deflection and the enemy aircraft went into a steep spiral dive. I attempted to follow, but the dive was too steep. I noticed that the escape hatch above the pilot's seat was open, due either to my fire or the crew escaping. I did not see any crew bale out as a large formation of Me110s appeared and I escaped into cloud.

No damage to own aircraft. Took off at 14.15, Landed at 15.35.

Soon afterwards 611 Squadron was sent west, to undertake operations from the airfields that protected the area around Liverpool, which had also come under attack. Peter remembers the squadron's move:

I flew with the Wing again later but during the second half of September we were temporarily based at Tern Hill, a Flying Training station in Shropshire to give day protection to Liverpool as there had been a few Luftwaffe aircraft flying round the west of England to attack the port by day. It was at this time that I had a very unusual experience when I was leading a section of three aircraft patrolling the Liverpool area to improve morale. The Ops Room kept us up too late and when they ordered us to end the patrol it was getting quite dark. I expected to be given a course back to Tern Hill, which was to the south, but instead I was being given vectors of 90 degrees, which is due east. I couldn't understand this and kept querying the instruction but was simply told to fly on the vectors given. It gradually got darker and our fuel was getting seriously low. I was getting ready to consider the need for us to bale out because there was nowhere we could land. At ground level by then it was quite dark, so that with the blackout we were effectively flying over black velvet. I had allowed myself another five minutes before I took the crucial decision when suddenly, without warning, directly in front of me in the blackness, there appeared two columns of lights; they seemed to be like diamonds in the sky.

It was quite miraculous and I realised in fact that they were the

lights of a runway, which had just been switched on. I'd never seen
a runway like that before; they either had glim lamps or paraffin
flares. Within a few minutes we had landed on Manchester's
civilian Ringway airfield, one of the few runways that could have
illuminated and let us land in an emergency. I realised afterwards
that Ringway had probably refused to switch on their lights until
we were almost virtually overhead in case there were German
bombers around. As soon as we had landed the lights were hastily
switched off. I have always remembered the 'diamonds in the sky',
which appeared when I was getting ready to bale out. If the
controller had simply said that there was an airfield waiting for us
it would have saved us a great deal of anxiety.

Towards the end of September, policies were made at Fighter
Command to organise different grades of squadrons with the
transfer of operational pilots. 611 Squadron which had only seen
limited action in the battle, was then denuded of pilots who had
significant experience as Spitfire pilots, and as a result I was posted
to No. 41 Squadron.

On 28th September 1940, Flying Officer Peter Brown received a signal telling
him of his posting to travel south and report to 41 Squadron based at RAF
Hornchurch; this squadron had played a significant part in the Battle of
Britain during that summer. Peter was happy to be joining this distinguished
squadron:

41 Squadron was based at Hornchurch on the eastern edge of the
London balloon barrage. It was a very experienced squadron and
had been in action over Dunkirk. It had already served one tour of
operations at Hornchurch in August returning then to its base unit
at Catterick and coming back again to Hornchurch in September
for another tour. Casualty reports after the war show that it was the
third highest squadron for enemy aircraft shot down but the second
highest in the number of casualties incurred. 41 was a great
squadron, highly professional, with very experienced pilots, all
with a great sense of humour. I was truly lucky with this posting.
The commanding officer was Squadron Leader D.O. Finlay who
had taken over with little experience in battle. The squadron had
lost two previous commanders in earlier fighting; these were
Squadron Leader 'Robin' Hood, who had been killed and Squadron
Leader Robert Lister who had baled out wounded. The Air
Ministry were still thinking in peacetime terms; they were posting
squadron leaders to lead squadrons in battle conditions simply by
rank and sometimes direct from desk or instructor duties. This was
acceptable in times of peace but fatal against the battle-trained
Luftwaffe. Flight Lieutenant Norman Ryder who was my flight
commander in A Flight, often led the squadron. We also had Pilot
Officer 'Benny' Bennions who was shot down a few days after I
arrived, having been seriously wounded in the head with a cannon
shell. He was certainly one of the aces of the Battle. One of our

pilots was Pilot Officer Eric Lock who is now acknowledged to be the highest scoring English pilot of the battle. He was awarded a DSO and a DFC and bar for his work but was seriously wounded in November. Others such as Flight Lieutenant Tony Lovell, Flying Officer 'Mac' Mackenzie from New Zealand, Flying Officer Guy Cory and Pilot Officer 'Hawkeye' Wells, were some of the people that I was very privileged to fight with.

The day after I arrived at the squadron my wish to get into the real war was granted. On that day I took off with my fellow pilots, and according to my logbook I went into action and damaged a Dornier 215. I can't remember the action, but that is what my combat report claims. I was very lucky as Norman Ryder said that I could fly with him for my first few flights, as that was the most dangerous time. Although I'd been a fighter pilot for 12 months and had a considerable amount of time on Spitfires, the transition from 12 Group to 11 Group was totally traumatic. The speed of events was so fast that for the first two or three trips I saw nothing. Norman had said *'just stick to me and you will be all right'*, which I did. Soon after he asked me to fly regularly as his number two which suited me very well.

Peter's combat report against the Dornier 215 states:

At 14.00 hours, off Dungeness at 15,000 feet I followed Mitor Leader into attack and fired three bursts into the No.2 of rear section. Heavy black smoke came from the port engine, but when I broke away the aircraft was still in enemy formation. Slight fire from rear gunner.

Peter claimed the enemy bomber as damaged. The bomber that he had shared in shooting down was a Dornier17Z of 2/KG2, which eventually crash-landed at Conifer Hill, Starston. Of the crew, Leutnant Ermecke was killed, while the remaining three NCOs baled out and were captured. Peter continues:

In 12 Group we had sat at readiness for days and sometimes weeks with no real action, although there was no shortage of convoy patrols and occasional X raids. On the third day with 41 Squadron I did five sorties, which was certainly a different intensity of battle. By October, the pattern of fighting had changed significantly. The Germans had realised that their bomber attacks on London by day were too costly, the plans for invasion in 1940 had been cancelled and with increasing cloud conditions they effectively ceased by the beginning of October. The Luftwaffe then changed their offensive attacks to Me109s coming over at 30,000 feet escorting Me109s with bombs. The speed of operation of course was much faster and we were then operating at heights, which had not been envisaged before.

It was incredibly cold at 30,000 feet; the temperatures were minus 40 degrees Centigrade. We had no heating in the cockpit, no heating for the guns and no heating for the windscreen; everything froze up. Sometimes half of the guns wouldn't fire, sometimes when we dived in to attack the windscreens froze up and we had to break off the attack because we could see nothing forward. After this had happened two or three times, I decided to carry out my own scientific development and I asked the flight sergeant for some neat glycol fluid. I took a very large rag soaked in neat glycol with me up in the cockpit, ready for the next interception. Fortunately, at about 30,000 feet we were ordered to intercept and as we dived down once again the windscreen froze up. I felt that this was my great chance because I would be the only man in the squadron that could see what was happening and go into action. I reached down for my glycol rag to clear the ice but it was as solid as a piece of plywood. So much for my scientific development! But it does indicate how very cold it was up there.

It seems that somebody had missed a very important design factor because with all the effort involved in getting us into action, to see the enemy and to attack sometimes with an advantage, we were unable to fire because they had forgotten to put heating into a Spitfire. As far as I know all American aircraft had heating in the cockpit. However, in spite of these difficulties I had some personal success.

On 20th October 1940, both 41 and 603 Squadrons were scrambled during the afternoon and at about 2.00 pm they intercepted a formation of approximately 60 Me109s at an altitude of 25,000 feet. Peter Brown was flying during that sortie and shot down one of the enemy as he now describes:

On 20th October 1940, we were vectored on to Me109s, about 30 of them. I attacked one, shot it down and saw the pilot bale out. He landed near West Malling in Kent. I decided that I would land and collect evidence to prove that I had shot him down. The intelligence officer drove me out to the village of Wrotham, where the pilot had been picked up, and was being held in the 'Bull' hotel cellar. I had a chat with him and then took away with me his schwimmvest and also his wings badge and returned back to Hornchurch.

Peter's actual combat report for that engagement read:

I was Red 2 in formation and I singled out one of the rear 109s. After one short burst from 150 yards astern and slightly underneath, glycol streamed out from the enemy aircraft. I gave him another short burst from 100 yards, using slight deflection. The enemy aircraft then dived down, apparently out of control; I followed him down several thousand feet. He then recovered from the dive and climbed up again. I gave him two more short bursts from 100 yards astern and underneath. The enemy aircraft then half rolled and I followed him down. The aircraft crashed in woods northwest of West Malling aerodrome and the pilot baled out and landed at Wrotham. I landed at West Malling. Two of my guns did not fire, presumably due to the cold.

The Messerschmitt 109E that Peter Brown had shot down belonged to 5/JG52 and was being flown on that day by Feldwebel (Sergeant) Bielmaier. The remains of this aircraft were recovered in 1973 and are now on display at the Lashenden Air Warfare Museum at Headcorn in Kent. The German schwimmveste (mae west), which Peter Brown took from his German opponent as a souvenir, is now displayed in the Hornchurch Wing Collection at the Purfleet Heritage & Military Centre at Purfleet, Essex. On 25th October, Peter was again involved in combat against Me109s, this time southwest of Ashford, Kent:

> Five days later, again unusually, we were able to bounce a wing of Me109s. I attacked one and opened fire without great success. He rolled over and dived away. I then climbed up higher and saw at least eight or nine 109s in formation at a slightly lower height. I dived into the attack, opened fire on one of the Me109s and saw white glycol streaming from the engine. I gave it another burst before it rolled over and disappeared into cloud. I claimed this as a probable, but later it was confirmed. I chased another one out over the sea, but my ammunition had run out so I returned to base.

Peter's combat report written that day stated:

> I followed Red leader and attacked a 109 with no apparent results. Having lost the squadron, I climbed up to 25,000 feet again and saw about 9 Me109s on my starboard beam. I turned to attack them and was involved in a dogfight. After two short bursts, glycol poured out of one of the 109s. I gave it two more bursts with slight deflection. The enemy aircraft rolled over on its side and dived straight into cloud. I then attacked another 109 and followed it over the sea, but after one burst my ammunition ran out. The first enemy aircraft I believe crashed within the vicinity of Rye. Two of my guns did not fire due to the cold.

It was in October that 41 Squadron upgraded their aircraft to Spitfire Mk IIs and carried on flying sorties against German fighters although the weather was worsening as the winter drew near. Peter again:

> Towards the end of October, we received Spitfire Mk IIs from my former squadron, No.611, who took our old Mk Is back with them into 12 Group. Why couldn't Fighter Command have done this a month earlier? As an example of the air activity at the end of October, on the 27th, the squadron operated three patrols during the day and on the 29th again three patrols, so the battle was still going on. The Germans lost 311 aircraft in October, most of them Me109s for little purpose. It is worth noting, that I did as many operational sorties in the month of October with 41 Squadron in 11

Group, as I did with 12 Group from July through to September. This I think clarifies so clearly the difference between the load carried between the two Groups.

Fighting against Me109s continued well into November in spite of the bad weather. On 7th November, four patrols at squadron strength were sent up. In spite of the worsening weather the squadron still carried out patrols, occasionally intercepting 109s. A memory for me was that Norman Ryder and I took off on the last patrol of the year on 31st December 1940.

By that time Air Vice-Marshal Keith Park had been relieved of his command of 11 Group and his place was taken by Air Vice-Marshal Leigh-Mallory. Air Chief Marshal Sir Hugh Dowding had already been relieved of his position without due recognition of his great achievement in the Battle of Britain and replaced as Chief of Fighter Command by Air Marshal Sholto Douglas in November.

With the new year of 1941 came new orders from the heads of Fighter and Bomber Command to take the fight back across the Channel to the enemy in Northern France. There were to be many various operations planned all with new names, Sweeps, Circuses, Rhubarbs and Ramrod. Peter now reflects on the positive and negative benefits of such operations:

When we entered the new year of 1941 the two new commanders started their strategic plans of 'leaning forward towards the enemy' and flying sweeps over France. 11 Group decided to set up an operation called a Rhubarb, in which pairs of Spitfires flew across the Channel at very low level, and then attacked targets of opportunity inside France. This was done when the weather was fairly bad with low cloud and it was felt that pilots could hide over the French coast in the cloud, and then come out to attack targets in front of them. Anyone with knowledge of the defence of German airfields knows that for Spitfires making *ad hoc* attacks this could be very dangerous. The pilots hated these Rhubarb attacks and the cost in the lives of pilots far outweighed any benefit or effects that were achieved. Flight Lieutenant Eric Lock was killed on such an operation on 3rd August 1941. What a terrible waste of the pilot's life.

I was Norman Ryder's 'number two' and he and I practiced flying in and out of cloud and beating up the Southend new arterial road. We sat ready for take-off on a couple of occasions, but the operations were cancelled because of the weather.

Throughout January we continued to carry out standing patrols, except on 10th when we were included in the first Big Wing operation over France. Three of the Hornchurch squadrons took part in the Circus with Wing Commander Broadhurst leading the Wing in 41 Squadron. There was no serious action except that Sergeant Beardsley of our squadron was severely shot up by a Me109, having left the main formation to chase two 109s in the distance.

The weather in January continued to be poor. Sadly for the

squadron, but good news for him, Flight Lieutenant Norman Ryder was posted to No.56 Squadron at North Weald to command. This was a promotion which was long overdue, and he should have been commanding 41 Squadron many months beforehand and decorated for his two tours in the Battle. We were all very sorry to lose him.

The date of 20th February 1941 was a day that Flying Officer Peter Brown would remember for the rest of his life. He had flown a patrol earlier that day and during that afternoon led another patrol over the southeast coast. He now takes up the story:

I led a patrol of three aircraft in the morning over the Dover area, which was quite uneventful. Later on in the day, I led a flight of six Spitfires to patrol the Dover line at 25,000 feet. After about 40 minutes of patrol, at 3.54 pm we received a single message from the Operations Room to the effect that 'Bandits' were in our immediate vicinity at 'Angels Six', which translated meant enemy at 6,000 feet. We were at 25,000 feet, and there was very little we could do without further information and instructions, except keep a very alert watch out for the enemy aircraft below in case they were climbing up. If we had seen the 109s on the climb that would have given us a tremendous advantage.

One of our pilots had left us, the top cover, and returned to base with engine trouble. Two or three minutes after this single warning from the Ops Room, I intuitively looked up at the three-o-clock position and I saw some 109s, four or six, diving down to attack from about 1,000 feet above us. I shouted a warning and immediately pulled into a steep climbing turn to the right to meet them head-on and open fire. Immediately there was a large bang in my tail and a metallic rattle along the fuselage. I blacked out completely and came to some 5,000 feet lower and in a spin over Dover Harbour. My control column was completely ineffective and I believed that having no control, my aircraft had been seriously damaged in the tail by one of the attacking Me109s.

Peter Brown had in fact unwittingly pulled the aircraft into a high-speed stall, a disturbing 10G manoeuvre, which happened to other experienced Spitfire pilots in the middle of combat action. Peter continues:

I opened the hood and prepared to bale out, but when I realised I still had plenty of height, I decided to stay in and managed to recover the aircraft from its spin. I closed the hood and as I climbed up again, I saw a pilot on a parachute.

When I circled around, I realised it was Sergeant John McAdam, but to my horror there was a hole in the front of his Sidcot suit with white smoke coming out. I realised that he had been shot by an incendiary cannon shell. He was unconscious and obviously very seriously wounded and I decided to stay circling around him, advising the Ops Room where we were, the height, and making certain that they knew where he was going to land outside Dover Harbour. I stayed with him until he entered the water and then I continued circling to guide the rescue launch. I then received another warning from the Ops Control, telling me that there were hostile aircraft in my immediate vicinity and to be very careful.

They were quite right, because a few minutes later tracer bullets shot over my wing. Although I had been flying immediately below the cloud base, the Germans had managed to find me. I instantly pulled up into cloud and when I broke cloud later I saw four Me109s making their way back across the Channel to France. The rescue boat quickly picked up Sergeant McAdam, but sadly he was already dead.

When I landed back at Hornchurch, I was very angry at having been given such an appalling height of 6,000 feet for the enemy aircraft who must have been some 20,000 feet higher at that time. I also learnt on landing that Sergeant Angus had also been shot down, had baled out and had landed in the sea, but had not been picked up. The enemy must have known where we were and had been extremely close to, if not above our height and position when the first and only warning was given. When I saw Wing Commander Broadhurst, the station commander, in his office I expressed my views very forcibly, saying that the Operations Rooms' appalling and belated warning was responsible for the loss of two of my pilots. My comments were accepted by the Wing Commander and Squadron Leader Finlay, my CO, who was present, but had not taken part in the sortie; the matter was never discussed with me again, and I continued as flight commander. It was reported later that the German ace, Werner Mölders, had shot them both down. Mölders' own flying logbook gives the time as 3.56 pm, just two minutes after our warning of 6,000 feet. Sergeant McAdam had been shot in the back by a cannon shell while he was on a parachute. Who was responsible for that? Why was our formation given such unreliable and belated information?

The tragedy was that we had been due to fly north to Catterick, our base station, for a rest two days previously. Instead of taking off then we had to stay on because Catterick was snowbound and 54 Squadron was unable to take off and equally we would not have been able to land there. If it hadn't been for the snow, which delayed our departure, then this misadventure would not have hit the squadron. On 23rd February 1941, 41 Squadron flew north to Catterick, which was to be our base for the next six months.

Catterick was a small airfield with a single runway with poor approaches and surrounding high ground. At the end of the day of the 3rd of March, Group control wanted an X raid to be investigated by a section. Flight Lieutenant John Mackenzie, the other flight commander, and I protested to the commanding officer Squadron Leader Finlay against sending off a section. It was dusk, the weather was bad with low cloud, and a section of aircraft would have been useless. However, Finlay insisted that we three would comprise the section and ordered us to take off with him. He was airborne first, followed by Mackenzie and myself within a few seconds' intervals, by which time the runway lights had been switched on as by then it was quite dark. As soon as Finlay was airborne, he realised that the conditions were impossible and there was no point in staying up; he landed in a hurry. He completed the circuit, overshot the runway, went through the boundary hedge and crashed 400 yards into a field, writing off his Spitfire but he was uninjured.

Mac and I were both still airborne, but apparently flying control did not know that three aircraft had taken off and so switched off every light, the runway, the circuit and lead-in lights, and the hangar and obstruction lights. The night was so black it was like having a cloth of black velvet thrown over the windscreen. I prepared to fly on instruments to climb up into the cloud just above to get height to bale out. I knew that to attempt to land without lights was impossible. Mac however, using some very powerful language, ordered flying control to put the lights on again. The landing conditions were difficult and Mac came in next and finished up stuck in the hedge at the end of the runway. I was then faced with a very low, slow approach in a Spitfire at night, possibly down wind. I switched off and stopped some 50 feet short of the hedge. This was a flight which should never have taken place, and we nearly lost a commanding officer and two flight commanders for nothing. Mac and I never forgot this incident and it was always a first point of discussion when we met 40 and 50 years later. As a point of interest that was the third time that I was ready to bale out. I was never nervous about having to do it; there would have been no alternative.

Although it was supposed to be a rest period, Fighter Command started to disintegrate the squadron. Flight Lieutenant Tony Lovell had already been posted to an operational training unit in February, but returned later. In early March Flight Lieutenant John Mackenzie and Pilot Officer Edward Wells were posted away and other experienced pilots were posted to central flying school, OTUs and other units. A number of new pilots came in from operational training units. This meant a greater load for me including night-flying patrols. On occasions I was on duty for 36 hours out of 48.

Squadron Leader Pat Meagher joined us as a supernumerary. He had been an instructor at No.5 FTS when I was under training there. On patrol one night he shot down a Heinkel bomber which was quite a feat. Tony Lovell shot down a Junkers 88 over the moors. I intercepted a Junkers 88, which rapidly disappeared into the cloud before I could get into firing distance. Apart from that there was very little happening operationally except convoy patrols and night readiness. At the time Al Deere of 54 Squadron and our own Benny Bennions were our controllers, which was very comforting. Our squadron doctor Ernest Anthony invited me down

to Upminster for the weekend. I decided to take the Station
Magister, a monoplane trainer and to land at Hornchurch. The
weather was so bad that all operational flying was cancelled but
somehow I managed to get Control to let us take-off. We followed
the main railway line south with the cloud getting lower and lower.
At Grantham I accepted that we had to give up. With my local
knowledge from previous flying at Cranwell I knew that Grantham
airfield was two miles southeast of the town and some 200 feet
higher. Flying at roof-top level over Grantham, I altered course,
and landed in and out of cloud on to the airfield, which was
officially closed in. The duty pilot was more than surprised and I
was more than relieved. We finished the journey by train, a much
more sensible way of travelling. Nil marks for airmanship.

Peter's time on squadron operations finished when he received a signal from
11 Group notifying him on 28th June 1941 of his new posting and duties to
No. 61 Operational Training Unit at Heston on the outskirts of London. His
experience with the distinguished 41 Squadron had come to an end; he had
been at readiness in Spitfire squadrons continuously for 21 months and had
carried out more than 200 sorties, of which more than 70 were during the
Battle of Britain:

I was posted at the end of June 1941 to 61 OTU to serve as
commander of No.1 Squadron. OTUs had been set up by Fighter
Command in 1940 as a means of training pilots to fly Spitfires and
Hurricanes and give them the basic rudiments of flying in
formation, battle climbs, low flying and carrying out air-gunnery.
When they arrived at a squadron, they would have at least 40 hours
of experience. During the Battle of Britain some of the pilots had
arrived on squadrons with as little as ten hours experience on
Spitfires.

Heston was situated a few miles west of the London balloon
barrage, and this presented a serious hazard to flying. It was a grass
airfield and the accident rate as at most OTUs was very high. The
courses lasted for six weeks to nine weeks and the students varied
significantly. Sometimes a course would be a mixture of people
from flying training schools or other flying units. I had one course
of Polish pilots and the only thing they wanted to do was to train to
fly Spitfires as quickly as possible, so that they could get to a
squadron and kill Germans. They could not understand that a very
thick haze was a reason not to fly from our airfield, so close to the
London balloon barrage, and sometimes it could almost be a battle
with them to prevent them flying just because the weather was
atrocious.

The Poles were the most dedicated pilots that I trained. The
pilots that I liked training best were the Australians with their sense
of humour and their broad attitude to life. I arranged that whenever
a course of Australians came in, they would come to my 'squadron'
or flight for training. The other flying instructors at Heston were

also pilots from the Battle of Britain.

For a period of time Wing Commander Sailor Malan, one of the outstanding pilots in the Battle of Britain was our Wing Commander Flying, but he stayed only a few months. Although I enjoyed being at Heston, one of my main memories of the OTU was the consistently high number of accidents and fatalities that we had. But I understand that this was a common factor, and that the highest rate of training accidents in the RAF took place at OTUs. For the first time in their training young pilots were being given adult responsibility.

There was one memorable occasion when we had an unexpected visitor to the flight. One of our planes arrived with someone standing on the wing being taxied across the airfield. When I went down to see who it was, it turned out to be Prince Bernard of the Netherlands, who with his wife Princess Juliana, was exiled in England. He held the rank of air commodore in England and was a very qualified pilot. He had come over to borrow a Spitfire for an hour or so. I found him a very charming relaxed person and his visit was a pleasure to us all. I gave him a quick cockpit check and briefing with maps carefully marked with balloon barrages, restricted areas and the safe route out via the Staines reservoirs. He took off and to my great relief he arrived back at the airfield an hour or so later and landed safely.

I would like to mention another special day, a very personal day. My young brother, a cadet airman awaiting a transfer to Canada for pilot training, visited me at Heston. I took him to my flight and I let him sit in a Spitfire, which was a great event for him. I then asked the already prepared flight sergeant if he had an aircraft that needed an air test. 'Fortunately we have Sir,' he said, and so my brother was kitted out, fitted with a parachute and off we went in a Miles Master advanced trainer. I gave him his first ever flight lasting an hour and let him take over the controls for most of the time. I am sure that the memory of this flight stayed with him for the rest of his short life until, at the age of twenty-one, he was killed on a bombing raid over Italy. The great advantage of Heston to most of the ex-Battle pilots and others was its proximity to London and the nightlife, even though air raids were taking place nightly at the time. We were only a short distance from Hounslow West underground station and so it was possible to get into the centre of London and have a good night out and be back home at Heston in time for breakfast.

In one of the hangars there was a Messerschmitt 108, a very pleasant peacetime German aeroplane that seated four. Flight Lieutenant Bell-Salter who had been badly injured in the Battle and was one of the flight commanders got permission for us to borrow it. We flew it down to Bolt Head on the Channel coast in Devon. We landed on a field at the end of which was a cliff with a sheer drop into the sea and tied it down. After a most enjoyable weekend with his family we started up the Messerschmitt, took off over the cliff edge and flew low and landed back at Heston.

At most of the stations I was posted to, I was able to take my dog, a Labrador bitch with me. She loved being at the flight dispersal because all the ground crews spoiled her. She would always beat them to be first in the queue when the NAAFI wagon arrived, and you had to be very fast to beat the airmen. Suddenly she would leave them and walk out to meet one of the Spitfires taxiing in; it was always my aircraft that she had picked out. She had this ability, without seeing me take-off, to know I was in that aircraft. The ground crews were totally amused by it. When newcomers asked how my dog did it, the old timers said 'It's quite simple, she goes into the flight room and checks on the authorisation board to see which aircraft he is flying.'

In April 1942, we received the news that 61 OTU was moving from Heston up to an unknown airfield called Rednall on the Welsh borders in Shropshire. This was going to be entirely different from being so close to London and all its nightlife, and there was great gloom and depression. Anybody who had any influence was trying to get a posting to somewhere else. I led a flight up to Rednall and on approaching the area I saw three crossed runways in a field of mud, and not very much else. It was one of the newly built airfields that had been designed with dispersal in mind, and everything was dispersed in the woods; each building was about 100 yards from the other and unless you had a bicycle you couldn't move around at all. The WAAF quarters were well protected with wire fencing. I can't say that I have met any colleagues who were at Rednall who have any happy memories of their stay, there was really nowhere to go. Fortunately, I was transferred to the satellite airfield at Montford Bridge which was much more pleasant, and life was more acceptable as it was close to the county town of Shrewsbury.

While flying there I had the only mechanical failures I had in the whole of my RAF service. While I was flying in the circuit, my engine caught fire but all I had to do was to switch everything off and carry out a dead-stick landing on to the runway and all was well. The two others occurred in quick succession. I was taxiing out to take off when the brakes failed on the perimeter track, but I was able to steer the aircraft off and stopped safely on the grass. I walked back with my parachute to the dispersal and started another aircraft. I took off on the runway and after about 150 yards the engine failed. I managed to swing it off the runway onto the grass without incident and I left it parked clear of the runway. I went back to my office and told my flight sergeant 'I am superstitious and will not be flying again today. I can accept two failures out of two, but the third one could have my name on it.' Because the OTUs were equipped with old squadron Spitfire aircraft serviceability was always a major problem for the maintenance teams.

On 15th July 1942, Peter was posted to the Empire Central Flying School at Hullavington in Wiltshire. When he arrived he found it was regarded as the university of the air, and students were sent there not only from all the commands in England, but also from America, New Zealand, Canada, South Africa, and so there was a very international group of students mainly of Flight Lieutenant or Squadron Leader rank. Peter was on the second course and he graduated successfully:

> I found it a very interesting and even fascinating course. Those who weren't already qualified flying instructors were given training instruction on single and twin-engine aircraft. I qualified as a single-engine instructor. We flew aircraft that we would never have flown before which for me included Oxfords, Ansons, and Blenheims. We worked in groups and helped to write the new textbooks on flying instruction. We went to all sorts of places including Bomber Command stations; we went to Farnborough to see the research that was going on with wind tunnels, and what they were doing in the water tanks to study the effects of ditching Hurricanes and Spitfires in the sea. This was a procedure not to be advised. While there I flew an aircraft called a Snargasher, which was a twin-engine Ab Initio aeroplane. ECFS was a very great learning centre as far as I was concerned.
>
> I also specialised on Blind Approach flying and I qualified as a Blind Approach Instructor, which I regarded as a very important asset for my own flying.
>
> There were two of us from Fighter Command, two from Bomber Command, two from Coastal Command, all ex-operational pilots, and we had to give presentations of our experience. I had probably the best report that I ever had in the RAF from the chief ground instructor A C Kermode who later became an Air Vice-Marshal in the Royal Air Force as Director of Education. He wrote: 'Flight Lieutenant Brown has learned a great deal from the course and in return has made his own contribution'.
>
> In all my experience in Flying Training Command I felt that there was a barrier between instructors and staff who had not done operational flying and pilots that had. It never came to the surface, but it seemed to me that that there would be some difficulty for an ex-operational pilot to achieve success in Flying Training Command. It may have been simply that ex-operational pilots had a more relaxed attitude to life and did not relate easily to the different disciplines.
>
> At the end of the course I was posted to 56 Operational Training Unit at Tealing on 16th October 1942, which was north of Dundee in Scotland. It was equipped with Hurricanes, but I didn't find that a problem. I had not flown a Hurricane before but I soon realised that it was ideal for fighter training. We carried out standard OTU courses there. The only problem was we had a hill about 1,000 feet high near the end of the runway but while I was there everybody managed to avoid it.
>
> There was however, one incident while I was there that I was involved with. One day I was cycling round the perimeter track

near the end of the runway, when a Hawker Hurricane aircraft overshot, carried on into a ploughed field and turned upside down. I was at the aircraft within seconds, but the pilot was unconscious. The only people nearby were some farm labourers and I realised we had to get the pilot out immediately in case the aircraft caught fire. I could see that the cockpit hood was open and so I explained to the farm labourers who had come over to help, how to lift up the wing to shoulder height, to allow me enough room to crawl in and release the trapped pilot. I am totally claustrophobic and hammered home to them that even if the earth moved, they had to hold up the wing until we were out, otherwise we would be flattened. When I reached the cockpit, the pilot was still unconscious. I carefully released his Sutton harness, then his parachute. One of his feet was trapped in the rudder bar and I had to undo his shoe in order to release his foot. With some strenuous effort I managed to get him out of the cockpit and clear of the wing with great relief. The RAF ambulance soon arrived with a fire tender and the pilot was taken to the local hospital. I resumed my cycle ride to my flight dispersal. All RAF cycles had a built-in head wind.

The following morning I received a telephone call from the wife of the pilot who was a student flight lieutenant. She asked me if I was Flight Lieutenant Brown, who had pulled her husband out of the crashed aircraft. With an inner glow I said 'Yes I am'. And she replied 'Good, what have you done with his other shoe in the cockpit?'

After she had hung up the telephone, I consoled myself by saying, 'Well shoes are expensive and clothing coupons are in short supply.' Her husband was not seriously hurt and soon recovered.

After I had been at Tealing for a couple of months I was transferred to the satellite airfield at Kinnell on 19th December. Kinnell was halfway between Tealing and Montrose and was situated out in the wilds. This is where we had our gunnery squadron where pilots practiced deflection firing at target drogues off the coast. I spent several months there as part of the air-firing training squadron.

Nothing outstanding happened there, except that on one occasion after I had got to know the people in the village I was invited to a séance. Out of curiosity I attended and in the half darkened parlour, with perhaps about six of the villagers sitting in a semicircle, the elderly lady medium said that somebody had come to see me and to show himself to me. I was very surprised but slowly this woman changed, quite visibly, into somebody I had known. It was in fact Pilot Officer Pollard of 611 Squadron who had been shot down and killed in 1941, and who had been my buddy in the squadron. I wasn't expecting to see anyone in particular, but he was as close and as clear as though he were alive in the room.

On 21st July 1943, I then had an unusual posting. I was sent to the RAF College at Cranwell, for special duties. This was for the training of Turkish pilots to become operationally trained Spitfire pilots, and we were formed into a special unit for this purpose. Another flight lieutenant was responsible for ground training and I ran the flying programme. The first course was very good indeed; I felt the pilots could have taken their place in any RAF fighter squadron after they had finished the course. I was also somewhat surprised to learn that at the same time Turkish pilots were being trained in Germany to fly Me109s.

At the end of the second course on 1st January 1944, Peter's promotion to squadron leader came through and he was then sent to the School for Flying Instructors at Montrose in Scotland. Although he was a qualified single-engine instructor he was required to qualify as a twin-engine instructor on Oxfords. After completion of the course he was posted to an airfield at Fraserborough on the northeast coast of Scotland, a satellite of No.14 Advanced Flying Unit at Banff:

My appointment was as squadron leader flying, but I was also the commanding officer of the satellite airfield. The unit was equipped with twin-engine Oxfords that were established training aircraft. I had excellent flight commanders working with me and apart from the east wind blowing hard and permanently it was quite a pleasant station. I was re-assessed as a flying instructor and awarded an A2 classification.

Reorganisations were taking place in Training Command, and some months later I was posted to Dallachy, which was the other satellite airfield of the parent station doing the same sort of job. The main hazard in these areas was the weather because of the surrounding hills and mountains. If I say that nothing very traumatic happened at AFUs it is because that was one of the main targets of the training programme. This low accident rate discipline may however have been be related to the very high accident rate at OTUs where the casualties in men and machines were so much more costly. During this time, I attended a Junior Commanders Course, basically on Royal Air Force Administration, and managed to achieve top place.

Further changes were occurring at Training Command and units were being closed or moved. 14 AFU was closed down as a training unit at Banff on 1st September 1944, to be replaced by Coastal Command attack squadrons. I was posted as Squadron Leader Flying to No. 9 AFU for Royal Navy airmen, at Erroll, a few miles from Perth and on the edge of the River Tay, which passed Dundee on its way to the sea.

We were equipped with Harvards, which I hadn't flown before. While I liked nearly every other aeroplane I had flown, I was unimpressed with the Harvard. It had a tendency to have carburettor problems, and carelessness in landing could result in ground looping. Worst of all for a training aircraft was that it had very bad spinning characteristics. When you put it into a spin and

then took the correct recovery nothing happened for some seconds
and you began to wonder whether you had done the right thing.
Then suddenly without warning it would stop spinning but unless
you were quick it would immediately spin in the opposite direction.
If you caught it in time you successfully recovered from the spin. I
thought this was a serious defect in a training aircraft.

A significant part of my work there was to test borderline pilots,
when the flight commanders were not really sure whether they
should be passed or taken off the course. So I had many flights at
night sitting well up in the back seat of a Harvard, probably in wet
weather. I would be desperately trying to keep a close eye on the
runway lights but at the same time allowing the pilot to go as close
to mutual destruction as possible in order to give him every chance.
I had to be ready to take over in the last second should it not work
out properly.

As the station was so near to the sea, it was decided that a Walrus
seaplane should be added to the inventory for air-sea rescue
purposes. This duly arrived under the charge of Flying Officer
Boddy, so naturally as Squadron Leader Flying I decided that I
should be the first person qualified to fly the Walrus. We took off
from the runway and Boddy did the first landing on the River Tay,
a fast flowing tidal river, with no problems. He then said to me; 'OK
you take over and take off'. But when I tried to taxi into position for
the take-off, the Walrus wouldn't move. Boddy said; 'you had better
go out onto the wing and see if we are caught up somewhere'.
Nervously climbing out on to the lower wing, I looked down and to
my horror I could see sand. We were stuck on a sandbank with the
tide going out fast and weren't going to get off. There was nothing
we could do about it except wait until the tide came in. After many
hours waiting and walking on the sandbank, anxious about dusk
coming up, we were afloat again. After a pause to ensure adequate
depth of water I started the engine by the hand crank and we were
soon back on the runway with very red faces.

With further reorganisation taking place the unit was then
moved south to No. 5 AFU Atcham near Shrewsbury to carry on
with the training programme. As by then the war in Europe had
finished the trainee pilots felt that they had little chance of
operational flying, and my major task was to keep them occupied
and keep up their morale.

At the beginning of August 1945, Peter Brown received notice of a posting to
the Far East to join a glider wing to take part in the operations against the
Japanese. In most actions of the war, glider wings suffered very high
casualties. A few days later an official message was received that the
Americans had dropped atomic bombs on the Japanese and that they had
surrendered:

This was wonderful news for me. As the satellite commander, I felt
we should celebrate and we had a very great party that night.

I then had to make a decision about my future. The RAF had been advising that a number of permanent commissions were to be awarded and applications were requested. I duly applied. They then published the first names of those who had been awarded the commissions, all of whom had numerous decorations and I had none. I realised my chances of getting a permanent commission were remote. I therefore decided to leave the service and start a new life and career in the civilian world. I little realised how difficult this would prove to be.

On 1st January 1946, I received in the post my Air Force Cross, which was awarded to me for my intensive and extensive work in training in many aspects of RAF flying and particularly with the Turkish pilots.

On demobilisation, Peter aged 26 was sent to the Demobilisation Group Centre on 26th November 1945 where he could be fitted out with a suit, or sports coat and trousers to wear for his entry back into civilian life. To Peter's horror, the authorities would not let him go through the demobilisation process without him first handing over his flying logbooks. Official instructions were that all logbooks were to be handed in. The fact that Peter was still a reserve RAF officer made no difference. So Peter decided to hide his first logbook, which by a miracle covered his flying up till the end of October 1940, which was the end of the Battle of Britain. After the war, RAF officers were awarded gratuities, which were based on the length of service and rank. Peter was given the grand sum of £300, which by today's standards would be about £15,000. He remembers his early days back in civilian life and his attempt to carve out a new career:

It seemed quite lot of money, but I had a wife and two children to keep. I then made the decision that I would go into the plastics industry and applied to attend a three months course on plastics that was just starting. This meant that the gratuity could be used to keep the family going while I was studying. At the same time they were also running evening classes in first year plastics technology and a second year in plastics technology, so I did both of these at the same time. For some three months, I was doing plastic technology from early in the morning until late at night, five nights a week, writing up my notes at the weekend. My hard work paid off and I was awarded the Bronze Medal First Prize in the Plastics Technology Examination. As a result of this, I was recommended for a job as an assistant editor of the industry journal called *British Plastics*, part of the Iliffe Group. The editor was a wonderful man who had served in the Royal Air Force in WWI, and the senior assistant editor had an MA from Cambridge. With his help I acquired a knowledge and a love of the English language which I had not had before, which I cherish to this day, and has been so useful to me in my later life.

It was a developing industry in 1946; it had just started to grow. Everything was new, new inventions, new developments, and new technology and so I was in the Plastics Industry right at the beginning. After three years I had an opportunity to join the Distillers Company in their plastics and chemicals division on the marketing side in London, and this seemed to me to bring a better long-term opportunity than as an assistant editor. So I joined the company and after a year the managing director rightly decided that I was far more interested in technical matters than straight selling and so I was appointed Technical Manager of the group. I had to build up a team and I travelled around the country calling on companies that had trouble either with our material or their plants. I also had control of large laboratories down in South Wales and so I was involved with a great deal of technological research. As a result of this and the papers I presented, the Plastics Institute awarded me their Fellowship, which was rather unusual because the normal route was first of all a degree and then an Associateship, and finally a Fellowship by nomination. With later American takeovers during 1970, I moved to an independent materials handling group in the north of England.

This was again a time when new things were happening and after being a general manager I was given the task of setting up an industrial mail order business, which was fully computerised and I believe was one of the first to be so in England. We made a significant profit in the first year. What seemed to help enormously was the postcode, which the Post Office set up and was unable to use themselves for several years for general mail, but was absolutely invaluable for mail order businesses. I was given the task of specialising in the legal aspects of the business and the acquisition of new companies. I went out to America, to Chicago, to look at a company and having recommended that we should buy it, I was then advised that I would be running it as its President for the next two years. This was totally unexpected, but I loved it. It was absolutely traumatic, there was drama every day. Chicago was certainly larger than life; but it was a very great experience and I wouldn't have missed it. But as Churchill once said, I wouldn't go through it again.

After my two years, I then handed over to a younger man, came back to England and decided to take early retirement. Having retired I then set up as a management consultant advising on new and existing businesses and particularly on commercial litigation. Although not legally qualified, my experience was such that I was able to call in the solicitors and barristers only when they were needed. I never lost a case, I didn't win them all, but on the other hand I always managed to settle outside of court if we weren't going to win. After ten years as a management consultant I decided that it was time to retire.

Six years ago I met Richard Smith, the author of this book and a friendship started which has continued to strengthen throughout the following years. Richard knew of my very great interest in the Big Wing controversy and the Battle of Britain and has given me many opportunities of publishing and lecturing on my special views. I have one ambition left and that is to complete the work I started six years ago. This is the book called *Honour Restored* in which I will expose and present all the evidence that Air Chief Marshal Sir Hugh Dowding was unfairly and disgracefully dismissed by very senior officers in the Royal Air Force. In 1997, I presented a thesis on the subject at the Purfleet Heritage Centre. I hope that I am granted the time to see that the book is finished and published.

Peter is a very modest person but his story would not be complete without mentioning the help he has given many people over the years with the amazing gift that he possesses, the gift of healing:

It would not be possible to talk about my life without referring to the fact that more than 20 years ago I was given the gift of healing. One day I found that I was able to put my hands on someone in pain and that the pain could be eased especially from certain ailments that doctors were not very good at handling. For four to five years of my life I worked in the second largest hospice in the country, giving healing and comfort to the terminally ill patients, not that I could heal their cancer, but I could help them to die with dignity, which is what hospices are all about. I also gave healing to the nurses, who permanently suffer from bad backs from lifting patients who can't help themselves.

I was there as a member of the caring team, accepted by the Matron, the GP doctors, and the nursing staff. I have given healing to hundreds and in fact thousands of people over the years without charge. I like to feel that it is one of the contributions that I have been specially privileged to make in my life. It doesn't need any religious faith or belief, it is not available only to any one sect, it is just a gift that I was given and which I have passed on to people of all creeds, races and colours without distinction.

Apart from his gift of healing, which he has undoubtedly used to the benefit of many, Peter's own hobbies over the years when time allows have included playing sports such as squash and badminton, which he continued to play until a back operation forced him to retire from playing at the age of sixty-five. His other favourite pastimes include: listening to music and playing the piano, painting in oils, collecting paintings and antiques and reading which is Peter's passion with a collection of over 2,000 books, some of which he has read several times. Today, Peter Brown spends much of his time lecturing and writing about the Battle of Britain and specifically the 'Big Wing' controversy. He has lectured at various schools and museums, where captivated audiences of varied ages listen to a man who knows his subject extremely well. His reward? To know that future generations will understand the sacrifice that his generation made to the world over those few months during the summer of 1940. At the age of 83 years, Peter still retains his zest and enthusiasm for knowledge and life. I am honoured to know Peter Brown as one of Churchill's 'Few,' as a historian and researcher and as a special friend.

CHAPTER 2

AN AMERICAN EAGLE
Flight Lieutenant William 'Tex' Ash MBE

During the year of 1939, the United States of America was a neutral country in an ever-increasingly hostile world. But a few individual brave Americans at that time felt that they could no longer stand by and watch as Nazi domination began to take hold over Europe. These few adventurous souls packed up their belongings and headed across the American border into Canada to join the Royal Canadian Air Force. Many would join the famous Royal Air Force 'Eagle' squadrons and some would later rejoin their own United States Army Air Force, when America entered the Second World War in December 1941. One of these young men was 'Tex' Ash. This is his story.

William Franklin 'Tex' Ash was born in Dallas, Texas, on 30th November 1917, the only son of William Ash and Margaret Porterfield. Two years later the family was enlarged with the birth of a daughter, Adele.

His father was a travelling salesman who made his living by selling women's hats and he had to travel considerable distances around the states of Texas, Oklahoma and Kansas, to earn enough to keep the family fed. It was also a desperate time in America with a depression looming just over the horizon; times were tough, but they were about to get even tougher.

At the age of eight, William would often accompany his father on his business trips helping to carry some of the boxes of goods from their vehicle to the stores, in towns like Waco and Muskogee. Many a time after a long journey, his father would come away without making a sale, having nothing to show for all his efforts.

The family home was never a fixed one, always changing from a succession of apartments or small houses, living in whatever they could afford at that time. William's education was obviously affected during this period, and it was as a temporary pupil at a school in San Antonio that he first tried to settle in. His main recollection during this time, was the amount of school fights one had to try and avoid during the school-lunch period. Not being of an aggressive nature, William found the prospect of having to fight other boys quite disconcerting. His first real school was the James Bowie Grammar School in Oak Cliff, situated in a residential part of Dallas. The school was named after the famous frontiersman and Indian fighter, who had made a last historic stand at the Alamo mission during the State's fight for independence against Mexico; he was also famous for the large hunting knife which bore his name.

Once William had started on the road of education there was no holding him back. His mother was also a great influence and helped coach him after school in English grammar. For the next few years, he would receive various merits and even a scholarship award for his outstanding academic skills from Dallas's largest jewellers Everts and Linz, who held an annual Encouragement of Academic Achievement Competition. He also excelled on the sporting front, picking up awards for swimming, fencing and horseshoe pitching.

Because the family's income was never able to rely on a steady weekly pay cheque, the young Ash decided it was time at the age of ten to broaden his horizons and earn some money for himself. He undertook work by himself to wash cars, do yard work and sell newspapers and magazines in the lobby of the Medical Arts Building. It was with the money he saved from these various jobs, that he hoped to pay his way through college. In fact, he eventually collected over several hundred dollars. Unfortunately, he would lose some of his money, when a family friend convinced them to invest in shares on the stock market. Soon after, the infamous Stock Market Crash of 1928 happened and young William lost two hundred of his hard-earned dollars.

It was a tough lesson to learn, but did not hinder his dream of reaching college. His education continued through Highland Park High School until he was selected to attend the University of Texas. Once there, he continued to support himself, at one time having four jobs at once; these included writing essays for other students, and organising a social register for the more prominent scholars for which he would charge five dollars. During the summer break, he would often travel to New Mexico with a friend, whose parents owned a small cabin in a place named Ruidoso. The cabin was situated near the Mescalera Apache reservation; and this is where William's fondness and imagination of the old west was allowed to run wild. He visited the Lincoln County Jail, from which Billy the Kid had made his escape, the walls still marked with bullet holes from that fateful day. Indeed, he would later recall, that during this time he had met and talked with an elderly gentleman, who had told him stories of the Kid. This kindly old man had been one of the Coe brothers, either Frank or George, who had ridden with William Bonny alias Billy the Kid, during the Lincoln County range war and had his trigger finger shot off.

Back at the university, his educational career was to follow a series of ups and downs. The first three years, he achieved A grades, and was one of the youngest students to receive an honorary scholarship award. He afterwards took the award, a golden key, to a pawnshop and with the money received, used it to buy his sister and himself breakfast for a whole month. The following term, for some reason, he failed to pass on any exam taken. But by the end of four years at the university, he had majored in English, classical languages, literature and philosophy.

After graduating, he worked for a short while at the Republic National Bank in Dallas, serving behind the cash desk, but his restless spirit got the better of him and he set out, drifting around various American states for a few months. He would make his way by jumping freight trains or thumbing lifts. On arriving in Kansas City, he managed to find employment with the man's furnishing department of Emery Bird Thayers, but his stay with them was short and he was sacked due to inexperience.

With the coming of war in Europe in September 1939, and after viewing many cinema newsreels of the Nazi mistreatment of the Jews, Tex decided he could not sit on the sideline in America and not help in some way. So he decided to enlist by crossing the border into Canada, to join the Royal Canadian Air Force. He arrived at Windsor, Ontario, but was told by the medical officer at the recruiting centre that he was underweight and to come back when he had gained the extra pounds needed. Undeterred, he travelled back to Detroit and spent the next couple of weeks eating as much weight-gaining food that his body could hold. One month later, back in Ontario, he weighed enough to be selected for aircrew training. From Ontario, he was then sent to be kitted out at the Eglinton Hunt Club in Toronto; while here he also undertook the usual basic air force square bashing and discipline.

Several weeks later, he returned to Windsor to start the elementary flying course at the training school. The first aircraft that he would learn on was a small biplane called a Fleet Finch. After many weeks of training he finally went solo and was sent to the Royal Canadian Air Force Station at Kingston to continue his service training.

The station was mainly staffed by Royal Air Force personnel, and the aircraft consisted of Fairey Battle fighter-bombers, which had even by that stage of the war become obsolete, being underpowered and out-gunned by the enemy fighters in Europe. The other aircraft at the base were North American Harvards which were used for aerobatic training. They were rugged aircraft and had the excellent Pratt and Whitney radial piston engine rated at 600 horsepower.

After completing the training, he was awarded his wings badge and commissioned as a pilot officer. Soon afterwards, he boarded a troop ship and set sail for England and on arrival was sent to the main RAF personnel depot at Uxbridge.

A week later, he was posted to an operational training unit at Hawarden in Wales, where he continued his flying instruction on Miles Master aircraft. After completing the course on the trainer, the next big step was to fly the RAF fighters, either the Hawker Hurricane or the Vickers-Supermarine Spitfire. For Tex it was to be the Spitfire. He recalls:

> I well remember my first close sight of a Spitfire. It was so much smaller than I expected. Particular features were the gracefully curved elliptical wing and the long nose accommodating such a powerful in-line engine. The Spitfire had no bad habits that I ever discovered. Even throttled back to 140 mph on the clock it simply mushed down through the air on an even keel. The dihedral made it possible to side slip almost like a biplane, so that one could do nice tight landing circuits just outside the aerodrome perimeter, slipping off height with a clear view of the field, unobstructed by the nose of the aircraft and straightening out the moment before touch down.

After completion at the Operational Training Unit, Tex was posted to an RAF squadron in 11 Group, No.234, but almost immediately his posting was changed, to join a new Royal Canadian Air Force squadron, 411 which was forming at Digby in Lincolnshire and nicknamed 'Grizzly Bear'. Once the squadron had been given operational status, its main role at that time was the unglamorous duty of convoy patrols, protecting the vessels as they sailed up and down the east coast of Britain. A few of the pilots in the squadron Tex had previously known during his training days in Canada; one of them was a chap named Robert 'Buck' McNair who would later distinguish himself as an ace in action over Malta. Tex remembers one incident with McNair while at Digby:

> I was flying back to Digby in the squadron's Miles Magister, with 'Buck' as a passenger. He then suddenly decided to try and find out what it would be like to use a parachute. I said to him I was against this idea, as it would look like a reflection on my flying capabilities. We both then wrestled with the double controls, as I decided to try to land and he tried to gain more height, so that he could jump. He dropped out and landed safely. He then immediately put in a claim for a Caterpillar award, the award given to pilots whose lives had been saved by use of a parachute. He claimed that a landing with me at the controls of the aeroplane had represented a dire threat to his life.

Settling in to the Officers' Mess, Tex was told one day to make a trip into Lincoln; the reason was to purchase some gramophone records for the Mess and to liven the place up. A few hours later, he came back having purchased Bach's *Toccata in C* and other classical pieces by Mozart, Beethoven and Brahms. The other members of the squadron were not impressed at all, and Tex was accused of misuse of communal funds to satisfy his own musical tastes. He ended up taking all of the recordings back to his own room, where he listened to them on his own portable wind-up machine.

The squadron received its marching orders during November 1941; it would move south to 11 Group. On 22nd November, therefore 411 led by Squadron Leader Paul Brooks Pitcher, flew down to RAF Hornchurch in Essex to start offensive sweeps.

On 14th January 1942, the squadron was up early as usual for early morning readiness. The early morning ritual of being woken by the batman with a cup of hot tea, getting into flying kit and then walking in the cold morning air over to dispersal still half asleep was not agreeable to every pilot, but everyone had a job to do and they got on with it. Tex was scheduled that morning for the first patrol with A Flight. They were scrambled, but then ordered back to land before sighting any enemy aircraft. Convoy patrols took place during the rest of the morning. Pilot Officer Sills reported he had seen a Junkers Ju88 some 5,000 feet above him during one of the patrols; he gave chase but lost the German in the clouds.

During the afternoon A Flight consisting of Flight Lieutenant Boomer, Pilot Officer Sills, Sergeant Gridley and Tex took off on a Rhubarb sortie over France. Taking off from Hornchurch at 3.00 pm, they stopped at Manston briefly; they then crossed the Channel at low level going into France east of Dunkirk. After crossing the coast, they headed for the canals around Furnes. Here the section split into two, Red section with Flight Lieutenant Boomer leading followed closely by Tex. They whizzed low and fast along a canal, shooting-up goods barges along the way. Returning to the coast, they saw some 100 German troops on the beach, so Flight Lieutenant Boomer sprayed them with machine-gun fire causing casualties. At that moment a German anti-aircraft flak ship, which was moored off the coast opened fire on the two Spitfires. Tex peeled off to attack the ship, but was hit by the light flak, which caused some very minor damage to his port wing root. He managed to get in a long burst of fire with his cannon along the bridge house of the vessel, causing damage. The two Spitfires then headed out over the Channel and for home. Tex landed back at Hornchurch with a few holes in his aircraft to show for his efforts, but he was otherwise unhurt. During this time, the two other Spitfires of Yellow section had managed to shoot up barges, canal locks and some gun emplacements. They too returned safely back to Hornchurch. Tex recalls his early days at the airfield:

> The accommodation at RAF Hornchurch was rather good. I started out being billeted in the Officers' Mess, but soon afterwards I managed to get a room of my own in the married quarters block. Here I had a very nice room and bath all to myself. As I liked listening to classical music, I could crank up the old gramophone player without disturbing my mates who preferred other types of music.

The squadron's next busy day came on 28th February 1942. During the morning the pilots carried out their normal routine of convoy patrols, but during the late afternoon, six of 411's aircraft were scrambled to protect aircraft and boats of the Air Sea Rescue Service, who were picking up pilots and returning commandos who had made a landing in France and destroyed a radio location station earlier in the morning.

During the operation while twenty miles off Manston, Flight Sergeant R.H. Gridley somehow collided with Squadron Leader R.B. Newton's Spitfire; the collision tore part of the squadron commander's port main plane out, as well as leaving a large gap in the fuselage behind the cockpit causing the wireless equipment to drop out. Endeavouring to bale out, Newton could not release his canopy and only when just above sea level did he manage to regain control of his aircraft.

Escorted by Pilot Officer Green, he managed to fly the Spitfire back to Manston, where he crash-landed uninjured. No hope was held out for Sergeant Gridley; two of the pilots had seen his aircraft go into the Channel, but did not see Gridley bale out. He was reported as killed and his wife who lived outside the airfield was informed by the Padre of the accident.

Fortunately, while the squadron adjutant Flight Lieutenant R.N. Whalley was busy compiling the casualty list, a signal came through that Sergeant Gridley had been picked up by a rescue boat from Dover and was only slightly injured. He had been taken to Ramsgate hospital suffering from shock and exposure.

Meanwhile, on returning Tex found he had a problem with his Spitfire and decided to land at Manston. Unfortunately, on his approach, he overshot the runway and pranged his aircraft. He ended up by entwining it in the barbed wire at the end of the airfield. Luckily the damage was light and he was unhurt. Such were the day-to-day trials and tribulations of a fighter pilot.

During March 1942, Tex and the squadron were moved down to RAF Southend, one of Hornchurch's satellite airfields. The weather during mid-March was very bad and over the period of the 17th–21st, no flying operations were conducted. Tex remembers the move to the airfield and their new accommodation:

> When we moved down to the satellite aerodrome at Rochford, near Southend, I recall that the new Mess was somebody's old country house and was quite stately. But by the time we had finished using it, I'm afraid it wasn't up to the standard that the owner had left it; especially when the guys would let off a little steam in the evening after flying the day's missions. They even rode a motorbike through the building on one occasion.

On the 19th, Tex along with Squadron Leader Newton, Flight Lieutenant Weston and Flying Officer Curtis were all invited to represent the squadron at the 'Guest Night' held at Hornchurch. The Guest Nights gave the pilots time to relax and mix with other pilots from various squadrons as well as guests invited from the other services, along with wives, girlfriends etc. Unfortunately for Tex, at the last moment he was detailed for duty and his place was taken by Pilot Officer Green; no doubt Tex felt somewhat disappointed at missing the party. However two days later, the squadron held a party in return at Southend, with Group Captain Harry Broadhurst and Wing Commander Peter Powell in attendance with many other guests.

The day of the 24th of March was a black day for both Tex Ash and 411 Squadron. It had started very cold with heavy fog, but by mid morning the weather had cleared rapidly. The squadron was detailed to act as close bomber escort on a sweep to Comines. Ten Spitfires of 411 took off from Hornchurch at 2.35 pm; Tex Ash was among them flying Spitfire AB281. The journey to the target was uneventful apart from the usual German flak. Once over the target the bombers released their bomb load and started to head for home; it was then that 411 was attacked. Yellow section led by Tex broke off away after the Focke-Wulf 190s who had dived away. The Squadron Operations Book reported:

> Yellow Section, P/O Ash, W/O Gridley, Sgt Taylor and Sgt Semple broke into the attackers who dived away. The squadron was forced to slow down in reforming. Shortly after, the whole squadron was forced to break into several enemy aircraft who were attacking from the rear, which put the squadron further behind the Hornchurch Wing. The squadron again attacked and turned sharply to engage the enemy. During individual dogfights P/O Sill's aircraft was hit in the glycol tank and he broke off engagement, diving sharply. The aircraft believed to be P/O Sills's was later seen crossing the French coast at 2,000 feet. He may have force-landed or baled out over France. The aircraft flown by P/O Ash was seen to be hit by fire from an FW190, but no information is available. P/O Sills, P/O Ash and W/O Gridley failed to return.

Of W/O Gridley, nothing is known as each flier was fighting off two enemy planes and had no time for observation. F/Sgt Randell flying as Blue 4 as top escort was separated from the squadron with Blue 3. Blue 4 tried to return to Manston, which was closed in with fog. He tried to make Hornchurch, but due to shortage of petrol, he crash-landed Spitfire AB284 in a field at South Ockendon. Sgt Taylor in Spitfire AB183, landed with a bullet in his leg at Rochford aerodrome (Southend) and overshot his landing; he was not seriously injured. On this day the squadron flew some 20 hours, 35 minutes of flying and claimed three enemy aircraft damaged.

Tex Ash recalls that fateful day:

I did a tight 180-degree turn in time to see a Focke-Wulf 190 going away below me to my right. I then did a three-quarter downward roll to the left and to my delight came out right behind the 190 at a range of about 200 yards. I started firing and kept on firing as I saw the hits from my cannon shells exploding along the wing root of the German. Bits of his engine cowling began to fall away and then he completely disappeared in smoke. I then pulled away and turned back towards our formation, which was already some distance away. I noticed to my left another Spitfire, presumably from my own section; he too was making his way back when I noticed a FW190 closing in on his tail. I shouted a warning to him over the R/T and began to turn towards the 190 myself. I came up on the enemy's beam and began to fire using a deflection shot. I then managed to get astern of him firing again at about 100 yards. Suddenly there was a thump and my guns were not operating anymore. I had been hit! I jerked around in a left hand turn with lots of bottom rudder to slide me out of the enemy's range. I then noticed that the engine was not sounding too good and that the engine revs were dropping and I was losing speed. Suddenly I noticed two FW190s coming in on me from two different directions. I rolled the Spitfire over into a dive, and decided whether to pull the cockpit canopy back and jump. I decided in an instant not too. Jumping out from a great height, I would be seen miles away by any Germans, and on landing I would probably have a German reception party waiting to capture me. I decided to try and force-land my aircraft instead, which if I survived would give me a better chance to remain free and escape.

When I was down to about 10,000 feet, the propeller had more or less stopped. The 190s kept passing by me, trying to finish me off, but they overshot with their greater speed. By the time I was at 1,500 feet I switched off the engine to avoid any fire breaking out. Down below the French fields began to loom up and I searched around and picked a suitable field to land in. I turned my aircraft to the right to avoid a church, which I had suddenly become aware of, then my Spitfire hit the ground, digging in its wingtip and cartwheeling across the field.

After coming to a sudden jerking halt, I was left hanging upside down in my Sutton harness. I released myself and crawled out from my shattered aircraft, which now lay in pieces. One of the wings was practically ripped off and the main fuselage was broken in half, just behind the cockpit. I looked up and saw a lone FW190 fly low over the crash-site of my wrecked Spitfire. I dived under the remains of my aircraft until the enemy aircraft had passed out of sight.

Tex was now alone and lost in occupied France. What was he to do next? Perhaps he could make his way to a friendly village, where contact with the local French resistance might be possible. Or perhaps the Germans were already on their way to the crash-site to capture him, and might only be minutes away. He had to think quickly and precisely on what his next move would be.

It could be a life or death decision. Tex decided to set off down a small narrow French lane, and continued walking until he reached the small village of Vieille Eglise. On entering the village, a small girl of about ten years of age grabbed his hand and led him up into a loft in a barn next to the side of her mother's house. The child's mother arrived and brought him something to eat and also some clothes so he could change out of his RAF uniform. While he was thanking the mother and child, a German patrol entered the village. Tex kissed them both quickly and ran out of the village as the Germans moved in:

> There was not much cover, but there was a little canal, which ran south. I jumped into it and waded along it low enough not to be seen. In my eagerness to get as far away as possible from the Germans, I continued until a very unpleasant smell told me I had wandered into a sewage ditch.
>
> While holding my nose, I opened and checked my RAF escape kit and found that it contained a map of the Pas de Calais, a tiny compass, assorted French money and some Horlicks tablets, one of which I ate. After walking for so long, by dusk I was too tired to carry on any further. In a field there was a haystack, which I thought would be an ideal resting place. I climbed on top and proceeded to crawl in, only to discover it was really a pile of wet manure covered by a few pieces of straw.
>
> I continued to walk all the next day, using some of my French money to cross a large canal by ferry. The following day, I avoided towns and using my map, made my way to an area which was sparsely settled. It was while walking through the village of Quercamps on the third night, that I heard some people singing First World War songs. I decided to take a chance and banged on the window shutters at the side of the building. The occupants came out and once I had established to them that I was a shot-down British pilot, their hospitality could not have been more cordial.

Tex was taken into the kitchen and given an enormous meal and cups of coffee. His host was the owner of a small restaurant. He had fought during the

First War and his left hand had been made useless in the conflict. He had two children, who would warn Tex whenever the Germans would pay a visit to the restaurant. When the Germans were making their searches, the children would lead him in the middle of the night to a large house, which belonged to a local mill owner named Emile Rocourt. Here Tex was hidden down in the cellar.

After a few weeks, a man known only as Monsieur Jean arrived at the restaurant and arranged for Tex to be taken to Lille. On arriving there, Tex was deposited at a safe house; the owner was a widow whose husband had been killed during the first few days of the German invasion. He stayed at the house for a week until Monsieur Jean arrived yet again, with the correct documents to travel to Paris. The trip was uneventful and on arrival, the two of them walked down the Boulevard Sevastopol and even visited Notre Dame Cathedral before Tex was taken to his next hiding place, a flat occupied by a young couple named Josef and Giselle. He would stay at the flat for two months while waiting for the necessary arrangements to be made for him to cross the Pyrenees into neutral Spain.

At dawn, one morning at the beginning of June, the Germans raided the flat. The door was smashed down and Tex and the other two occupants were dragged from their beds. Tex tried to explain that he had only come to the flat a day or so earlier, but before he could continue, he was stopped by a soldier's rifle butt to the face. They were taken to the Gestapo headquarters in Paris and then separated. Tex was then locked in a room in the basement for about one hour, then taken to a room upstairs and placed in front of an interrogator in civilian clothes. He tried to talk to the man in French, but was immediately shouted down and told to speak English. Tex recalls the events that then took place:

> I decided to come clean and told the man behind the desk, who I was. I repeated to him the date and place where I had crashed. He replied, 'It would not prove you were the pilot who had got out of it. You could have been dropped as a spy.'
>
> I replied, that surely the British would not be stupid enough to send in a spy with badly spoken French and no German at all. He said, 'there's only one way that you can prove who you are, and that's to give me the name of every single person you've had any contact with from the time you crashed.' I told him, 'I'm terrible with names.'
>
> The man got up from the desk and called the two soldiers waiting near the door. As the man left the room, one of the soldiers jerked me to my feet and stood behind me holding my arms, while the other hit me in the face with his fist. I turned my head away from the next blow and he then hit me in the stomach. His next punch winded me badly. I was gasping for breath and feeling sick, when he hit me again. The soldier then paused, took out a handkerchief which he bound tightly around his knuckles, and then proceeded to rain a whole series of blows at my jaw, cheek and eye.
>
> I was more or less unconscious, when I was allowed to fall back into the chair. I let my head fall forward till my forehead rested on my arms, doubled across my knees.

I remember lifting my face away from my sleeve and saw that there was rather a lot of blood on it. One of the soldiers pulled my head upright by my hair and I saw that the man who had interrogated me was back in the room. He placed an official looking document in front of my face, but I could not focus very well because one of my eyes was almost completely closed due to the beating. The man said it was from the Kommandantura and that it said, that if the person calling himself William Ash fails to provide satisfactory proof of his identity, he will be executed by firing squad at 6.00 am on June 4th. I replied. 'What's today?' 'June 3rd.'

After several more questions, Tex was taken back to the cell by the soldiers and left to ponder on his situation. The next day dawned, but it was not until noon that he was given any food, a hunk of black bread and some sauerkraut soup. Soon afterwards he was once again taken up to the interrogator, who started the procedure all over again. After yet another beating, Tex was again taken back to his room. His beating had left him unable to walk and with great pain on one side, where the blows had landed just over one of his kidneys. He managed to lie on the makeshift bed although badly bruised, and fell asleep.

This torture went on for about ten days, as far as Tex can remember, until one evening, there seemed to be a loud commotion going on outside his cell door. This turned out to be an argument between a Luftwaffe officer and the Gestapo. The Luftwaffe officer was tearing the interrogator off a strip, for not informing him of the captured RAF pilot. The officer insisted that he talk to the prisoner and after a few telephone calls to other military departments, Tex was escorted from his cell and taken by the officer and two Luftwaffe airmen to the nearest railway station. His destination, Germany.

After a long and tiring journey, the train finally arrived at Frankfurt. Here Tex was sent to a holding camp for captured air force officers, known as a Dulag Luft. On arrival, he was given an official Red Cross card to fill in, with details of his rank etc; this would be passed on and would inform the RAF and his family that he was still alive. It was here that he met another fellow pilot, Dublin-born Patrick 'Paddy' Barthropp. Paddy had been shot down on 17th May, while flying with 122 Squadron, who were also based at Hornchurch. He had been shot down over Audruicq, near St Omer, by Focke-Wulf 190s, while on escort patrol covering a raid by Douglas Boston DB.7 bombers.

Soon after, Tex, Barthropp and others were sent to Stalag Luft III at Sagan, where they found other well-known RAF prisoners of war, Norman Ryder, Roger Bushell, Robert Stanford Tuck and Douglas Bader. Tex reflects on the one-man war that Bader carried on against his jailers:

He regarded the Germans' insistence on taking his artificial legs away from him, when he was first captured, as a personal act of war. They did this to try and stop his escape attempts. From that time on, he never missed an opportunity to barrack or insult and torment them. They finally decided they had had enough of him and several months after I arrived, they finally removed him from the camp and sent him to Colditz Castle. We watched him as he was led through the gates, and we all jeered at the Germans.

When Tex first arrived at the camp, he found that they were not receiving any Red Cross parcels and so they had to survive on the slim rations supplied by the Germans. He was forced once again to make do with what was available, as he remembers:

> I suppose I was lucky, thanks to my teenage training during the depression years, in making do with what was available. I could eat anything – even the green, runny foul-smelling cheese, which turned most people's stomachs. The Germans also served up a rare delicacy called Klip Fish; this was a dehydrated food used in the First World War and was now dug up to serve as prison food in this war. It looked like wood shavings, but after soaking it in water it acquired the consistency and odour of wet dog hair and you could then fry it. I used to go around the huts with a basket and collect bushels of the stuff.

It was at this camp that Tex would meet another ex-Hornchurch flier, Pilot Officer William Stapleton. They struck up a friendship and they remain close friends still today. Stapleton had been shot down over Dunkirk on 2nd June 1940 while flying with 41 Squadron. Bill Stapleton recollects their time at the camp:

> I met 'Tex' as he was called throughout his time in the prison camp, in the east compound of Stalag Luft III, Sagan in Germany. I had been a PoW for well over two years, when Tex joined us. We lived in 'syndicates' of about sixteen in one room, sleeping in three-tier bunks. Tex and I were in different huts but, even then, we did meet and occasionally chat. Circuit bashing, or walking round and round the compound perimeter for hours on end, was occupational therapy and afforded the opportunity of mixing with others not of one's own particular fraternity.
>
> Life as a prisoner of war is not a pretty one; considerable self-discipline is required to combat the onset of self-pitying depression. Tex impressed me with his quite reasoned attitude towards most questions. Undoubtedly a well-read, cultured individual he was altogether different from the few Americans flying with the RAF that we had already come across. They were in the main, gung-ho fighter pilots, as brave and as dedicated as Tex, but not in the same league intellectually. Throughout our time together I cannot remember when I saw Tex Ash in any mood other than one of extreme optimism. He was a 'big' person with a very 'big' mind.

During his first few weeks at the camp, he was introduced to the escape committee. They had to give their overall approval to any escape ideas, before the plans could be put into operation. The senior officer at this time was Lieutenant Commander Buckley. Tex and Paddy Barthropp went before the committee with their own idea of a plan. This was to hide in the Vorlager shower hut after the weekly wash, and lift the small trap door, which led to the small compartment, which housed the stopcocks for the water supply. While this was being done the main bath party would somehow manage to arrange for the German prisoner count to be correct, so nobody would be missing. They would then emerge from the shower at night and only have one fence to cut. Tex recalls:

> We were kitted out with a compass, a rough map of the area and most important of all, 'the mixture', a concoction of chocolate and cereal which was supplied to those about to make an official escape. The truth of the matter was that getting our hands on some of the 'mixture' was a vital consideration for us. On the day of the escape, it did not prove possible to fix the count. Paddy and I, hiding in our tiny chamber underneath the shower room, were soon aware of the searching Alsatian dogs and their prison guards, blowing whistles and dashing around looking for us. They were bound to find us and it was only a question of whether we would be able to finish off the 'chocolate mixture' between us to keep it from falling into enemy hands. Soon after, the trap door of our hide was flung open and looking up at the guards who were pointing their rifles at us, were two grinning chocolate-smeared faces. We were hauled up and marched off to spend time in the cooler.

After his time in solitary, Tex along with Bill Stapleton, Paddy Barthropp and others, was then sent to another camp, which was situated at Schubin in Poland. This camp was not under the control of the Luftwaffe, but the Wehrmacht (German Army). While here, Tex tried a number of escape attempts that were unsuccessful, but there was one, which almost worked.

The prisoners had dug a tunnel, which started from one of the camp latrines. This ran for more than one hundred yards under a potato patch and past the camp wire. Over fifty prisoners escaped, Tex being one of them. Hundreds of German troops were tied up combing the area for several weeks trying to round up the escapees.

Tex was on the run for almost a week before being recaptured in a small town named Hohensalza. He was then returned to Schubin for another spell of solitary confinement. While there, Tex witnessed the brutality of the Nazi regime, when looking out of his cell window one day:

> Conditions in my cell were bad enough, but looking out of my cell window one day, I saw twenty or thirty German soldiers and Volk Deutcher armed with whips. They were herding up some two hundred Polish women of all ages along the road and sending them to the railway station. They were loaded up in cattle trucks and sent to the Ost front, for the use of the German troops. This was the first time I had actually seen it happening. It made me so furious I thought I would choke.
>
> I started screaming abuse at the men with the whips. After a while the guards came rushing into my cell and pulled me away from the window by smashing my hands with their rifle butts. Afterwards they boarded up the window, so I could not see out at all.

Tex and other air force escapees were eventually sent back to Stalag Luft III, where now there was also an American compound set up. Rumour around the camp spread that sergeant pilots were going to be sent to a camp in Lithuania. Tex decided that it might be an easy place to try another escape attempt. He persuaded a New Zealand sergeant pilot named Don Fair, to exchange identity. Fair took his place among the officers, while Tex started on his journey to the camp at Hydekrug in Lithuania.

At this camp another tunnel was excavated and an escape attempted. Forty prisoners were selected for the attempt, but on the night only twenty managed to break free before the guards discovered the escape hole outside the perimeter of the camp. Tex was among the twenty that did manage to get out. He takes up the story:

> I went bounding along in that excess of energetic excitement that one feels on finding oneself outside the wires or walls. There can be no sense of freedom like the first few minutes of a prison break. For several days I kept going east across low, marshy ground avoiding the more treacherous areas by plotting a course that took me wherever cows were grazing.
>
> I was a bit confused about how I was going to get back to England. I should have headed westward for the port of Memel. There I could have tried to stow away on a neutral ship. Instead, I headed east, stopping at a broken down farm where the peasants provided me with something to eat and drink. I stayed with them for a few weeks.

Tex then decided to make his next move. He would have to find a small boat to try and make his way to Sweden. He came across some boathouses on a river, but found that getting one of the boats out was too difficult. He had noticed some men working on a nearby vegetable garden and called out to them to help give him a hand with the boat. Unfortunately, they turned out to be German soldiers in work clothes. He was quickly over-powered and then taken by car to a Gestapo office in Hydekrug.

After more interrogation and the threat once again of being shot, the Gestapo quickly received information about the identity of their prisoner from Stalag Luft III. Sent back to Luft III, he spent a longer than usual time in solitary. Fortunately he was allowed to read in the cell and a number of books had arrived, which he devoured including the complete works of Plato in French.

It was during this time that the famous escape from Stalag Luft III took place. In all seventy prisoners managed to break free before the tunnel was discovered. Paddy Barthropp was among the intended prisoners to escape, but was found before he could climb out. The escapees managed to remain free for a few days, but all of them except three, who evaded capture, were rounded up.

On the direct orders of Hitler, the Gestapo murdered fifty of the prisoners. The men shot included: Roger Bushell, Kirby-Green and Cross, and a few others whom Tex had known well. Wing Commander 'Paddy' Barthropp DFC comments:

Tex was one of the great escapers of World War 2; he never gave up trying. We had both escaped together twice, the last time at Oflag XXI B in Poland, but we didn't make it home. When he eventually returned home he was awarded an MBE, it should have been the Military Cross or Distinguished Service Order (or both) especially after the hard time he had with the Krauts in Paris.

With the Germans in full retreat on both western and eastern fronts, the prisoners' hopes for a quick ending of the war were uppermost in their thoughts.

But during the winter of 1944-45, the Germans decided to move the PoWs and began marching them into central Germany, away from the advancing Allies. Tex and his comrades were ordered into line, with guards on either side of the column and began their trek through the deep snow. On the first day they reached the town of Muskau, and here he met up again with his friend Barthropp. They were then herded aboard railway trucks and eventually arrived at a prison camp, which was situated between Bremen and Hamburg. Tex was now the worse for wear, suffering from jaundice. He was left behind at the camp, while most of the other prisoners were sent north to a camp named Marlag. A few weeks later, with the British advancing on all fronts, a battle developed near to the camp. Tex remembers:

I watched as the white-clad German soldiers from a mountain division began to ring the camp with their 88mm self-propelled artillery guns. They were preparing to engage the Guards Armoured Brigade which was advancing up from the south.

They no doubt hoped that the advancing British would not fire at them for fear of hitting the camp. Unfortunately for them, this was not to be and the battle began.

We moved the sick and injured to a fairly safe part of the compound and then I slipped through the wire to escape for the last time. On reaching our lines, I was able to assist the Armoured Brigade by helping them to pinpoint the location of several Tiger tanks.

A week or so later, I and many others were assembled on Luneberg Heath to be flown back to Britain. We were then sent to hotels on the south coast and given all the food we could eat until we resumed our normal size and shape. Some months later, a large brown envelope was sent to me. It contained my dossier from Stalag Luft 3, with all my escapes and punishments marked in it. There was also a letter from the War Ministry saying that I might like to keep the record of my prison experience as a souvenir.

On returning to Britain, Tex applied for British citizenship. This was finally accepted and he received an official certificate from the Home Office department dated 4th July 1946. While awaiting his naturalisation, he had to find a way of living, so he applied for a job as a school teacher. He was accepted and was sent to a school near Ashford in Kent, where he taught children in class sizes of up to fifty of all ages. One of his greatest challenges at this time was taking the boys in cricket; a game he knew nothing about, and had never witnessed being played.

After a short while Tex decided that the teaching profession was not really his forte and he soon decided to try and obtain a grant and return to college to study for a degree. A grant was made available from the Canadian government and Tex entered Balliol College, Oxford, studying Modern Greats. While here, he also found time to work as a reporter for the *Oxford Mail* newspaper.

It was during this time, that Tex married Patricia Marlande Rambaut. Tex's relationship with her had started a few months before he had been shot down in 1942, and had continued by letter while he was in the prison camp. Coming to the end of his college time, Tex took up employment with the British Broadcasting Corporation's external services, broadcasting to North America in 1948. Tex and his new wife moved to London into a flat in Putney, which overlooked the River Thames.

After only a short while, Tex began to make his mark in the company, becoming senior producer for the overseas service. Later, in 1950, he applied for the post of BBC representative for India and Pakistan. He was not chosen initially, but was then given the job and sent to India. Here, he took up residence in the Maidens Hotel in Old Delhi, but was then given a more comfortable and convenient new apartment near the government buildings in New Delhi, before finally moving into a very nice bungalow. During his time in India, he became a father with the birth of a son named Francis and also a daughter, Juliet.

Making many Indian friends, Tex was introduced to many of the Indian cultures and religions. One friend, Narayana Menon introduced him to the Hindustani music of the north and Carnatic music of southern India. Here, he also met musicians like Ravi Shankar who would later make his mark on western music in the late 1960s, when visited by the pop group, The Beatles.

Tex also took an interest in Tantrism and various Yogas. But his attitude to religion was only fleeting; he recalls a verse he used to sing as a child, which he then translated as he walked the streets of Calcutta.

> I don't care if it rains or freezes
> I'll be safe in the arms of Jesus;
> I am Jesus' little lamb.
> Yes, by Jesus Christ I am.
>
> (translated)
>
> I don't care if it rains by golly,
> I'll be safe in the arms of Kali;
> I am Kali's little goat,
> Well, shut my mouth and slit my throat.

Tex's interest in music and the arts was put to good use again, as a wide range of activities became available to him; this included writing a play for the amateur dramatic society in Delhi. He also helped the Indian Prime Minister at that time, Pandit Nehru, in organising the political broadcasting for India's first general election. He returned from India and was transferred to become the assistant head of the BBC's Transcription Service in Maida Vale.

During this period he had a novel published, which also included his own political views regarding the armed struggles of Vietnam and Malaya against imperialism. The book was titled *Choice of Arms*.

When a young West Indian man named Kelso Cochrane was murdered in North Kensington in the 1960s, for no other reason than that he was black, Tex drafted his own leaflet on the shame of it for Britain. He then had thousands of copies printed and distributed around the local London area. For many West Indian people it was a very frightening time, especially for the black women who were too frightened to leave their homes even during the day. Tex helped organise, with others of good will, a group of people to escort the women.

Sadly, Tex and his wife separated during this time and he later married again to a beautiful and well-educated woman he had met in India. Her name was Ranjana Sidhanta. Tex and Ranjana are still together today, although he has always maintained that from the start he was never the marrying type:

> What I am really and have always been, from my earliest attempts to run away from home is a born escaper. A born escaper is bound to go through life, quite unconsciously creating situations to escape from. It almost seems to me now, that when I volunteered at the beginning of hostilities in 1939 it was to become a prisoner of war in order to try and escape. That approach of mine to the married state may have been taken in a similar spirit.

Over the years, Tex has helped to fight the cause of freedom, anti-racism and oppression. In 1967, he helped form the Communist Party of Britain; it was also during this time that the Vietnam War was now making headline news in most British newspapers. Both Tex and his wife Ranjana were against the United States of America's political and military involvement and invasion of Vietnam. They together launched the first appeal in Britain for medical aid for Vietnam. Tex was also able to put together a forty-five minute documentary detailing the facts against American military involvement in the war. Using film stock shot by Joris Ivens in Vietnam, Tex wrote the narration for the film, which was spoken by Lindsey Anderson. The documentary appeared under the title of 'The Threatening Sky'.

Tex continued his job with the BBC; but now to a lesser extent, he was working as a script editor in the radio drama department. He also continued with his own writings, which included two books *Ride a Paper Tiger* and *Take-Off*.

In 1969, he journeyed to Albania for the first time; while here he collected material for a new book he was about to write. The book, titled *Pickaxe and Rifle*, was written to give the British worker an idea of what life was like in a socialist country.

Tex's friend Bill Stapleton remained in the Royal Air Force after the war, and achieved the rank of Wing Commander; he was also awarded the CBE. His friendship with Tex continued during the post-war years and he recalls:

> Tex had now become a United Kingdom citizen and subsequently became a very political writer of novels and features. He was tremendously successful in left-wing theatre groups and in the

Writers' Guild. Notwithstanding his honestly held strong views politically, he maintained the same quiet, considerate and reasonable attitude in discussion, even with those diametrically opposed to his views. I know because I found myself sometimes in that position and still do. I regularly meet Tex and have done so for many, many years. We go months without meeting, then one or the other will make a call and a lunch will be arranged. Unlike so many others of our breed, one will never hear him bragging of (highly suspect) deeds of daring do; one will never hear the reasons for his leaving a (then) safe, well fed and enjoyable life in the United States of America to join someone else's war. He is a man I feel privileged to know and who I enjoy knowing; he is, indeed, a very honourable man.

Today at the age of 85 years, Tex Ash has still got his finger on the pulse and is still very active with regard to helping others. He still attends the prisoner of war reunions and keeps in contact with dear friends. He continues to support the museums and historical groups who keep alive the memory of RAF Hornchurch and the sacrifice of the men that flew from there. This Texan who decided to come to Britain and fight for freedom in its darkest hour, deserves this country's respect and thanks. On behalf of the United Kingdom, thank you William.

CHAPTER 3

TOP GUN
Flight Lieutenant Eric Stanley Lock DSO, DFC & Bar
1919–1941

Among the many wartime air aces of the Second World War, there is one who stands out against the rest, whose aggressive fighting skills would see him rise very quickly to become one of the Royal Air Force's top scoring fighter pilots by the end of 1940. He was basically a hunter; he was also a loner when it came to air fighting. Although he would take off with the squadron, once the enemy was sighted 'Lockie' was gone and would not be seen again until he would land some time later with one or two enemy aircraft claimed destroyed. This is his story.

Eric Stanley Lock was born on 19th April 1919 at Bomere, Bayston Hill near Shrewsbury in the county of Shropshire. He was the youngest son of Charles Edward Lock and Dora Lock née Cornes who farmed Bomere Farm and worked the adjacent Sharpstone Quarry. Both of his parents' families had been involved in farming for generations; his mother's family, originally from Cheshire, had moved southwards in the nineteenth century.

Eric's early years were happy. He would have many adventures playing in the nearby woods, which stood at the edge of the family farm; where he would play with his sister Joan, sometimes gathering primroses. By the age of seven, Eric was sent to a boarding school at Clivedon, Church Stretton that was run by a Mrs Pearson. It was during his time here that he won a book prize after entering a painting competition, which had been organised by a county newspaper. His painting of wild flowers drawn from memory won him the prize and he was awarded this on 13th April 1928. A few days later on his eighth birthday, the lady reporter of the newspaper put in a message of good wishes to Eric also adding: 'The men who move the world are those who don't let the world move them'.

From the boarding school, he moved on to the old Shrewsbury Boy's High School, but his stay there was short, the school closing down after the death of its Principal. He was then sent to Prestfelde School situated in London Road, Shrewsbury to continue and complete his education. He became popular with both students and teachers alike and distinguished himself in both track and field sports.

His parents would recall later the spirit of boyish fun that Eric possessed:

He had won five cups at the school sports and had brought them home in triumph. Before displaying them he put them in a bag with another trophy on the sideboard; he was then ready to display them. He said, 'That's for running, that's for swimming, that's for boxing, that's for throwing the cricket ball, that's for the long jump' then putting his hand back into the bag, he cried out, 'and that's for walking the best hound puppy in South Shropshire.' The young Eric certainly had a sense of humour.

Another of Eric's favourite pastimes was horse riding. He was a member of the South Shropshire branch of the Pony Club and also rode at meets with the South Shropshire Hounds. It was while at one of these meetings that he fell and broke his left arm, which although was set correctly, never recovered its normal strength.

But when did the seed of aviation and aircraft in general first appear in young Eric's imagination? At High School, fellow pupils recalled that he was fond of building aeroplanes from 'Meccano' and that the margins of his exercise books were often filled with sketches of flying machines. Eric's sister Joan Statham remembers those early days:

He did go to Prees Heath; there he had a five bob flight, when Alan Cobham's flying circus was travelling around the country. Eric was about twelve at the time. He liked speed, motorcycles and sports cars; he later bought a Norton motorcycle, which had been ridden in the Isle of Man TT Races. The rider had been killed and Eric bought it from the widow. He loved to ride it. He would get it up to a certain speed and then stand on the saddle and do all sorts of gymnastics and spread his arms wide to balance; he used to do that daily I think. Sometimes he would take my little terrier dog, which he would include in the activities. Eric was a law unto himself. Once he scared us because he did not come home from school on time. We went to look for him and there he was walking across the fields.

Eric Lock finally finished his schooling in 1933. By the early thirties, his parents had finished farming at Bomere Farm and were now working on Allfield Farm near Condover. Eric would for the next few years work on the farm or help out at the quarry works, where he got the opportunity of learning to drive the lorries.

By the mid-thirties, Eric Lock's interest in flying had grown such that he would often make the trip to Longmynd airfield to watch gliders. And it was at one of these gliding meetings that Lock would meet and talk with one of the contemporary celebrities of the air, the record-breaking pilot Amy Johnson. Eric's sister recalls:

He wanted to join the air force because he was mad on flying, but my father would not sign the papers when Eric was seventeen. In those days a farmer expected his sons to follow him into farming. But Eric would never have made a farmer.

Eric Lock's ambition to become an airman turned to reality, when aged eighteen he joined the Royal Air Force Volunteer Reserve in February 1939, as an Airman-under training Pilot, serial No. 745501. He undertook his part-time training at Meir, near Stoke-on-Trent, which consisted of weekend flying instruction on Tiger Moth aircraft and attending evening classes. His progress was outstanding and by 3rd March 1939, he had taken his first solo flight. After receiving further experience, which included night-flying training, he was awarded his pilot's certificate in May and given the rank of sergeant pilot.

With the outbreak of war against Germany almost imminent, he was sent to join No. 41 Squadron based at Catterick, North Yorkshire. During the early part of the war, its pilots saw no action and Eric was given the task of ferrying fighter aircraft across the Channel to Abbeville in France.

In July 1940, Eric Lock married Miss Peggy Meyers, the only daughter of Mr and Mrs J.A. Meyers of London, Ontario, Canada. Peggy had been a former Miss Shrewsbury. They were married at St Julian's Church in Shrewsbury.

It was at this time that he acquired his RAF nickname of 'Sawn off', given to him by his fellow squadron friends, because of Eric's small dumpy stature (he was only 5ft 6ins) when wearing a Sidcot flying suit; but most of the time he was just known as 'Lockie.'

On 15th August, while operating from Catterick with 41 Squadron, Lock claimed his first enemy aircraft. When flying Spitfire R6885, he destroyed a Messerschmitt Bf 110 fighter-bomber over the Bishop Auckland area. But it would be down south in No.11 Group Sector during the Battle of Britain that his skills would come to the fore. Having returned with 41 Squadron to RAF Hornchurch on 3rd September 1940, two days later Lock was to achieve considerable success.

At around 2.15 pm, 41 Squadron were ordered to patrol Maidstone. At 2.30 pm, a large formation of Messerschmitt 109s was sighted at 25/27,000 feet. In his combat report of the action Lock states:

> I was Yellow 1, patrolling with 41 Squadron on the Maidstone patrol line. We dived through cloud, when my section became split up. When we came through the clouds I found myself about 2,000 feet above and behind the squadron formation. My No.2 and 3 were missing, so I remained in this position. The squadron then turned northeast. I then saw a large formation of Me109s come between the squadron and myself, so I climbed back into the sun to gain more height. I then sighted several formations of Me109s in line abreast, so I joined one of the last formations of 109s. I waited for quite a while and then had a short burst at one on the extreme left. He went into a dive with smoke and glycol coming from the engine. I then gave the next aircraft a short burst, and he started to sideslip. I gave him two more short bursts and he went into a vertical dive with flames coming from the engine and bits and pieces flying off. It crashed between West Malling and Ashford.

Lock claimed the two 109s as destroyed and a probable. He had fired just 300 rounds of ammunition. Half an hour later over Sheppey, he was in action again against a raid of enemy bombers with fighter escort at a height of 15,000 feet.

After landing back at Hornchurch, the squadron was immediately scrambled again just after being rearmed and refuelled. Once in the air, the pilots were vectored to intercept a formation over Sheppey. Eric Lock reported the following encounter:

> I was Red 2, flying in formation with the rest of the squadron when we intercepted a formation of enemy aircraft. We attacked the bombers first. After we engaged we broke to port, I then saw Red 1 shoot down a Me109, which exploded in mid-air.
>
> It then developed into a dogfight. I then engaged an enemy Heinkel 111 which crashed into the river and I followed this down. I climbed back to 8,000 feet and saw another Heinkel, which had left the main formation. I engaged same, and his starboard engine was set on fire. I closed in to about 75 yards and fired two long bursts and smoke came from the fuselage. The enemy aircraft then put his wheels down and started to glide. I then stopped firing and followed him down. I was then attacked by a Me109, who fired at me from below and wounded me in the leg. As he banked away, he stall turned. I fired at him and he exploded in mid-air.
>
> I then followed the bomber down which landed on the sea, about 10 miles from the first one in the mouth of the river. I circled round a boat, which was at hand. I also flashed my downward light – I saw the boat go to the enemy aircraft. I was then joined by Red 3. On our return we saw the first bomber, which was still floating. I saw a small rubber boat.

Pilot Officer Lock's aircraft had suffered only minor damage in his tangle with the Me109; he landed his Spitfire N3162 back at Hornchurch and was immediately taken away to receive medical attention for his leg wound, which was not serious. In that one day, Lock had claimed two Me109s and two Heinkels destroyed with one Me109 probably destroyed.

On the morning of 6th September, 41 Squadron sent up twelve Spitfires on a patrol. Lock was flying in A Flight, Yellow section as Yellow 3 when he began to suffer from lack of oxygen. In his report he stated:

> I was patrolling with 41 Squadron in Yellow section. We climbed to 20,000 feet when for some unknown reason I passed out. I gained control of my machine at about 8,000 feet. I climbed up again hoping to find my squadron, but without success. I sighted a Junkers Ju88 at 18,000 feet, which I attacked. I opened fire over the Channel when it started to dive. I fired more bursts as we crossed the French coast. I saw it crash about 20 miles inland.

The 11th September would prove to be another very busy day for the Royal Air Force. The Luftwaffe that day launched three major raids against Portsmouth, Southampton and London. The third raid against London was picked up coming in near Folkestone at 3.45 pm. At RAF Hornchurch, eleven Spitfires of 41 Squadron had been ordered off to patrol over Maidstone at 3.15 pm. Sergeant I. Howitt flew one of them and was sent to carry out a spotter patrol over the coast, which was a dangerous duty for any pilot. At 4.10 pm, after almost an hour on patrol, the rest of 41 Squadron's Spitfires met the incoming German raid, which consisted of between 60 and 70 Junkers Ju88s and Messerschmitt Me110s at 4.10 pm. They went into the attack led by Flight Lieutenant Norman Ryder who broke up the enemy formation by diving his aircraft down through the centre of the Germans at 20,000 feet. 'Sawn off' Lockie was again in the thick of the action:

> I was patrolling with 41 Squadron as Yellow 2, when we sighted enemy aircraft. We went into echelon starboard and peeled off to port and dived on the enemy bombers, which broke up. I attacked a Ju88 from astern giving him several bursts. This had little effect, so I then did a quarter attack on the same. Having carried out this attack the Ju88 dived. I did not see any effect from the quarter attack so I attacked from below.
>
> This attack must have killed the pilot because the aircraft crashed in a field about 17 miles south of Maidstone. I circled it for a few minutes and saw it explode. I climbed back up to about 6,000 feet, when I was attacked by a Me110. After a dogfight, which lasted for twenty minutes, he crashed with his starboard engine on fire, about ten miles southeast of the Ju88. I received heavy fire from the rear gunner. I noticed that the Ju88 had white and black stripes painted on the tail fin. I force-landed at West Malling as I had run out of ammunition and petrol.

On returning to Hornchurch, Lock claimed both aircraft destroyed but his Spitfire had suffered some minor damage to his port wing from return enemy fire. The squadron also claimed two enemy aircraft damaged, with two Spitfires damaged and one lost. One pilot was wounded; Pilot Officer George 'Ben' Bennions suffered a wound to his left heel, when a shell splinter came into the cockpit. His aircraft's pneumatic system which controlled his brakes and guns, was also knocked out. Bennions managed to get his aircraft back to Hornchurch despite his wound and carried out a good landing. Pilot Officer Gerald Langley was shot down and forced to bale out over Sevenoaks, Kent. He landed safely. Sergeant Howitt's Spitfire was also damaged by enemy fire and he was obliged to carry out a forced landing at Hornchurch.

On one of his few visits to the family home during this busy period, Lock's sister Joan remembers how the fatigue of the constant aerial fighting was beginning to show on her brother:

> I remember Eric coming home for just a few hours around midnight. I remember when he came in the look of his face, he seemed to have aged considerably, and I think that was because a pal of his had been shot down over London. His parachute had been shot at while descending, and he had obviously fallen like a stone. Eric went to see this poor fellow's mother, it turned out that she was blind and a widow. I think that's what made him think he'd shoot down as many Germans as he could.

During the afternoon of 14th September 1940, Eric Lock was flying his
Spitfire on a lone spotter patrol between Dungeness and Ramsgate, when he
sighted an enemy fighter formation coming over at a height of between 25-
30,000 feet. His report again shows the determination that Eric had in getting
to grips with the enemy:

> I was out on patrol to the south coast to give information. I was
> flying at 31,000-33,000 feet, when I saw a formation of 12
> Me109s, travelling east of the coast between Dover and Deal. I
> attacked the last section of the formation; they were flying in a
> diamond formation. I was just about to close in, when I was
> attacked from above by some other Me109s. They peeled off from
> about 3,000 feet above me and carried out a head-on attack on me.
> I waited until one was in range and gave him a long burst. He
> passed a few feet above me; I carried out a sharp turn to the right
> and saw him in flames. Just then, I was attacked again from head-
> on. I waited till he was at point-blank range; I saw my bullets go
> into the enemy aircraft, and as he went past underneath me, I gave
> him a very long burst of fire. I saw some more enemy aircraft
> coming down on me, so I half rolled and dived through the clouds.
> I had just passed through the clouds when I saw someone who had
> baled out. I followed him down to the ground. I am pretty certain it
> was a Me109 pilot, I saw the troops rush up to him and he appeared
> to be holding his arms up. I flew low over the field and he waved
> back. This was afterwards confirmed by the police.

Eric Lock's combat report claimed the two Messerschmitt 109s as destroyed.
   On the 15th September (Battle of Britain Day) 41 Squadron were ordered
at 2.10 pm, to scramble on their second sortie of the day and told to patrol over
base at 25,000 feet. At 2.30 pm, an enemy formation of 50-plus Dornier
bombers and their escort fighters was sighted. The pilots were led that day by
Flight Lieutenant Norman Ryder, who formed them into a line astern
formation. They then peeled off to port and dived down to engage. During the
twisting and twirling confusion that was aerial combat, Pilot Officer Lock
claimed an Me109 destroyed as did two other fellow squadron pilots, Flying
Officer Boyle and Flying Officer Mackenzie. During the fighting, 41 were
joined by Hurricane aircraft from other squadrons who shared in the
destruction of a Heinkel bomber with Pilot Officer Baker. 'Lockie' reported:

> We delivered our attack and I broke away to starboard. I started to
> climb again and sighted a formation of three Dornier 17s escorted by
> three Me109s, just above the clouds. I saw a Hurricane attack the
> Me109s, so I joined him. He shot one down in flames as I was
> attacking. I attacked from behind and underneath, firing a rather long
> burst. He went into a vertical dive on fire. The Hurricane pilot then
> beckoned me to attack the three Dornier 17s, so we selected one
> each. We both delivered an astern attack, to stop the rear machine
> gunner, this seemed rather effective. We then carried out our attacks.
> When I delivered my second attack, the starboard engine burst into

flames and the aircraft dived into the sea. By now the two other Dornier 17s had dived to sea level. We carried out a quarter beam attack on the remainder. After a while, the starboard engine caught fire and he also landed in the sea by a convoy. But this was shot down by the Hurricane 30 to 40 miles southeast of Clacton.

I left the other Dornier 17 being chased by the Hurricane, as I had no ammunition. I was later joined by a Hurricane over the coast; he went north then. His code letters were US-O or UR-O.

Back at Hornchurch, Lock reported to the Intelligence Officer and claimed one Me109 and one Dornier 17 destroyed.

It had been the turning point of the battle. Never in one day had the German Luftwaffe encountered such large RAF fighter opposition over London and the southeast. Air Chief Marshal Hugh Dowding's battle tactics had finally paid off and by bringing into action squadrons from 12 Group on that day, the Germans were in total disbelief. The Luftwaffe, convinced by their own leaders that the RAF were now a depleted and demoralised force with very few aircraft serviceable, were totally shocked by the number of Spitfires and Hurricanes that came out to meet them. The Germans suffered heavy losses that day, losing 56 aircraft; the RAF lost 27 aircraft with 12 pilots killed. Two days later Adolf Hitler postponed the proposed invasion of Britain indefinitely.

The weather over the next two days was poor, with flying operations only required during the late afternoon of 17th September by the Hornchurch-based squadrons. No doubt the tired pilots took full advantage of the lull in the fighting to catch up on much needed sleep, Eric Lock among them. But the next day, on the 18th, it was back to readiness at dispersal as usual. The first enemy raids of the morning were picked up over Calais at 9 am, which consisted of mostly Me109 formations at 20,000 feet.

41 Squadron were ordered off and at 10.10 am sighted the Me109 formations at 7,000 feet above their own position. Lock reported:

When ordered to patrol base with Mitor (41 Squadron's call-sign), we were attacked from above by many Me109s. I had a full deflection shot at one enemy aircraft and it was seen to go down in smoke. The squadron then broke up. We were ordered to reform over Gravesend. I climbed to 29,000 feet, but could not see any sign of the remainder of the squadron. I climbed up to 31,000 feet, when I saw a lone Me109. I chased it towards Kent. I got in an astern attack and fired a short burst, but could not see any effects. I closed in to about 100 yards this time, attacking from below. I gave it two short bursts, when it exploded and went down in flames just off Margate.

This aircraft, Lock claimed as a probable.

The squadron was again called to action in the afternoon at about 1.00 pm. Eric Lock with his section was acting as rear guard when at 1.15 pm, he noticed three pairs of enemy fighters coming in from behind and below. He informed his squadron leader and broke away to make certain. By the time he had done so, the last pair had passed underneath him. Turning back, he saw a large formation of friendly fighters ahead. When the enemy aircraft sighted these, they turned back. Lock in turn attacked one of the last pair from out of the sun. He gave the enemy fighter a long burst of two to three seconds of machine-gun fire, which caused the enemy machine to go into a vertical dive with black smoke and glycol streaming from the engine. As the 109 continued its dive earthwards, Lock attacked the second Me109, but could see no positive hits on the machine although it was trailing smoke as it dived into cloud to escape. Lock followed, but could find no trace of the German. On his return to Hornchurch, he claimed one 109 destroyed and the other as a probable.

Squadron Leader Cyril 'Bam' Bamberger was a sergeant pilot when he joined 41 Squadron from 610 Squadron on 17th September 1940. He flew alongside Lockie in the same flight and recalls the following:

> Lockie always seemed to me to be the shining light of the squadron. While he would come back from a sortie claiming another enemy kill, I would have been lucky to manage to hit anything in the melee up in the sky. I had arrived at Hornchurch being posted from 610 Squadron, who had been based at Hawkinge. I was then put into the same flight as Lock. He seemed to me to be an extrovert character and a friendly person, although I never really got much time to know him due to the segregation of the sergeant pilots and officers once operations had ceased at the end of each day.

Eric Lock was the only pilot in 41 Squadron to make enemy claims on 20th September, when flying on a reconnaissance patrol over Maidstone, Dover and Boulogne. At 11.45 am, he encountered a Me109 and later a Henschel HS126 army-co-operation aircraft, and shot both of them down into the Channel. In his combat report, Lock only records the shooting down of the Me109, which he in fact wrongly claimed to be a Heinkel 113 fighter. There is strangely no mention of the Henschel combat in his report except on the first page to say he had shot it down. As the following combat report states:

> I was Red 3 in 41 Squadron, when we were ordered to patrol Maidstone at 20,000 feet, where we joined up with 603 Squadron. We climbed to 25,000 feet, when we were attacked from above by 109s. I saw a Me109 attack Mitor leader from above. As he delivered his attack without success, he did a steep turn to port. He was then in my line of fire, so I gave him a short burst. He went spinning down with black smoke coming from his engine. He could not have managed to reach his base.

On 1st October 1940, Lock's award of the Distinguished Flying Cross was gazetted. The citation read: *This officer has destroyed nine enemy aircraft, eight of these within a period of one week. He has displayed great vigour and determination in pressing home his attacks.*

For Eric Lock it was a well-deserved award for his outstanding achievements in the air, during the last few weeks. His wife and family were understandably proud as well as the local people in his hometown.

On 5th October, the Germans carried a series of fighter-bomber sweeps over Kent, with Me109s fitted with a single bomb slung beneath the fuselage, weighing 250lbs. Their mission, to cause as much havoc as possible on coastal targets and those just inland. Then they would race back across the Channel and home. 41 Squadron was again heavily involved that day flying three sorties. On his second patrol of the day, Lock claimed a 109 south of Maidstone and one probable. On his third patrol, he took off in the late afternoon to patrol over the Dungeness area. At 4.00 pm, his section sighted a formation of between 12 and 15 Me109s at 27,000 feet. As they had the advantage of height and surprise, they dived down onto the formation from slightly behind. Lock picked out one of the enemy and attacked from astern and above. He fired one burst of fire for one second. The 109 climbed vertically and then fell forward into a vertical dive with glycol leaking from under the right wing. He watched it go down to about 7,000 feet, where he left it. The German did not make any attempt to recover and crashed somewhere in the Tonbridge, Maidstone and Sevenoaks area. He claimed this as a probable.

Again the next day the squadron was heavily engaged with formations of 109s. At 2.45 pm, both 41 and 222 Squadron were involved. 41 had just sighted four Me109s over Maidstone and were going down into the attack, when a force of 20 Me109s who had been waiting unseen above bounced them. Fortunately 222 Squadron was on hand to give support and a furious dogfight ensued. Pilot Officer Lock claimed one of the enemy fighters destroyed, as did Flight Lieutenant Eric Thomas of 222.

The morning of 11th October saw the aerodrome at Hornchurch fog-bound, it was not until about 11.00 am that flying operations could be resumed. Luckily, the Hornchurch squadrons were not needed and it was not until 4.00 pm that they were scrambled when a German raid was plotted coming in. Both 41 and 222 Squadrons were vectored on to the approaching enemy formation. But it was only 41 Squadron who made enemy contact, sighting Me109s above them at an altitude of 30,000 feet. Not the sort of position that a fighter pilot would like to be in, with the enemy above. Climbing up to engage, two of 41's pilots collided in mid-air. One pilot was killed, but the other landed safely by parachute. Battle was joined with the enemy fighters as Lock's combat report now shows:

> I sighted 12 109s passing above and behind me, and at the same time I saw another five 109s diving at me in echelon. As they started to open fire, I did a steep climbing turn into the sun. I turned with the sun in my favour to look for my squadron, but instead I saw the five 109s going away to port. So I dived behind them, as I had 2,000 feet on them. I closed with the No.5 of the echelon and when in range I fired two bursts of two seconds from underneath and astern. He did a flick roll and then started to dive with smoke and glycol spewing from his engine. I left him at 20,000 feet diving steeply, his machine a mass of flames. This was over Dungeness.

At 9.35 am on the morning of 20th October 1940, the first enemy raids were picked up on the radar. But it was not until 11.15 am that any of the Hornchurch squadrons were called to take off. At 2.00 pm, both 41 and 603 Squadron intercepted a formation of 60 Me109s flying at 25,000 feet. Eric

Lock and his section were acting as rearguard when the enemy was sighted. The pilots positioned themselves into line astern, while Lock was still about 2,000 feet above them, and decided to remain in this position. He saw a small formation of 109s pass underneath him in line abreast, between him and the squadron. He attacked one of the enemy machines on the port side and fired two bursts from behind causing it to dive steeply with glycol streaming from underneath its starboard wing. Lock continued to dive, and then pulled his Spitfire into a steep climbing turn, managing to get in another burst on the same 109; immediately its engine began smoking and it dived into the sea about 10 miles from Dover.

Returning, he sighted five more Me109s crossing the coast, south of Dungeness. Lock attacked one of the 109s, which was lagging behind. He fired three bursts from behind and underneath the enemy machine. The Messerschmitt spun down towards the sea.

Lock then opened up on another enemy aircraft and left it smoking in a shallow dive, as he had expended all of his ammunition. On his return to Hornchurch, he claimed one of the 109s destroyed.

On 22nd October, Eric Lock was invited by the Empire News Service to do a radio broadcast, along with a Hurricane fighter pilot, Pilot Officer Tom Francis Neil of 249 Squadron based at North Weald. During the broadcast Lock related the following to the announcer:

Eric Lock: What happened to me was this. Our Spitfire squadron was over London, when the battle began and pretty soon we were all split up into a series of dogfights. When you are tearing about the sky you don't see much, and sometimes find yourselves alone when you do get a chance to look around. That is what happened to me. I could see no sign of my squadron or of the enemy formation. There were plenty of clouds about, I remember. I looked around and saw about 2,000 feet above me and away to the northeast of London, three Dorniers and three Messerschmitts being dogged by a Hurricane. I decided to go up and give whatever help I could, but before I could get up there the Hurricane was milling around with the 109s and two of them were walloping down through the clouds, absolutely done for in my opinion. When I got up there, I shot away at the other Messerschmitt. Then I saw you (the Hurricane pilot) blaze away at a Dornier. He did a somersault – a couple of somersaults. As he whirled over, bits of his wings fell off and he went crashing down through the clouds. After that I drew alongside the Hurricane and you pointed forward (Hurricane pilot).

I looked where you were pointing, and saw a Dornier about a mile ahead, heading off for the sea. I opened up and drew away, then made an attack and the Dornier went down through the clouds. We both followed him through, and took it in turns to attack him. By the time he had reached the coast, he was at 1,000 feet and still going steadily. He was only 50 feet when I passed down the middle of a convoy, well below the tops of the masts of the ships. Then, about 40 miles off Clacton, I gave the Dornier a final burst and in he went.

He alighted on the water tail first, quite comfortably, you might say. Then a wing cracked off, his back broke and down he sank.

Announcer: Well your story certainly shows that it doesn't matter to the Germans, I mean – whether a Spitfire or a Hurricane attacks them.

The Hurricane Pilot: There's no doubt about that at all. Nevertheless, I'm used to the Hurricane, so give me a Hurricane every time.

Eric Lock: And give me a Spitfire. By the way, a Spitfire is a lot easier to handle than some of the old trainer aircraft I learnt on. I hope that my old instructor is listening in to this, for he always said I was the world's worst pupil in any kind of aircraft.

Lock was awarded a Bar to his DFC on 22nd October 1940. The citation read:

In September 1940, while engaged on a patrol over the Dover area, Pilot Officer Lock engaged three Heinkels, one of which he shot down into the sea. Immediately afterwards, he engaged a Henschel 126 and destroyed it. He has displayed great courage in the face of heavy odds, and his skill and coolness in combat have enabled him to destroy 15 enemy aircraft within a period of 19 days.

The Luftwaffe continued with its fighter-bomber sweeps on 25th October, the first raid starting at around 8.00 am that morning. At 9.00 am, 41 and 603 Squadrons were ordered up to patrol between Hornchurch and Rochford and were later vectored over Kent. At 9.50 am, southeast of Biggin Hill, they sighted an enemy formation of Me109s at 28,000 feet. With the sun directly behind them, 41 Squadron and 603 dived into the attack. Sergeant John McAdam claimed a 109 destroyed, while Eric Lock claimed a probable. He singled out one of the enemy machines and did a quarter attack, which developed into an astern attack. Once hit the German aircraft went up into a steep right hand climbing turn with flames coming from its engine. It stalled at the top of its climb and spun downwards, crashing north of Biggin Hill.

41's only casualty was Pilot Officer Aldridge, whose aircraft was damaged, but repairable.

Eric Lock's luck however was to run out on 17th November 1940, when as part of a formation of 12 No.41 Squadron Spitfires, they encountered about 70 Me109s over the Thames estuary at 25,000 feet. During the engagement, Lock claimed two Me109s destroyed before being set upon himself by an enemy fighter of JG54. He was badly wounded in the left arm and in both legs, but managed to crash-land his Spitfire P7554 near Martlesham Heath in Suffolk. For two hours, Lock remained trapped in his aircraft unable to free himself due to his injuries. Luckily, he was finally rescued by two soldiers who carefully removed him from the Spitfire's cockpit. They constructed a makeshift stretcher and carried him for two miles negotiating ditches and dykes until they were able to find further assistance, and transport him to hospital for medical attention. The squadron record book filled in by the squadron intelligence officer in Lock's absence states:

> Pilot Officer Lock destroyed 2 Me109s (in sea) before being shot down himself. He crashed at Alderton with extensive injuries and is in Ipswich Hospital. His combat report will be sent later.

Joan Statham, Eric's sister, recalls her visit to see her brother at the hospital:

> I remember when he was in hospital in Ipswich and visiting him in his room. He was lying there with drips protruding everywhere and he looked terribly, terribly ill, and his face was so white because he had lost such a terrific amount of blood. Later on when he was fit enough he was transferred to Halton, which was the big RAF hospital. He was put in a saline bath every day; his left arm was in plaster. I can even still recall the smell, the horrible smell of the wound, which was seeping through the plaster.

It was while in hospital that Lock gave the details of his combat and crash on 17th November to the intelligence officer:

> Whilst on patrol with 41 Squadron on Sunday 17/11/40, we intercepted about 70 Me109s about 2,000 feet below us on the left. Being at the rear of the squadron I picked out an enemy aircraft and gave him a two-second burst from below and behind. The enemy aircraft emitted smoke and flame and went into a steep dive, I followed and watched him hit the sea. I climbed back to 20,000 feet and did another astern attack on another Me109, firing two two-second bursts, which set the enemy machine on fire and he too dived into the sea. I was then about 20 miles off the coast, when the next thing I remember was diving towards the sea. I tried to open the hood, but could not do so and crash-landed near Martlesham Heath.

After spending time in Ipswich Hospital, Lock was moved to the RAF Hospital at Halton in Buckinghamshire. Here, his 41 Squadron colleague Flying Officer Peter Brown, visited him:

> I took him the best wishes from all in 41 Squadron and brought him up to date with the news at Hornchurch. He was cheerful and recovering from his serious wounds. We talked about his progress, but did not discuss his return to flying. I felt at the time that the very serious injuries he had suffered and his exceptional achievements in the air would put a return to operational flying out of the question for a long time.

The official notification of the Distinguished Service Order award was bestowed upon Eric Lock on 17th December 1940. It read:

Pilot Officer Eric Stanley Lock DFC has been appointed a Companion of the Distinguished Service Order in recognition of gallantry displayed in flying operations against the enemy. Pilot Officer Lock showed exceptional keenness and courage in his attacks when engaged last month with his squadron in attacking a superior number of enemy forces. He destroyed two Messerschmitt 109s, bringing his total to at least 22. His magnificent fighting spirit and personal example have been in the highest traditions of the service.

Eric Lock was to spend the next four months in hospital undergoing 15 operations to remove shell splinters from his body. It was during this period that he was moved to the Queen Victoria Hospital, at East Grinstead, where he came into contact with another fellow RAF Hornchurch pilot, Richard Hillary, who had flown with 603 Squadron and had suffered grievous burns during the Battle of Britain and was now undergoing reconstructive surgery to his face and hands. Along with Lock and Hillary in Ward 3, were Squadron Leader Tom Gleave of 253 Squadron and Pilot Officer Maurice Mounsdon of 56 Squadron. In Hillary's acclamied wartime book *The Last Enemy*, Lock was mentioned as being prone to the odd outburst of anger and sarcasm towards the nursing staff. Richard Hillary noted:

Opposite me was Squadron Leader Gleave with a flap graft on his nose and an exposed nerve on his forehead. In Ward 3 he had been unable to sleep, nor could the night nurse drug him enough to stop the pain. Next to him was Eric Lock, a tough little Shropshire man who had been with me at Hornchurch and collected twenty-three planes, a DSO, a DFC and a bar. He had cannon shell wounds in the arms and legs.

Our heads were shorn and our scalps rubbed with special soap and anointed with M & B powder. We submitted to this with a varying amount of protestation; the squadron leader was too ill to complain, but Eric Lock was vociferous and the rest of us sullen. The nurses were efficient and not unfriendly, though the enforced wearing of masks and rubber gloves made them a little impersonal. Our language was always rough and sometimes offensive; Eric with an amiable grin on his face would curse them roundly from dawn to dusk, but they seldom complained.

While at East Grinstead the fun side of Eric Lock also showed itself, when he undertook to be master of ceremony for a show given by Celia Lipton, who arrived to entertain the burned pilots. From all accounts he made a very good job of it.

On 1st April 1941, Eric Lock attended an award ceremony at Buckingham Palace, to receive from King George VI, three medal decorations for his gallantry in the air. It was the first time that one individual had been conferred this honour in wartime. When receiving his awards, the DSO, DFC and Bar, the King asked him if he would be flying again soon, to which Lock replied, that he thought he would.

The next day, Lock received a large package with a telegram from RAF Hornchurch; when he opened it, it read:

> *Air Officer Commanding Group and all ranks on this station send you heartiest congratulations on the DSO awarded to you yesterday by the King. The news of the progress you are making and the award of this well won decoration has made the whole station happy.*

Eric Lock was a quiet, reserved young man and soon after the announcement of his triple awards, the press began to make use of the RAF hero. Even across in America, he was recognised and was one of only eleven RAF pilots to be selected to receive a coveted eagle's feather from Chief Whirling Thunder of the Red Indian Organisation in Chicago, for having specially distinguished themselves in flying operations against the enemy. A letter accompanied the feather from Sir Walter Monckton.

Eric spent most of May on sick leave, staying at the home of his parents at 'Eastingham,' Lyth Hill Road, Bayston Hill. As he grew stronger and more confident, he was asked to make a public appearance at a Sunday concert arranged in aid of the Sentinel Works' Spitfire Fund. Again he was presented with gifts subscribed by members of the staff. Mrs Woodvine, wife of the Works Director presented him with a silver tankard, while his wife was given a monogrammed silver jewel case. It was also one of the few occasions when Eric made a speech. In his reply to the workers he said:

> I want you to hasten with this Spitfire; I know you will succeed by the enthusiasm you have shown in already raising £1,600. Nothing would give me greater pleasure than to fly that Spitfire with 'Sentinel Works' on it, in action against the enemy. I hope that honour will be mine, and I promise you that I will do my best to bring victory to this country of ours, which I am so proud to serve.

On 27th June 1941, Eric Lock returned to his old airfield at Hornchurch to take up duties as flight commander of A Flight 611 Squadron. Cliff Broadbent was a ground crewman with 611 Squadron at RAF Hornchurch, and he can recall the arrival of Lockie to the squadron:

> I was the engineering NCO in charge of A Flight in those days. Pilots were coming and going when the news arrived that Lockie was joining us that week. Eventually this little fellow came staggering down to the dispersal not knowing which aircraft he was going to get. So I said, you are down for FY-F if you want to go and have a look. Anyway he wandered off to have a look at his aircraft and came back about an hour later and gave me the thumbs up; it was just what he'd wanted.

As soon as Lock had received his Spitfire, he asked another NCO Sam Prince to paint something special on the aircraft. Prince recalls what this special request was:

I met him when he had just been posted as Flight Lieutenant. The first thing he asked me to do was to paint a Churchill V-sign hand on the cowling of the aircraft. He always reckoned he was one of Churchill's Few, so he wanted this put on.

On 6th July, the day dawned with fine weather for operations over France and 611 was involved with another Circus operation with the target being Lille. The squadron was to escort a formation of Short Stirlings to and from the target. A Flight known as Charlie section consisted of Flight Lieutenant Lock, Flying Officer Peter Dexter, Pilot Officer Wilfred Duncan Smith and Sergeant Jock Gilmour.

It was while just passing out over the target northeast of St Omer that Eric Lock sighted enemy fighters:

> I was leading my section at 2,000 feet over Lille having split into pairs and having circled Lille. When on the way out a Me109F passed behind me. I suddenly saw him flashing past my mirror. I did a steep turn to the left, and then having completed about 180 degrees of my turn I saw the Me109 straight in front of me. I gave him a two-second burst of cannon fire, whereupon about a quarter of his starboard wing and an article about the size of a large suitcase came away from his aircraft. This may have been his cockpit cover. He then went into an amazing sideslip cum slow roll.

On returning to Hornchurch, both Lock and Sergeant Gilmour each claimed a Me109 destroyed, Gilmour also claiming one damaged.

The late Group Captain Wilfred Duncan Smith was flying with No.611 during this time and fondly remembered Lockie when interviewed by the author:

> He was quite a chum and a remarkable bloke altogether. He was a first class shot, but people used to discredit him saying he couldn't have shot down that number of aircraft. I can assure anyone, that if he claimed he'd shot it down, he had alright, because he was an excellent shot with an aerial gun.

Sam Prince again recalls:

> Eric Lock would not have had the swastikas put on his aircraft, if they were not confirmed. They were his twenty-six, which he had shot down. He had courage, a pint-sized pilot with gallons of courage, and a great pilot.

On 8th July, the Hornchurch Wing carried out a sweep during the morning. During this operation Lock added another Me109 to his score, as his following combat report records:

> I was leading Charlie section and having crossed the French coast at 18,500 feet, saw 5 Me109s a few miles north of the target, up sun

and above. We turned to get behind them, when I was attacked from astern by some more 109s. Evading these, I attacked the last one in that formation, giving a short burst of cannon fire, but missed.

I then realised that I was boxed in by 109s, so I spun down in an aileron turn. When pulling out of my dive at 4,000 feet, I observed a Me109 converging on me and did a beam attack with cannon. The enemy aircraft belched smoke and I continued to follow him down to 2,000 feet. I saw him go into the ground near a wood.

As there were some enemy troops in the vicinity, I kept on diving and sprayed them with machine-gun fire. On climbing back I was attacked by three more 109s, so I pulled the boost plug and came home at zero feet.

His last visit home was on 25th July, and it was during this brief stay that the residents of Bayston Hill showed their special respect for the young pilot. The local Women's Institute had opened up a subscription fund in the village and from the response the local population raised enough money to buy an airman's watch and silver cigarette case, which was inscribed *To F/LT E.S. Lock DSO, DFC – In recognition of his gallantry and skill from the inhabitants of Bayston Hill*. Unfortunately, he was late in arriving home, so the gifts were presented to Eric's wife Peggy in his absence. He had only been at home a few hours, when he received a telegram recalling him to Hornchurch for flying operations.

During those last few days of July, Eric Lock took time to write to his mother, and this would turn out to be his last letter.

A Flight No.611 Sqdn
RAF Hornchurch

Dear Mother

I am sorry not to have written before, but really we have not had even the time to shave, I expect you've seen the results of our efforts in the papers though. We start at 4.23 in the morning and finish at 11.18 at night, so you can see its pretty tiring. Yesterday I got my first Hun since I got back; I blew him to pieces while over Lille. We make on average three trips a day, anything from sixty to eighty miles over the coast which believe me is not all fun.

How is the harvest going on, you can see them when we're going over France, then you realise how bloody stupid this war is. We had rather a bad time yesterday; two of my boys were shot down, the rest of us escaped by the skin of our teeth. But believe me, we've got those Jerrys on the run.

I hope to fly up the day we get released, but it will only be for a few hours.

We are just about to go on our second raid now, so I'll have to go. Please don't worry if something happens to me, because nine times out of ten our boys are prisoners of war.

So see you soon
Eric.

On 3rd August 1941, the day dawned brightly as the Hornchurch squadrons prepared to get ready for the day's missions. 611 Squadron was to be involved in carrying out Rhubarbs and Sam Prince remembers this, Eric Lock's last day:

> It was a gorgeous day; I was at A Flight dispersal point when Eric and the rest of them went off. Some of them returned and we waited for Eric; I think the aircraft he was flying was coded FY-V. But he didn't come back.
>
> We waited until late evening, thinking he's probably been picked up by the air sea rescue launches. It was around the Pas de Calais area where they had done the Rhubarb at the time. When we found out that he had been shot down, we thought it was probably ground fire from around the beaches that had got him. The Channel was searched but there was no sign of him.

Eric's sister Joan recalls when they received the news that her brother was missing:

> I remember his wife answering the phone and they told her that he had failed to return from operations that day. My parents were out at that time; of course we were obviously devastated by the news and we hoped very much that he would be a prisoner of war. Mother and I spent days listening to Lord Haw Haw, the German radio propaganda newscaster, but I'm afraid the news wasn't good.
>
> After reading his last letter home I felt Eric was very despondent and very weary; and I felt in my innermost soul that he'd had this premonition that he wasn't going to make the end of the war. I also felt that I would never see him again.

The 611 Squadron Operations Record Book recorded the following for 3rd August 1941:

> Slightly cloudy morning turned to lovely sunny afternoon. Six pairs of the squadron indulged in Rhubarbs, one in the morning and five pairs in the afternoon, but there was insufficient cloud cover over France so everyone came back except 'Lockie' (F/Lt E.S. Lock DSO, DFC) who went in with F/Lt Cathels (403 Squadron) at D'Hardelot and was last seen streaking down a road at the back of Boulogne, brassing off soldiers on bicycles and whooping over the R/T, '*Ha-ha, look at the bastards running.*' It seems a ruddy awful waste to lose so great a pilot on so trivial an expedition. It is anticipated that the German Press will make much of Lock's capture or death. His aircraft was a Spitfire Vb W3257.

So what did happen to Eric Lock? After he failed to return, it has always been accepted that he lost his life as a result of attacking German troops in the Boulogne area. This Rhubarb action was highly dangerous and he or his aircraft may have been hit by return fire from the ground troops, resulting in a bale out or crash in the Channel. He might also have been damaged by

German anti-aircraft fire when crossing out over the French coast at low level on his return and ditched in the sea. No trace of his body or aircraft wreckage was ever found.

Eric had taken off from Hornchurch with Flight Lieutenant Cathels of the newly arrived 403 Canadian Squadron; they had flown in from Ternhill the previous day. Cathels flew in a 611 Squadron aircraft and his flight was recorded in that squadron's Operations Book. It is possible that this was arranged so that Lock could introduce him to the special tactics of Rhubarbs, so that Cathels could be better equipped to lead his own 403 sections.

They took off together at 2.45 pm and Flight Lieutenant Cathels is recorded as having landed back at Hornchurch at 3.45 pm. Lock was last seen diving down to attack the German troops. Allowing for a return flight of 20 minutes, the latest time for Lock's attack on the ground troops and any R/T message would be 3.25 pm.

If Lock had survived his attack against the ground troops without serious damage, he would have returned to base with or soon after Flight Lieutenant Cathels.

During the course of the day, the weather had improved and fine weather was not suitable for Rhubarbs. To stay in the area alone, close to German Me109 fighter airfields would have been suicidal. Lock made no radio contact after his comments on attacking the German soldiers.

Two years ago, it was publicly claimed that Eric Lock was shot down by a German Messerschmitt 109 pilot named Oberleutnant Johann Schmid of JG26. This claim appears to have been made on the simple basis that as the RAF had lost one Spitfire over France on that day, and the Germans only claimed one Spitfire shot down on that date, then *ipso-facto* Oberleutnant Schmid must have shot down Eric Lock. The claim however fails to identify the time of the actions. Clearly, Lock was over France at approximately 3.25 pm. However, Christopher Goss, an aviation historian and researcher with a special knowledge of Luftwaffe operations, has examined German documents and the JG26 war diaries which show that Oberleutnant Schmid claimed to have shot down a Spitfire at 6.32 pm (5.32 pm British time). Schmid's claim was unsubstantiated and no geographical position was given.

This was some two hours after Lock had been reported as being in action against the German troops and 2¾ hours after he had taken off from Hornchurch with Cathels. Two important factors to be taken into consideration are, firstly a Spitfire's fuel limitations would not allow such a lengthy stay over France, and secondly why should Eric Lock stay over hostile territory for such a long time on a Rhubarb, on his own putting himself at such great risk?

Our detailed research has failed to provide firm evidence as to where or how Eric Lock was killed. The official report made at the time notes that Lock and Cathels set off at 2.45 pm on a Rhubarb. On approaching the French coast, Lock informed his wingman (Flight Lieutenant Cathels) that he was to fly high and that he (Lock) would fly low. This report and others assume that Lock fell victim to ack-ack fire and this has been accepted for 60 years. We believe this to be the truth. One thing is certain. On a time basis alone Flight Lieutenant Eric Lock could not have been killed by Me109 pilot Oberleutnant Schmid.

Squadron Leader Peter Brown AFC, who had flown with Lock in 41

Squadron reflects on the tragedy of his death:

> When I heard that he had returned to fly with my old squadron
> No.611 so quickly and was flying on operational sweeps over
> France, I was very concerned. Later when I heard of his death on a
> Rhubarb flight in unsuitable weather, I felt that an outstanding
> young fighter pilot had been needlessly sacrificed on a sortie of no
> significance.
>   Who had allowed this to happen? Why did Eric return
> immediately to a front line squadron fighting over enemy territory?
> I don't know if Eric was physically and mentally fit to return to
> such a testing duty, but surely his fighting skills and experience
> could have been passed on to trainee pilots at an operational
> training unit.

Eric Lock was one of the Royal Air Force's youngest and gifted aces, and he
had been lost at a time when they could ill afford to sacrifice such experienced
flight commanders and squadron leaders. One can only assume that had he
lived through the war, Eric Lock would have no doubt have been
acknowledged as one of the most respected aces in the same way as Johnnie
Johnson, Robert Stanford Tuck and Adolph Malan.

Lock's final tally for enemy aircraft was as follows; 26 destroyed and 8
probably destroyed. Although only small in stature, in the air Eric Lock was
a giant among men.

What memorials are there to the memory of Eric Stanley Lock? He is
remembered on the Royal Air Force Runnymede Memorial, Panel 29. A
plaque hangs inside Condover Church and two memorial bench seats with a
named panel have been sited, one inside the grounds of Shropshire Castle, the
other at Bayston Hill. In Hornchurch itself, near the airfield, one of the roads
is named after him. Recently, the Shropshire Aero Club situated at Sleap
Airfield near Wem opened its newly re-furbished restaurant and bar and
named it 'The Eric Lock Bar.' The opening ceremony took place on Friday,
8th February 2002, and was declared open by Eric's nephew Ken Lock, along
with Battle of Britain veteran Squadron Leader Peter Dawbarn. Eric's sister,
Joan, donated a framed portrait of her brother drawn by the famous artist
Cuthbert Orde in July 1941.

I have left the last few words on Eric Lock to one of his contemporaries,
Peter Brown, who flew with Eric on a number of occasions:

> Eric had a quiet personality in the squadron, but he would always
> join in the fun. He was certainly dedicated to getting a high number
> of victories and to achieve this he flew on his own whenever
> possible, and many of his kills were away from the squadron. He
> was always very modest about his success. He was instinctively a
> hunter and a very good shot. His results were exceptional, but the
> risks were high with no one to help scan the sky for unseen
> Me109s, as in November 1940 when he was shot down and badly
> wounded. After all these years, following the war, I am glad he has
> finally been acknowledged as the top-scoring pilot during the
> Battle of Britain.

CHAPTER 4

THE FLYING SCOT
Squadron Leader Iain Hutchinson TD

At the outbreak of the Second World War, the Royal Air Force had been shown to be wise in their decision to enlarge their ranks with the help of the Volunteer Reserve, established a few years earlier. With this, came an influx of trained non commissioned officers, whose rank was sergeant pilot. During the next 18 months of war, especially during the Battle of Britain, the role played by the sergeant pilot in defending Britain's freedom was crucial. The mythology built up about the Battle of Britain over the last fifty years, has given the visual impression of dashing officer types. The fact is that one third of the men who fought during the battle were sergeant pilots and some of them went on to achieve high rank status and become aces. This is the story of one such sergeant pilot.

Iain Hutchinson was born at the family home in Glasgow, Scotland on 13th November 1918, just two days after the end of the First World War. He was the only son of Edward Gayton Hutchinson and his wife Gertrud (née) Marriott. His father's occupation was an insurance inspector, a job that entailed visiting other insurance agents to check on their procedures and work. The family expanded with the birth of a daughter christened Betty Elizabeth. Iain's earliest childhood recollection was when he saw one of his aunts taking his sister out in her pram and coming back later to tell the family she had lost her. Iain had the instant feeling of delight that his rival had gone, but this would not last for long as his sister was found and brought home.

As a young lad, Iain enjoyed cycling and when he was able, music, which was a great hobby with him. Later, he progressed to tinkering around with constructing elementary radio sets and got as far as building a single valve set.

The first school he attended was Craigton elementary school, which was only temporary, while awaiting the final construction of the new Mosspark School to which he was eventually transferred. He was six years old at this time. He subsequently passed the eleven-plus examination and went to a school named the Albert Road Academy, a grammar school in Pollokshields, a district in Glasgow. He stayed there until he qualified with the Scottish Higher Leaving Certificate, leaving at the age of sixteen to start work initially in a shipping office; he then passed an exam and got into a local government office job. His main hobby at this time was swimming for which he became club junior champion.

So when did Iain Hutchinson become interested in aviation, and what sparked his interest in aircraft? He now recalls:

I became very interested in aviation at the age of eighteen. I had a friend who did some flying and he took me up once or twice and from then on I became fascinated. He would take me up in an old Gipsy Moth at the Scottish flying club at Redruth. I learnt to fly there and got my private pilots licence in 1938. Subsequently, I joined the Royal Air Force Volunteer Reserve down at the enrolment centre in Glasgow.

After joining the Royal Air Force Volunteer Reserve as an Airman-under training-Pilot in May 1938, serial No.741639, Iain who stood at six foot three inches must have been one of the tallest pilots to join that year. He went to Prestwick, where he undertook his flying training at No.12 Elementary Flying Training School on 5th June, learning to fly on Tiger Moth and Hawker Hart biplane aircraft. On 1st September 1939, Iain along with the rest of the RAFVR, signed up to be embodied into the regular air force.

It was on 29th September that Iain married his sweetheart Margaret Sutherland at the main registry office in Glasgow. Iain had known Margaret since she was thirteen; both had attended the same school. They decided that as the future looked a bit precarious, they would get married. Her father was Lieutenant Colonel Sutherland MC, DCM, who had fought in both the Boer War and the First World War. After Prestwick, Iain was sent on 6th October 1939 to No.12 Flying Training School at Grantham, undertaking flying training on Avro Anson aircraft. He completed his course on 6th January 1940, and received notification of his first posting to 236 Squadron on the same date, the squadron then being based at Martlesham Heath, Suffolk. The airfield was also being used as a research establishment at that time. No.236 Squadron was flying Bristol Blenheim aircraft and was about to be transferred to Coastal Command. Iain was only with the squadron for about one month, but remembers his time flying the Blenheim:

> The aircraft was very nice to fly, although it felt like being in a greenhouse; there were all these square glass panels around you. When you were used to flying an aircraft with very good vision around it, which even the Anson had, the Blenheim felt very closed in. But you got used to this and they flew very well; they had a nice broad undercarriage and the sound of the air-cooled rotary engines had a deep reassuring sound. It was a little bit heavy to handle at times. At that time we only had a crew of two, the gunner and myself.

He left 236 on 9th February 1940, travelling to RAF Duxford to join 222 Squadron and was equipped with 16 Bristol Blenheim Mk I light-bombers at that time. The squadron had been reformed in October 1939, the task undertaken by Squadron Leader Herbert Waldemar Mermagen known in RAF circles as 'Tubby'. He had arrived from Usworth to take command. The new squadron were given a solitary hangar and office, which had been vacated by 611 Squadron.

During March, the squadron were re-equipped with Spitfire Mk Is and became operational within a month. Convoy patrols were the main operations during this period of what was known as the 'Phoney War.' The squadron would fly to the airfield at Horsham St Faith early morning to undertake these patrols then fly back to Duxford in the evening.

It was in April 1940, that Iain became the proud father of a baby girl, who had been born prematurely, and was named Anne.

While on patrol on 10th April 1940, Iain was forced to return and make a forced landing at Martlesham Heath in Suffolk; this he did successfully without injury to himself.

Owing to the news of the German invasion of Holland and Belgium on 10th May 1940, the squadron personnel were recalled from leave and ordered at short notice to move to RAF Digby, Lincolnshire, taking off at 4.50 pm.

On 28th May, Iain and his fellow pilots were ordered down to Essex, to operate from RAF Hornchurch. The very next morning, they flew an early morning patrol with 19 and 41 Squadron, taking off at 4.15 am. But the patrol was uneventful and no enemy aircraft were seen. Iain recalls their time over the beachhead:

> On the 31st May, we did three offensive patrols over Dunkirk; we then went back to Manston and refuelled and continued with another patrol over the Dunkirk area. You couldn't really see much down below, because we were at a fair old altitude, but you could see the pall of smoke that rose from the burning fuel tanks. I didn't see any enemy fighters, but we ran into some light anti-aircraft fire when we came in fairly low. You could see the troops on the beaches and the ships waiting to take them off. I was flying Spitfire P9379 during this time.

1st June 1940 saw 222 in action during an early morning patrol, when they engaged a formation of Messerschmitt Me110 twin-engine fighters and Me109s. Flight Lieutenant A.J. Robinson, Pilot Officer T. Vigors and Sergeant S. Baxter each claimed a Me110, while Flight Lieutenant D. Bader and Pilot Officer H.P.M. Ederidge destroyed a Me109 each. But the action was not without casualties to the squadron. The following pilots were listed as missing: Pilot Officer Falkus, Pilot Officer Morant, Pilot Officer Massey-Sharp and Sergeant White. Fortunately Pilot Officer Morant returned the next day by boat with soldiers of the British Expeditionary Force. It appears that while engaged in combat with an Me109, east of Dunkirk, he was shot down with a cannon shell through the glycol tank and had to make a forced landing on the beach with wheels up. After destroying his machine with the help of men from the BEF, he walked along the beach and boarded a ship for Dover, arriving back at Hornchurch the following day. Pilot Officer Falkus was later confirmed as a prisoner of war, but Pilot Officer Massey-Sharp and Sergeant White were both killed.

With the completion of the Dunkirk evacuation, 222 Squadron were sent up to the RAF aerodrome at Kirton-in-Lindsey, Lincolnshire. Here the squadron would carry out the rather boring routine patrols needed to protect the shipping convoys around the Wash area of the North Sea.

It would not be until the end of August that Iain and his squadron would again move south, by which time the Battle of Britain would be at its height and every squadron would be needed in the Royal Air Force's struggle against the Luftwaffe to keep Britain free from invasion. Iain remembers the move back down to Hornchurch:

We came down to relieve No.264 Defiant Squadron, who had also been up at Kirton-in-Lindsey with us, so we knew some of them. It was very sad to find out that they had been shot to pieces. We arrived on 29th August and on the 30th, I was shot down for the first time. The sky was clear from horizon to horizon and my squadron was climbing to our allocated altitude. Now flying in line astern formation, we entered into the fight. I then saw three Me109s sweeping by underneath me; while I was fumbling for the firing button control, somebody got me from behind. I was going to bale out, but my aircraft seemed still capable of flying so I decided to try and make it back to Hornchurch. It would not make the airfield, so I put the Spitfire down wheels-up in a field in Rainham. As the aircraft came down I saw a farmer ploughing the field drawn by two horses. He was no doubt shocked as I flew past him, hit the ground and eventually came to a halt. The only injury I sustained was a bruised and cut nose from bashing myself on the gun-sight. The aircraft was repairable though I remember Sergeant Pilot Reg Johnson wasn't very happy with me when I was shot down, because I was using *his* aircraft which was a new one.

The Spitfire Iain had been flying that day was R6719; which was back flying the following day. He had crashed in a field at Damyns Hall Farm at Wennington, near Rainham, Essex. Indeed the very next day on the 31st, Iain was again airborne although wearing a plaster across his damaged nose; this time it would be very different and the Germans would be on the receiving end. The squadron were ordered to scramble and at 1.40 pm, just north of Maidstone, dived down on a formation of Messerschmitt 109s at a height of 26,000 feet. His combat report details:

At 29,000 feet, Pilot Officer Broadhurst and myself engaged some 109s. I delivered a quarter attack on one Me109, opening fire at 200 yards and ceasing fire at 100 yards. I fired seven bursts at him and on my second burst, white smoke commenced to pour from his engine. This got thicker and black smoke mingled with it as he went down. I could see flames from his engine cowling as I followed him down. But at 20,000 feet, having followed him from 26,000 feet, I was attacked by another Me109 and was forced to leave him.

On landing back at base Iain claimed the German aircraft as damaged, and the Messerschmitt 109 was later credited as belonging to 2/JG77. It had been flown by Oberleutnant Eckhart Priebe and had crashed at Elham Park Wood, the German pilot having baled out wounded and been captured.

During the morning of 3rd September, while operating from Hornchurch's satellite airfield at Rochford, 222 was ordered to patrol over base at 9.50 am at 20,000 feet. At 10.50 am, B Flight with whom Iain was flying, engaged a mixed formation of Dornier 215s, Me110s and Me109s over Rochford. He claimed a damaged Messerschmitt 110 twin-engine bomber during the action, as his following report confirms:

> I was at 27,000 feet by myself, when I noticed below a circle of Me110s with a straggler. I dived on him and allowing for full deflection, I opened fire at 400 yards. The rear gunner ceased his firing after my second burst. I re-opened fire at 200 yards as he went into a right-hand turn and closed to 50 yards, when I stopped firing and broke to the left and down.

Over sixty years later, Iain still remembers clearly the engagement:

> I can remember two actions specifically, one was when I got mixed up with seven enemy Me110s, and they went into a defensive circle. I remember thinking it was somewhat of a negative formation, so I started to blast off at them as well as I could. In some ways it was not an easy formation to attack, because you would be coming in rather fast and they are going quite slowly in a different direction.

The standard RAF formations at that time were based on the Vic formation of three aircraft, while the battle attack rules of engaging the enemy had been drawn up long before the war with Germany had begun. During the Battle of Britain it was found that the RAF fighters were at a disadvantage with the Germans while still using the old Vic formation. The Germans had developed a looser formation of four aircraft during the conflict in the Spanish Civil War. They could when required separate into two pairs; this being known as the finger-four position. Iain decided to try something different, rather than fly the standard formation:

> I remember our squadron commanding officer Johnny Hill; he was a good leader, but led in the conventional way, which at the time always did strike me as a bit dangerous. He led us in line astern formation which was called 'battle formation.' You were weaving up and down and you had to have your eyes looking at the chap in front, so that you didn't hit him, and this didn't give you time to look about. This was about the time that I decided that what I was going to do was drop back to the end of the formation and do a bit of weaving. At least I could keep an eye open for enemy fighters.

The Spitfire was an excellent fighting machine in the air, but on the ground one of its main disadvantages was its narrow undercarriage and its lack of forward viewing while taxiing to take off. This was due to the long nose of the aircraft and the restricted view through the armour-plated front windscreen, which also housed the reflector gun-sight. Most pilots would lean out of the side door and have to taxi the aircraft from left to right to get into position to take off. Iain remembers sometimes this did cause problems, especially during a squadron scramble:

> I recall once when we were scrambled, that Pilot Officer Laurie Whitbread was leading and I was following doing the correct procedure of swinging the aircraft's nose from side to side while taxiing. You just didn't taxi out in formation with the other guy, you had to check that there was nothing in your way. I swung to the left then swung to the right and there he was in front of me stationary and it was impossible to avoid him. I hit him and damaged his aircraft. I was reprimanded for the incident, which I felt was a little unfair.

With 222 now in the thick of the fighting, the pilots lived from day to day on a knife-edge. Every morning of that long hot summer, they would be up and at readiness at least by 5.00 am, ready for the morning patrol. In between sorties they would try and relax by reading books or listening to the radio, playing cards or chess; any second the alarm could sound, and once more they would be ordered aloft to engage the overwhelming formations coming across the Channel. What thoughts must have played on these young men whose average age was about twenty years? Iain Hutchinson was twenty-two at the time:

> I can't remember feeling terribly nervous, just reasonably apprehensive when we were climbing up, I don't remember ever feeling stressed at dispersal or when the alarm went; you just rushed to your aircraft and you had so much to do that you didn't have time to think about it. The only problem I had once, was after I had time off from being wounded by cannon splinters and I came back to fly. I had come back late and the squadron had already taken off, so I got permission to take off and join them if I could. So I took off and when I got airborne I found that some 'blighter' had switched off my oxygen at the bottle, and the bottle was behind the seat and armour plate. Luckily, I managed to twist my arm around and unscrew it, because I thought if I come back now they might think I was funking, after being shot down before.

During the battle it was formally recognised that the Spitfire squadrons would deal mainly with the Messerschmitt 109 fighter escorts, while the slightly slower Hawker Hurricanes would engage the German bomber formations. Of course there was never an ideal situation and at times Spitfires and Hurricanes would all mix in together to deal with the enemy. It has always been recognised in aerial warfare, that whoever commands the advantage of height and surprise will always be in a better position to direct the terms of engagement over the enemy. But there is also the element of luck; every pilot had to have some luck as well as the skill to survive. Iain Hutchinson certainly had his fair share of luck:

> You were led into the attack by your leader, once in the attack you had to choose your target, which meant therefore in a sense the

squadron split up. You then went for your target. If you only got up as far as the bomber height when you ran into them, then you would attack the bombers; but normally we were sent up to keep off the high level fighters. This is one reason why the attrition rate of Spitfires was greater than that of Hurricanes, because you are less likely to be shot down by attacking a bomber, than if you tangled with a fighter who was just as nimble as you are. So we had a slightly tougher deal in handling our share of the battle.

Another occasion I dived to attack four Germans in line astern, and I was going fairly fast. I shot at the leading one, but their No.4 began shooting at me and I could see his tracer bullets going past me and hitting the leading German as well. I then broke away, climbed back up and looked for another target. I remember one incident, which even at the time, was amusing. After the main engagement most of the aircraft had disappeared, so I climbed up fairly high, went to Dover, then flew back, and this was in the late afternoon against a setting sun. I flew back up into the sun and went through several formations of Me109s heading back across the Channel, home to France. Luckily nothing happened, I didn't see them until I was on them and they didn't pay any attention to me.

On Wednesday 11th September, Iain and the rest of the squadron were ordered to scramble and given instructions to patrol over the base, when operations control identified a mixed formation of Heinkels and Junker Ju88s with their fighter escort approaching from the south. In the following engagement, he claimed the probable destruction of a Heinkel He111. Iain takes up the story:

I attacked a Heinkel 111, and I remember seeing return fire from his rear gunner, so I fired back. Then I fired at his starboard engine and saw smoke starting to appear from it; then his undercarriage dropped. When I got back I claimed him, but I didn't get the claim approved. But what I expect had happened to him, was that another RAF fighter who was milling around at low level probably finished him off and could see where the German had crashed and got the victory. This probably happened numerous times; because often the guy who had initially started the attack at 30,000 feet would have no idea where the enemy aircraft had finished up.

I can recall seeing a Hurricane and a Spitfire trying to elbow each other out of the way to fire at a Me109, which was going vertically down, as dead as a dodo, and they were obviously trying to claim him. I never wasted my time trying to claim an aircraft, which I thought was likely to make it back. If not, I claimed it as damaged.

Iain's combat report written at the time states:

On another occasion after the squadron had delivered an attack upon the enemy formation, I noticed a He111 behind the formation on its own. As I went into the attack, another Spitfire delivered a short attack, whereupon the enemy aircraft lowered his undercarriage and black smoke emitted from its engines. The Spitfire broke away and I watched the enemy aircraft then commence to raise its undercarriage and the smoke ceased. I therefore delivered an attack myself. On the second burst his undercarriage dropped again and glycol and oily smoke poured from the starboard engine. I transferred my attack to the port engine with the same result. As the lower rear gunner was firing, I finished my ammunition at him; then as a Me109 attacked me I broke away. As I went down I could still see the He111 with both motors smoking and dropping down below the formation, its undercarriage still down. On landing, I noticed my aircraft was covered in dirty oil from his coolers.

As the heavy fighting increased, the pilots after returning from combat would find many familiar faces absent from dispersal chairs or the Officers' Mess. What were the thoughts that these young men must have had at the time? They knew that perhaps their next trip up into the summer skies might indeed be their last. Iain recalls how he adjusted to this stressful period:

You didn't dwell on these things. I think to be truthful my philosophy at that time, even from the beginning of the war, was that those who were at the sharp end were unlikely to see their way through to the finish, particularly those in the Air Force. So I had the feeling that I was just waiting for my ticket to come up, it was just a question of the sooner I got it over with, the better. A very odd philosophy, but that's what really kept me going, I had accepted the fact that I wasn't going to survive, so I just carried on flying every sortie. That was the sad thing about my friend John Ramshaw. We were rushing out for a scramble at Rochford, and he came up to me and said, 'you're always taking all the flights.' By that time I was the senior sergeant pilot.
    So I said to him, 'alright, you carry on then' and that was the flight in which he was killed. I always felt to myself afterwards, perhaps if I'd let some of the others fly a bit more, they would have got more experience and it wouldn't have happened, but that doesn't necessarily follow I suppose.

Of all the many facets of the Battle of Britain, perhaps the most understated was the tremendous effort and hardship that was undertaken by the ground crew. These men tirelessly worked throughout the long hours of the day and night to keep their squadron's aircraft in effective condition. Some of the crews worked over twenty-four hours in one go to maintain a fighting force of aircraft.

    They also were in the front line when the Luftwaffe changed their tactics in mid-August and began bombing the RAF airfields. Iain Hutchinson has only praise for those unsung heroes on the ground:

One particular incident I remember was when the airfield at

Hornchurch was under attack, and I landed and taxied to the dispersal area. It was quite noisy with the bombs dropping and the 3-inch and Bofors anti-aircraft guns firing; but these boys came rushing out with the fuel bowsers and the belts of ammunition and set about rearming and re-fuelling my Spitfire. I got out of the aircraft to give them access to the cockpit and to keep out of their way, but I was glad to get back into the aircraft and rejoin the scrap. They were brave men on whose skill in maintaining the aircraft you could rely unreservedly. They kept the aircraft in tip-top condition and I never suffered any problems caused by faulty maintenance.

On Saturday 14th September, 222 was sent to Rochford airfield near Southend at 1.30 pm, and the pilots were called into action at 3.25pm when they received the order to scramble with a large incoming German raid having been plotted. They were then told over the R/T to join up with No.603 City of Edinburgh Squadron (also based at Hornchurch) and patrol at an altitude of 14,000 feet. While over Canterbury, Kent, they sighted a large formation of Messerschmitt 109s at 21,000 feet. During the ensuing action, Iain Hutchinson claimed one of the German fighters destroyed, as his combat report for that day shows:

When we went in to attack a group of Me109s. I selected one as my target and opened fire at 250 yards, closing to about 100 yards, during which I fired three bursts of approximately three seconds each. Some parts of the machine fell past me. He went into a dive, which got steeper as he went down and I followed him, giving him a very short burst at 250 yards range. He went straight through a cloud and when I came out below it, I could still see him diving for the ground.

In turn, Iain himself was attacked by a German fighter and suffered damage to his Spitfire, which forced him to look for the nearest airfield to make an emergency landing. He found Detling and after landing was informed that the aircraft he had shot down had been seen diving to the ground. His own aircraft X4265 was not too badly damaged and was repairable. In later years, it has been documented that the German aircraft Iain had claimed belonged to 1/JG77, and had been flown that day by Feldwebel (flight sergeant) Ettler. He had managed to force-land his aircraft at Long Barn Farm, Boxley Hill, near Detling, and was captured unhurt.

As the sun rose and a new day dawned on Sunday 15th September 1940, very few at that time would have guessed what significance this day would hold in future years; to the pilots it was just another day's fighting in holding the German Air Force at bay. 222 Squadron was still based down at Rochford and after the previous day's hectic fighting had only seven serviceable aircraft available.

At 2.05 pm, the squadron were ordered aloft to patrol in company with 603 Squadron at 20,000 feet over Sheerness. Meanwhile, back on the ground Iain Hutchinson had been left without an aircraft to fly. Undeterred, and eager to get into the fight, Iain walked over to where 41 Squadron was dispersed and persuaded them to loan him one of their aircraft, and to allow him to fly with them:

> We were sent up and did an attack on some bombers; we were then split up. I was flying with another Spitfire, a chap I knew in No.41. I was looking around on my side of the two of us, but the next time I looked over my friend was gone and a Me109 had taken his place. The next thing I recall was that I had been shot down. I managed to bale out uninjured and I landed ok; several hours later I was back at RAF Hornchurch. It is not recorded in the official records of squadron aircraft losses, as I was not supposed to be flying that day.

In reality, there was very little time for pilots to take a break in the fighting, but on the odd day, when weather conditions restricted the Luftwaffe from mounting operations over the southeast coast and London, some of the pilots would venture up to town and take in a show or frequent the clubs in the West End. Here they could relax, let off steam and enjoy a few pints of beer. Iain remembers such visits to the capital:

> I went up to London on a couple of occasions; this was usually when the weather had closed in and you couldn't fly, so you could get a day off. I remember going up to the Hippodrome to see the show 'Black Magic.' I thought the bombing of London was terrifying. I remember falling flat on the pavement when I heard the bombs coming down, but you came to accept it. There'd be houses on fire and others that had been destroyed. I must confess that I was more terrified being in London during the bombing than ever I was when flying. I remember later, when I had to spend time in hospital, you couldn't go to the shelters, you were in your bed and they were bombing. A bomb dropped about 100 yards from the hospital and caused a fifteen-foot crater in the grounds.
>
> One amusing incident that I can remember was when at Hornchurch; I was playing the piano in the sergeants' mess during an air raid. A group of airmen had gathered around me and were belting out some of their favourite songs. We had all put our glasses of beer and tin helmets, upturned on top of the piano. Unknown to me, one of the pilots had poured his glass of beer into my helmet for a practical joke. Suddenly, the station attack-warning siren sounded, and everyone rushed for the door. I jumped up too, looking for my tin helmet, but it was missing. Some poor chap had taken mine in the rush to get out, and in the process had received a soaking.

On 18th September, Iain was once again on the receiving end, when he came out second best to a Messerschmitt 109 fighter over Canterbury, Kent at 1.53 pm. He again took to his parachute leaving his aircraft, Spitfire R6722, to plunge into a field at Clock House Farm, Challock. Iain was slightly hurt, but thankfully nothing too serious. On his return to Hornchurch, Iain records the response of one pilot on seeing him:

At Hornchurch, I used to share a room in the sergeants' mess with my good friend John Burgess. When I was shot down over Canterbury and I eventually got back, I crept into bed late that night. The next morning I went into shave in the Mess, in the washroom. Suddenly one of my fellow pilots saw me and jumped and said, 'you bastard, I thought you were dead,' I was blamed for being alive!

On Monday 30th September, 222 were scrambled for the second time during that day, this time at 1.00 pm. Taking off from Hornchurch, the pilots were quickly vectored towards the southeast of London. At the height of 24,000 feet, a German formation was sighted consisting of around twenty bombers with a large fighter escort. 222 dived down and on breaking up the enemy fighters, managed to engage the bombers. However, the 109s soon recovered and a succession of turning, twisting combats entailed. Sergeant Rainford Marland claimed two enemy fighters probably destroyed, as did Pilot Officer Eric Edsall. In the confusion of the fast and furious battle that was raging, Iain Hutchinson became a victim of what we call today, friendly fire. Iain can clearly recall the event:

I was keeping a lookout when I saw a Spitfire behind me, and I turned and banked to give him my plan form, and he shot at me. But this wasn't the first time that this had happened to me. Pilot Officer John Broadhurst had earlier in the battle, shot at me in the distance after one scrap; I can remember seeing his tracer coming over my bow. But thank goodness he missed me. But this other guy was quick on the trigger and he hit the petrol tank and tore a six-inch hole in it and it just went up in flames immediately. I then tried to get out as quickly as possible, but I didn't do the right thing in retrospect. If I had had my wits about me, I would probably have slowed the aircraft down and then baled out. But unfortunately I was still travelling at a fair speed. First of all my parachute became trapped against the hood, because my upper torso was bent back along the fuselage and my legs were still inside the cockpit. But suddenly within an instant, I was travelling free through the air and that was it. I couldn't see very well as my eyes were burnt. I pulled my ripcord and my parachute opened and I landed rather heavily.

Two dear old ladies came over to help me; I thought they were with the Women's Defence Force at the time. It turned out they had been having a picnic lunch and had seen me coming down. They had some brandy with them, but they wouldn't let me drink it, they just wet my lips with it, which didn't do much good. I don't really remember how long it was before I was picked up; I remember a doctor came and tried to help with my dislocated shoulder, but it was extremely painful, so he gave me an injection and then reset it. But my shoulder was broken as well as being dislocated. No wonder it was so painful. My right trouser leg was pretty well burnt away and I had burn marks up my leg.

I was taken to Uxbridge hospital and they sprayed the burns with

Tannic acid, I understand that I was the last patient to be treated this way. They sprayed all the burns with that; they then developed a crust or a scab. It healed alright on my face and my arm, but on my leg it went septic so they had to peel off the scab, which was a painful operation. It did heal up, but left a mark. I was in hospital for about a month, and then they sent me back on leave to Glasgow. They said that because I'd been a good boy and had done what I was told, they would not put my injured arm in an aeroplane splint and instead they would put it in a sling. I was told to report to the Queen Victoria Hospital in Glasgow. I was sent to the physiotherapist and he manipulated my arm; there was a terrible pain, he had broken it again. So I finished up in an aeroplane splint after all. An aeroplane splint is a wire construction and forms a continuous wire which is shaped to go around your ribs on one side, come up under your arm and then it runs along your arm to your wrist with wire on either side. It was slightly padded, which was never sufficient, and it was a painful business putting up with it because you had to sleep with your arm up at night.

After spending several weeks recovering from his wounds, Iain then went back to Hornchurch. He was still not fit for flying operations, so he was made a Duty Pilot. This entailed recording the arrivals and departures of aircraft and giving any clearances necessary on the airfield from aircraft coming from other airfields.

This he continued to do, until on 15th January 1941, he received his next posting to No.3 School of General Reconnaissance at Squires Gate, Blackpool as a pilot to fly the Blackburn Roc aircraft, where they were training navigators for Coastal Command. His main duty was to fly the aircraft with the trainee navigator seated in the rear, then fly over an area of the Irish Sea where the navigators would be tested for their ability to set various courses and headings. One of the main advantages for Iain at this time was that it enabled him to fly a variety of aircraft that were being used by the school; these included the Hawker Hurricane, Bolton-Paul Defiant, Westland Lysander, Bristol Blenheim and others.

While at the school, Iain was commissioned as a pilot officer on 4th August 1941. He remained with this unit until 6th January 1942, when he was posted to No.1 Photo Reconnaissance Unit at RAF Benson, near Oxford. He was first sent to Detling in Kent, to undertake training for photo-reconnaissance, mastering the technique of flying the aircraft at various angles to enable the pilot to position the camera for the best shot. He also learned the main functions and components of the aerial camera:

There was a technique for taking the pictures which seemed rather crude, but it worked. You flew towards the target, and then just as you were getting close, you then turned the aircraft over so the wings were vertical and the bottom wing was pointing at the target. You would then straighten up the Spitfire, switch on the cameras and photograph for a certain length of time.

I did some sorties over France. I started off with the simple

things like the Channel ports. Most of the time I was flying at
around 30,000 feet. My luckiest flight was when I was flying in
10/10ths cloud on the way out to Charleville and Le Mezières
where there were marshalling yards. By very good fortune there
was a gap in the cloud immediately over each of the targets, so I
managed to get photographs of each of them. My last flight using
the Spitfire was on 14th March 1942. I was then sent to No.2 PRU
and then on 25th March I undertook my first flight on a De
Havilland Mosquito. I had a short flight of one hour and then I was
sent off on my own to do solo and local reconnaissance for a couple
of hours.

Iain was sent up to No.2 Photo Reconnaissance Unit at Leuchars in Scotland
on 21st March 1942. His main operations with this unit involved covering the
areas of Norway and Denmark. Iain's first operational trip with his new unit
was on 27th March, when he flew to Christiansand where he spotted a
German shipping convoy. On returning, he reported his sighting to the
Operations Room and a squadron of Albacore torpedo aircraft was sent off to
attack the convoy. Iain continues:

I remember on one trip to Norway, one of the Mosquito's engines
failed. The port engine took fire, but we managed to put it out. I
then flew the remaining 550 miles over the North Sea on the one
engine and landed back at Leuchers. I was the first person to have
flown such a long distance on one engine. In a Mosquito it was a
very scary experience; it would have been pretty chilly had we
ditched into the sea.

My last trip was on 2nd April 1942 when I was doing a
reconnaissance over the port of Trondheim, where the German
battleships were lying. No.4 Group Bomber Command was
awaiting the results of my flight to enable them to determine if an
attack was feasible. We were doing a run over warships and as we
were going further in, I noticed some anti-aircraft fire was
following my track; there was a whole series of puffs of smoke
behind me. I thought they were just putting up some resistance; but
they were in fact indicating to their fighters where I was.

Two Focke-Wulf 190s appeared and attacked and hit one of the
engines; they demolished the cockpit instrument panel and part of
the cockpit hood. I could not give the 'bale out' order as my
navigator was in the nose bombsite position and his parachute was
stored behind the rear armour plate which had been raised just prior
to reaching the enemy coast. The attack continued and I had no
alternative but to carry out a forced landing on the snow-covered
island of Oerlandet. So I landed the aircraft on the island, and came
to rest not too far from the German airfield situated nearby.

We got out of the Mosquito and my navigator Sergeant Allan
took the Verey pistol and fired it at some petrol, which was dripping
from the aircraft, which then proceeded to go up in flames. As we
were walking away, we met a Luftwaffe chap carrying on his

shoulder, a single fire extinguisher, which we felt was a little inadequate as our poor Mosquito was a huge ball of flame by that time. We were then taken to the dispersal area of the airfield and greeted by the German pilot who had shot me down.

It was an interesting meeting because the pilot said to me, 'I'm sorry we have been waiting so long for you. The coffee's cold, but have a glass of Schnapps instead.' He continued: 'You are lucky, for you the war is over; we have to carry on. You will now be taken for interrogation but you do not have to answer anything.' It was an interesting introduction to our opposite numbers in the Luftwaffe.

Iain and Sergeant Allan were then separated, Iain spending the night in the Officers' Mess. They were then collected the next day by a German officer and taken down by railway carriage to Oslo. While there they were given a meal by the German Red Cross, consisting of a plate of butter beans and a small amount of ham. From here they were taken to a castle in Oslo, put into a room where they remained until they were transported down by a Junkers Ju52 transport aircraft to Denmark. They were then loaded aboard a train bound for Frankfurt and taken to a Durchgangslager Luft camp for interrogation. Here they spent three days in solitary being interrogated and then they were shipped into the main camp.

It was here that Iain cracked a rib while playing football in the compound; he was sent to the nearby hospital and after recovering he was asked if he would be the liaison officer between the camp and the hospital, which treated the sick and injured. He agreed to do this, but it wasn't a particularly pleasant job because he was locked in for twenty-three hours a day in the wards. Iain remembers that he assisted a captured British paratroop medical team perform an operation on a Polish pilot who had suffered burns and had gangrene on his fingers. On another occasion, Iain was asked to help an American flier, who had been in a crash in a B17 Flying Fortress and had suffered bad concussion. The American thought he was still in Iowa; a German officer asked Iain to try and talk to the American and explain to him where he was.

In June 1942, Iain received the wonderful news from his wife, that he now had a second daughter, named Patricia. On 5th August 1942, in absence, he was promoted to Flying Officer. Iain was then sent to another camp, Oflag 21 B situated in Poland until early spring 1943, when he was sent to Stalag Luft III at Sagan, Germany. Here he was billeted in the east compound of the camp. Of his time there, Iain comments:

The trouble was, there was a big long waiting list for escapes and I couldn't even get on to that. Some of the army other ranks serving as orderlies in the camp were going to be shifted to their own camp. So I arranged with one of them to change identities, because there was more opportunity of getting outside the wire of an army camp, as they would go to work on the land and so on. We were not allowed to work as officers at Stalag Luft III. So I was about to arrange the swap over with this army chap, when they had the Big Escape and the order went out that no more escapes were to be attempted until further notice. So my only chance at getting out had gone.

Within the camp I was able to do various things. I played the piano for the camp choir, we did the Messiah and Elijah; I helped produce a play in a double room which our chaps had made into a theatre, making the seats out of packing cases and so on. I also helped in the camp's selection of music, a bit like a disc jockey, changing the records over on the old gramophone, which was relayed over the loudspeaker system.

On 5th August 1943, Iain received a communication that he had been made a flight lieutenant. By mid January 1945, with a temperature of minus 23 degrees centigrade, snow on the ground and the Russians advancing, Iain and his comrades were marched out of the camp. They were allowed to pick up Red Cross provisions of food and cigarettes and were taken south initially. On the way, the column of prisoners stopped at a small village, an old lady appeared from one of the buildings and handed some soup to one of the German guards, who was standing near to Iain Hutchinson. The German refused the soup and told the old lady to give it to Iain, who had some then passed it on to somebody else. The column of prisoners was then marched to a place called Moskau.

From there they were sent to another camp at Luckenwald, which was near Berlin, in February 1945. Conditions and food were pretty poor. Eventually Red Cross parcels did arrive and the situation was eased and they carried on until the advancing Allied armies were near. The Germans then pulled out, leaving only a few guards who put on Red Cross armbands. Some of them occupied the open cells in the compound. To the Allied prisoners' dismay, a German SS light anti-aircraft battalion came and camped on the south perimeter of the camp. Their commanding officer, a colonel, sent a message into the camp stating that for every German he found in the camp in jail, he would kill ten of the prisoners. Not long afterwards, the German battalion disappeared and Russian tanks and cavalry were seen approaching the camp. Near to the camp the advancing Russians met some German resistance and the sound of battle was very noisy for a while. Iain recalls:

All of a sudden it became peaceful and once again we carried on for a while. The Russians then sent in guards, who were very good and foraged for food for us. We had some nice food for a while. Then their rear echelons came up and they were a bit of a shower; we got fed, but not nearly so well. Eventually, there was a camp organisation set up to run our side of the camp; this was under Squadron Leader Roland Beamont. I was put on his staff and helped organise the camp magazine.

One incident I can remember is when a jeep suddenly arrived and some journalists from the American side came over and they asked how we were doing. We told them that no one had come to take us away; they said not to worry that they would sort it. In a couple of days came a big convoy of American army trucks. We were loading up, when the Russians arrived with Tommy guns and they said that if any vehicle tried to get out of the camp with PoWs, they would shoot them. So we all got off the lorries and one or two people took off to try and walk to the American lines. But I've no idea what happened to them. We learned later that we were being held hostage pending resolution of the handing over by western forces of White Russians held by them. It was not a comfortable situation. The Russians eventually came up with trucks for us, and took us up to the autobahn out of Berlin to Magdeberg, where we were deloused and fed. One of the people serving the food said they had been told to be careful with us because our stomachs would be shrunk, and that we should not eat too much; but we were eating like flipping horses. We were then put aboard aircraft and flown to Brussels in Belgium. There, we were given five pounds in Belgian currency, which we couldn't do much with. We did manage to go out on the town and have a few drinks. We were flown back to Britain and then sent to the big de-briefing centre in the Midlands. From there, we were sent home on leave for a few weeks and then sent back again for demob; then that was it.

Iain returned to Glasgow and his family, where he had an apartment flat. With peace now declared he decided to go back to university and study. He managed to secure a place at Glasgow University and for the next three years undertook studies on the following courses: geography, geology, mathematics, and biology. He achieved a degree as a Bachelor of Science.

On 11th January 1947, he joined the Glasgow University Air Squadron, still retaining his rank as flight lieutenant. Here, he did the regular training on the old Miles Magisters. It was while with the university squadron that the commanding officer whom Iain had known in the Volunteer Reserve before the war, asked Iain if he wanted to rejoin the RAF as they were asking for pilots. He went before an RAF board and was accepted, and was then sent to Biggin Hill on 14th June 1949. He was then posted to RAF Finningley on 21st June, which was a flying proficiency school flying Harvard and Tiger Moth aircraft. He was then sent to No.204 Advanced Flying School on 13th September. Here he remained until 6th December 1949, when he was posted to 20 Squadron at RAF Valley. The squadron was basically an army co-operation unit and used the following aircraft: Spitfires, Harvards and Martinets. Iain also flew the Bristol Beaufighter, which was used as a target-towing drogue, and one of the early jets, the Vampire, when it arrived:

Even at this late date, dual training was not thought necessary. I was checked out by the squadron commander and more or less went straight on to the Vampire, having been given the run down on its controls and vices.

On 20th August 1951, Iain was posted to RAF Fighter Command Headquarters at Uxbridge. It was while serving here that Iain wrote a paper for the stationing of RAF rescue helicopters around Britain for rescuing pilots who had been downed in the sea. His recommendations were accepted and he also designed a droppable container, which held a dinghy and some survival equipment, which could be dropped from a Spitfire. It was made and tested at Farnborough, it worked, but for some reason the ministry decided not to go ahead with it. Iain also devised the search and rescue pattern, which became the standard Fighter Command regulation until the beacon system was introduced. He left Fighter Command Headquarters on 19th December 1954, and was sent to the Royal Air Force Staff College on 11th January 1954. Here his main duty was to write appreciations and staff papers to broaden the knowledge of the RAF service, but he also worked in co-operation with the Army and the Navy conducting joint exercises with them. On leaving staff college on 4th January 1955, Iain Hutchinson was promoted to Squadron Leader.

His next posting was to No.11 Flying Training School to learn to fly twin-engine Varsity transport aircraft, because he was going to take over a squadron based in Cyprus. Unfortunately, the squadron were disbanded before he could take up the position. However, he finished the flying course at 11 FTS and got his green instrument rating; he was then posted to the Air Ministry on 21st February 1955, taking up his position at Kingsway, London on 4th April 1955, where his main duties involved intelligence information gathering. After only a short stay at the Air Ministry, Iain managed to get transferred to the Operational Requirements Directorate on 20th June. Here, he became involved with the operational requirements for safety equipment, i.e. parachutes, dinghies, ejector seats etc. Iain finally decided to take early retirement at the age of thirty-nine and left the Royal Air Force on 1st December 1957.

He then spent the next six months teaching at a secondary school at Bracknell in Berkshire, which was quite an experience. Here he was given the lowest stream of pupils. He found the students an entertaining group, but he couldn't really teach them anything. He was trying to teach mathematics, but they were not that interested, as they were soon to leave and were more interested in earning money.

While at the school, Iain applied for a post with the United Kingdom Atomic Energy Authority, who had a vacant position for an experimental officer at Dounray. He managed to read up on as much information on atomic energy before he was interviewed and got accepted for the job. Starting his new position in April 1958, he was joined later in the year by his family. He was promoted to senior experimental officer while there, and became the nuclear material accountant, also responsible for preparing the experimental report for the establishment for sending down to the United Kingdom Atomic Headquarters.

Iain then went down to Winfrith in December 1960, where he remained as nuclear materials accountant. In 1969, he applied for an attachment to the International Atomic Energy Agency and was accepted. He was given a two-year leave of absence to go to Vienna, Austria, where he was initially in the nuclear accounting field and then moved on to looking after instruments and their development. He was promoted to diplomatic rank while he was there. He was subsequently given the job of organizing international training courses on national systems of nuclear materials and accounting and control. People from all over the world attended, from Japan, America, Europe and Russia and Iain was responsible for organising their training in the relevant disciplines. He was then given the honour of designing the course and specifying the topics for a training course for inspectors. This involved liaison with the atomic energy authorities in Moscow and Washington principally. They allowed Iain and his staff to go there and work at their facilities. Here Iain designed a practical course for inspectors so that they would get accustomed to inspecting different types of nuclear facilities, typical of those types they would expect to look after, and to confirm that the nuclear material was properly declared and actually there and not being secreted away. He remembers:

> We ran courses in Russia and the Ukraine; the ones in America were also interesting too. The amazing thing about being in the position I was, was that although I was relatively low on the totem pole as far as a UK atomic employee, over there I was one of the UKA representatives and we were able to meet the man at the head of the United Kingdom Atomic Energy Authority and put our points of view.

Iain Hutchinson left the UK Atomic Authority in 1971, but took on a long-term contract with the International Atomic Industry for five years. This was extended for another two years, and then he was given the job of doing the technical editing of a book on radiation fuel processing, which had been written by the Japanese and translated not too well into English. Eventually Iain was given the task of re-writing this book completely into understandable scientific English. He finally retired from working in 1981. He continued to pursue his hobbies, which included sailing and playing squash. Now, in his retirement Iain is still very active and attends squadron reunions, and supports various Battle of Britain events. This tall, blue-eyed and soft-spoken Scotsman is a true gentleman, and very modest regarding his RAF wartime exploits. But sixty years ago Iain and men like him, held tightly in their hands the freedom of the world against Nazi tyranny and won.

CHAPTER 5

BROADY
Air Chief Marshal Sir Harry Broadhurst
GCB, KCB, KBE, CB, DSO & Bar, DFC & Bar, AFC
1905–1995

Harry Broadhurst was born on 28th October 1905 at Frimley in Surrey. His father, also named Harry, had served as a regular officer in the South Lancashire Regiment. He was the Regimental Sergeant Major for many years and visited many places with the regiment, including the Indian sub-continent and Gibraltar. His mother's maiden name was Patterson. The young Broadhurst had one sister, Nora, who had been born in the Indian sub-continent, and was six years his senior. At the outbreak of the First World War, his father had purchased a house in Emsworth, Hants, so that his family would have a permanent home. Previous to that, they had always travelled with the regiment.

During his early years, the young Harry did what most young children do, having marvellous adventures at play and making mischief. One day, he craved a drum, so he took himself down to the local shop and told the shopkeeper that his father would pay him later. He then marched off home playing his newly acquired possession. However, his father reckoned he wasn't going to have all this noise and marched him back again. On another occasion, there was to be an important inspection at the regiment; everything had to be cleaned, polished and painted. Come lunchtime, the man who had been remarking the Officers' Mess tennis court went for his meal, but left the white paint marker behind. Young Harry came along and thought this was a marvellous toy and proceeded to put dozens of white lines all over the tennis court. On finding out about the young boy's mischief, his father locked him up in the guardroom to teach him a lesson.

It was during the First World War in France that Harry Broadhurst senior was commissioned, but he was later invalided out of the front line due to trench fever; he ended the war as a captain. The young Broadhurst undertook the usual primary schooling and was then sent to be educated at the Portsmouth Grammar School, which he attended from 1915 until 1922. After finishing his education, he entered into employment as an assistant to a surveyor and also spent a short time in the Territorial Army joining on 21st May 1925, and attaining the rank of 2nd Lieutenant in the 2nd Hampshire Heavy Brigade, Royal Artillery, TA. But on 1st October 1926 against his father's wishes, he resigned his commission as 2nd Lieutenant and volunteered to join and train as a pilot in the Royal Air Force. His application was, therefore, signed by his Territorial Army commanding officer. Harry Broadhurst would later recall:

Peter Brown

op left: A youthful Peter Brown aged 14 years.
eter Brown Collection

op right: Pilot Officer Brown seen standing next to a
Vapiti biplane at RAF Cranwell.
eter Brown Collection

Bottom left: Future Pilot Officers. Peter pictured at
Hanworth 1938, seen here with P/O Thompson (left)
and P/O Dennis David (right).
Peter Brown Collection

Bottom right: Portrait photograph of Flying Officer
Peter Brown 1940. *Peter Brown Collection*

Top: Pilots of 611 Squadron, seen here outside their dispersal hut at RAF Digby, August 1940. From left to right, back row: Sgt S. Levenson, P/O C. MacFie, Sgt A. Burt, P/O D. Scott-Malden, P/O C. Jones, ?, P/O D. Adams, Sgt A. Darling, F/O B. Heath,?. Front: F/O D. Watkins on F/Lt W. Leather's knee, P/O P. Brown, F/Lt K. Stoddart, P/O P. Pollard. Some of the pilots are also wearing revolver sidearms.
Peter Brown Collection

Bottom left: The German pilot Feldwebel Bielmaier of 5/JG52 whom Peter shot down on 20th October 1940; pictured on right, with his two ground crew.
L.J. Hickey Collection

Bottom right: Peter Brown seen here with Pilot Officer Guy Cory outside 41 Squadron's dispersal hut, Hornchurch, November 1940. Peter is wearing the German shwimmveste he took from Feldwebel Bielmaier. *Author via Mileham*

op: Up at Catterick! A Flight of 41 Squadron May
941. Left to right: Sgt Hopkinson, Sgt Fowler, P/O
Keeble, F/Lt P. Brown, Sgt Baker, P/O G. Draper,
gt R. Beardsley, Sgt T. Healey.
uthor via R. Beardsley

nset: Peter seen here in the cockpit of a Hawker
Iurricane at 56 OTU Tealing in October 1942.
eter Brown Collection

Bottom: At 61 OTU, RAF Heston, October 1941: front
row, left to right. F/Lt Hopkin DFC, F/Lt Brown,
F/Lt Rogers, S/Ldr Bateman, W/Cdr Malan DSO, DFC,
G/Cpt Parker DFC, AFC, S/Ldr Walker, F/Lt Bisdee DFC,
F/O Watkinson and F/Lt Holland DFC.
Back row: W/O Morfill DFM, F/Sgt Gooderham,
Sgt Crozier, Sgt Allen, Sgt Chiole, Cpl Simpson,
Sgt Miller and F/Sgt Chapman. *Peter Brown Collection*

Top left: Peter Brown pictured with some of his Turkish pilots at RAF Cranwell in August 1943. *Peter Brown Collection*

Top right: Peter Brown was Squadron Leader Flying at No.9 Advanced Training Unit, Erroll in Scotland 1944. *Peter Brown Collection*

Middle: Do you remember? Ex-41 Squadron Battle of Britain pilots meet up for a reunion in September 1949. Left to right: F/Lt Roy Ford, S/Ldr Peter Brown, S/Ldr Bob Beardsley, W/Cdr Don Finlay, F/Lt Cyril Bamberger and S/Ldr John Mackenzie. *Peter Brown Collection*

Bottom right: What a Birthday Present! In June 1999, always the pilot, Peter aged 80, took to the air and flew the light aircraft seen pictured behind him. *Peter Brown Collection*

William Ash

Top: Members of 411 'Grizzly Bear' Canadian
Squadron pictured at Hornchurch 1942. Tex is
pictured 7th from left in the back row.
Author via Ash

Middle left (top): Tex pictured in Spitfire AD281.
It was in this aircraft that he was shot down on 23rd
March 1942. *Author via Ash*

Middle centre: Three friends. Bill Stapleton (left),
Tex and Paddy Barthropp (kneeling on left) seen here
as prisoners of war at Stalag Luft III.
Author via Ash

Middle right: Tex with ex-411 pilot, Squadron Leader
Chuck Semple at the Memorial stone dedicated to 411
Canadian Squadron at Digby. *Author via Ash*

Middle left (bottom): Canadian Premier
Mr Mackenzie King congratulates Tex, after he had
returned from another sweep over France in late 1941.
Author via Ash

Bottom right: Paddy and Tex meet up again with the
Spitfire at the Battle of Britain Memorial Flight's
headquarters at RAF Coningsby, Lincolnshire.
Author via Ash

Eric Lock

Top left: Eric Lock aged 7 and his sister Joan on holiday at Rhyl, North Wales 1927.

Top right: Newly commissioned Pilot Officer Eric Lock standing outside the family home 'Eastingham'

in June 1940. This photograph was taken by his siste[r] Joan. *J. Statham*

Bottom: Eric with his Singer Le Mans sports car at Lake Vyrnwy, North Wales 1936. *J. Statham*

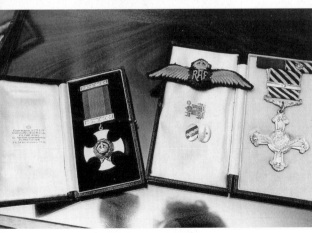

Top: Eric with 611 Squadron mascot 'Scruffy' at Hornchurch July 1941, before he was reported missing in action on 3rd August 1941. *IWM*

Middle left: Eric Lock's medal awards, (left) the Distinguished Service Order, (centre) his Wings and (right) The Distinguished Flying Cross with bar. *J. Statham*

Middle right: Pilot Officer Eric Lock climbs aboard the dispersal truck with a helping hand from Flying Officer Peter Brown at RAF Hornchurch, October 1940. *Author via Mileham*

Bottom right: The pencil portrait drawn of Eric Lock by artist Cuthbert Orde dated 19th July 1941.

Iain Hutchinson

Top left: Iain Hutchinson aged 6 months.
Author via Hutchinson

Top right: Iain on holiday in Scotland 1936 aged 18.
Author via Hutchinson

Middle left: With wife Margaret in 1948.
Author via Hutchinson

Middle right: Mid-1939, aged 21 Iain is seen here standing with Douglas Hogg in front of a Hawker Hart biplane. Hogg was killed by friendly fire during the Battle of Britain on 3rd September whilst with 25 Squadron. *Author via Hutchinson*

Bottom Iain whilst at Kirton-in-Lindsey. Note the Saint motif on his mae west life jacket.
Author via Burgess

Top: A touch of the 'Biggles,' Iain seated in the cockpit of a Hawker Hart, mid-1939. *Author via Hutchinson*

Middle left: Iain with pilots of 222 Natal Squadron out at dispersal at Kirton-in-Lindsey, July 1940. *Author via Burgess*

Middle right: Iain after graduation at Glasgow University 1949 aged 31. *Author via Hutchinson*

Bottom: Pictured in front of the immortal Spitfire, Iain is reunited with former 222 Squadron Battle of Britain engine-fitter Dave Davis (left) in 1993. *Author via D. Ringrow*

Harry Broadhurst

Top left: Harry Broadhurst aged 19.
Author via D. Lunn

Top right: Keeping a tight formation, Harry Broadhurst (centre) leads the 19 Squadron aerobatic team in their tied together Gloster Gauntlet biplanes during the Hendon air display in 1936.
Author via Broadhurst

Bottom left: The three members of 19 Squadron's aerobatic team; Left to right: F/O J.R MacLachlan, F/Lt Broadhurst and F/O B.G. Morris.
Author via Broadhurst

Bottom right: Broady and his WAAFs at RAF Hornchurch 1941. *Author via Broadhurst*

Top: Broadhurst shows an invited party of South American officers the oil-stained spinner of his Spitfire at Hornchurch. This was just after his head-on attack with a German ace on 7th July 1941, in which the German's aircraft exploded in mid-air showering Broadhurst's Spitfire with oil and human remains. *Author via Broadhurst*

Middle left: Broadhurst chats with a Desert Air Force pilot; the crashed aircraft is a RAF P40 Tomahawk. *Author via Broadhurst*

Middle right: Getting ready for the big push? Broadhurst with other senior commanders. Field Marshal Bernard Montgomery and Admiral Bertram Ramsey on his immediate left, discuss final plans to invade Sicily 1944. *Author via Broadhurst*

Bottom left: Broady seated in his Spitfire Mk IX. *Author via Broadhurst*

Bottom right: At 38, the youngest acting Air Vice-Marshal in the RAF, Broadhurst is seen here with Lord Trenchard in 1944. *Author via Broadhurst*

Top left: Harry Broadhurst in his captured German Fiesler Storch aircraft.
Author via Broadhurst

Top right: I'll drink to that! Harry Broadhurst (right) and Lord Louis Mountbatten toast each other.
Author via Broadhurst

Bottom left: Broadhurst (centre) and the crew of Avro Vulcan XA897 before its flight to Australia in 1956.
Author via Broadhurst

Bottom right: Broady in his Air Chief Marshal's uniform, at the wedding of his daughter Diana in 1956
Author via D. Lunn

Dave Glaser

Top left: The Glaser boys, Jack and Dave in 1933. *Author via Glaser*

Top right: Sergeant Dave Glaser pictured just after joining the RAFVR in June 1939. *Author via Glaser*

Middle: Jeffrey Quill's Spitfire seen here at Rochford, Hornchurch's satellite airfield, August 1940. *Author via Glaser*

Bottom right: Dave pictured in the cockpit of a 65 Squadron Spitfire at Hornchurch, August 1940. Note the glare cover attached to the Spitfire's cowling to stop glare from the exhaust stubs when flying at night. *Author via Glaser*

Top: Dave's 234 Squadron Spitfire
W3936 seen here at dispersal at
Warmwell aerodrome 1941.
Author via Glaser

Middle: Cine gun-camera footage from
Dave Glaser's Spitfire clearly shows an
engagement with a Messerschmitt 109
during 1941.
Author via Glaser

Bottom right: Flying Officer Dave
Glaser with his pet spaniel puppy
'Blackie' while with 234 Squadron
1941. *Author via Glaser*

Top: An excellent air shot of Dave Glaser flying his Spitfire Mk VIII in Australia.
Author via Glaser

Above: Dave Glaser seen here with 549 Squadron ground crew, while operating from the Darwin area of Northern Australia in 1944/45. The Spitfire is a Mk VIII coded ZF-Z.
Author via Glaser

Right: Dave Glaser seen with his Australian Blue Heeler 'Baron'. At this time Dave was with 54 Squadron. *Author via Glaser*

Top left: Dave marries Cora Ann Gillie on 10th December 1949 at St Andrew's Church, Hamble. *Author via Glaser*

Top right: Dave Glaser pictured whilst Senior Test Pilot at Hurn.

Bottom: Dave seen here seated inside the cockpit of a BAC 1-11 at Hurn aerodrome in the 1960s with fellow test pilot Chuck Thrower. *Author via Glaser*

Top: Finally laid to rest after 35 years! The remains of Flying Officer Franciszek Gruszka are buried with full military honours at Northwood Cemetery, Middlesex on 14th July 1975.
Author via Glaser

Right: Dave Glaser with his Rumanian wife, Rodica.
Author via Glaser

Eric Barwell

Top left: The young and adventurous Eric Gordon Barwell at play. *Author via Barwell*

Top right: Pilots of 264 Squadron pictured just prior to the Battle of Britain. Standing left to right: ?, F/Lt N. Cooke, S/Ldr P. Hunter, P/O M. Young, P/O G. Hackwood, P/O Barwell, P/O S. Thomas, P/O D. Whitley. Seated: P/O Goodall, P/O D. Kay, Sgt A. Lauder, ?. *IWM*

Middle left: Armourers of 125 Squadron load up the Boulton-Paul Defiant's gun turret with fresh ammunition belts. *Air Historical Branch CH 4606*

Middle right: Squadron Commander Eric Barwell (centre) pictured with fellow pilots of 125 Newfoundland Squadron in 1942. *Air Historical Branch CH 4610*

Bottom left: Flying Officer Eric Barwell soon after receiving his DFC in February 1941. *Author via Barwell*

Bottom right: Return to Hornchurch! Ex-264 Squadron Battle of Britain pilots and gunners gather outside the Officers' Mess at Hornchurch in 1993. Left to right: Eric Barwell DFC, Fred Gash DFM, Fred Barker DFM and John 'Ginger' Lauder. *Author via D. Ringrow*

William Crawford-Compton

Top: No.485 at Redhill 1941. Left to right on Spitfire: F/Lt R.H Strang, Sgt I.J. McNeil, Sgt Frecklington, Francis, Sgt W.M Krebs. Standing: P/O MacLoud, Sgt E.A. Cochrane, Sgt L.P. Griffith, Sgt Crawford-Compton, S/Ldr Knight, Sgt A.S.Kronfeld, P/O D.T. Clouston. Sitting: Sgt J. Rae, P/O R. Barrett and Sgt H. Sweetman. *Author/RNZAF*

Middle left: Presentation Spitfire 'Auckland I' flown by Crawford-Compton on a sweep over France, showing shrapnel damage inflicted during the sortie. *Copyright E.D. Mackie Collection*

Middle right: Sergeant Harvey Sweetman pictured in front of his Spitfire, which was publicly funded and named 'The Spirit of Redhill'. *H.N. Sweetman*

Bottom right: Sergeant Pilot Douglas Brown of 485 Squadron seen here in his Spitfire, December 1941. His memories of Crawford-Compton are featured in this book. *Author via Brown*

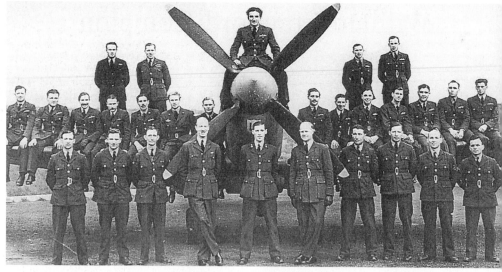

Top: Crawford-Compton sits astride a Spitfire Mk IX while this group photograph is taken of 64 Squadron at RAF Hornchurch in 1943. Left to right, front row: two unidentified ground staff, F/Sgt Lowe, F/O Mellersh (IO), Doc Dewell, F/O Farries (EO), F/Sgt Moon, two unidentified staff, F/Sgt Rose. Sitting on wing: Sgt Bilsland, Sgt Byrne, F/O Harris, F/O Poulton, F/O Mason, Lt Johnsen, F/O Harder, F/O Curd, P/O Dalziel, unidentified, F/O Patterson, P/O Kelly, Sgt Ledington, Sgt Burge. Standing on wing, left to right: unidentified, F/Lt Donnet, Sgt Coupland and F/Sgt Batchelor. *Copyright M. Donnet*

Middle left: Two of New Zealand's renowned fighter pilots, Bill Crawford-Compton and Edward 'Hawkeye' Wells relax with a game of cards. *Author via Brown*

Middle right: Standing next to his personally coded Spitfire Mk IX at RAF Hornchurch in 1943. Where did he get that pipe? *RNZAF*

Bottom left: Wing Commander William Crawford-Compton seen here at Hornchurch in October 1943 as Wing Commander Flying. *Copyright IWM*

Bottom right: Group Captain Crawford-Compton seen here with his wife Chloe (on left) during the 1950s. *D. Lunn Collection*

In those days it was possible to transfer across into the Royal Air Force, which I did in 1926, under a scheme whereby I only had to learn to fly and not learn all the disciplines of being in one of the other services, which was a lot more fun because I went straight to a squadron. Unfortunately at that time I was very much into racing motorcycles and I actually fell off my racing motorbike on the way to joining the RAF. This didn't do me a great deal of damage, but it immobilized me somewhat, so I started life in the RAF in hospital for a month; for which they docked me one month's seniority and made me pay for the hospitalisation and banned the remnants of the motorbike from the camp. My RAF number was 24035.

Broadhurst's parents had hated the idea of their son joining the flying service and his mother forecast disaster. This was in fact not long in coming when on 11th November 1926 their son was involved in an air accident. Harry Broadhurst remembers:

It was on Armistice Day, just six weeks after joining and I had just learnt to fly. I was sent to see a court of inquiry in the back of a bomber, which was the standard equipment in the squadron. The next thing I remember was waking up three days later in hospital. I never met the chap who was flying the aircraft and didn't know what had happened. My parents found out about the accident in the local paper at the weekend. They rang up to discover what had happened to their beloved son, but there was nobody in the camp at Netheravon to tell them, so that was a bad start to their opinion of their son going into the RAF. What had happened was that there was heavy fog and the pilot had tried to get the aircraft down on to the airfield, but there were no aids in those days. Unfortunately, he hit the high ground short of the airfield. He was killed and I was very lucky to survive, but I have no memory of the event whatsoever. Fortunately, this didn't put me off flying. The aircraft I learnt to fly on was an Avro 504K and the advanced trainers were fighters from the first war, Sopwith Snipes and the bombers were De Havilland 9As.

Diana Lunn, née Broadhurst, can recall her father telling her of his initial entry into the Royal Air Force:

My father had joined the RAF on a short service commission, and then later extended this, which meant he had abandoned hope of obtaining a permanent commission. He had difficulties with his initial medical to join the RAF, as his blood pressure was too low, the doctor sent him to run round the block a couple of times and then he passed. He was planning to go into partnership to run a garage in Emsworth, when his service career finished; however Hitler changed all that with the announcement of the formation of the Luftwaffe in the 1930s, leading to the build up of the RAF.

It was during his early days with the RAF, that Broadhurst met and fell in love with Doris Kathleen French, also known as Kay. Her father was a leather wholesaler in Portsmouth. They had been introduced to each other by one of Broadhurst's friends, Patrick Connolly, also at that time in the RAF.

After completing his flying training, he was awarded his wings on 8th August 1927, and given a short service commission. At the age of twenty-one, he was posted to his first squadron, No.11 (Bomber) Squadron based at Netheravon, Wiltshire on 3rd April 1928, as a pilot officer. In July 1928, the squadron were to have moved to India, but this was delayed until December, eventually sailing from Southampton on 29th December on the HMT *Nevassa* and arriving at Risalpur, India on 22nd January 1929.

The squadron was commanded by Squadron Leader P.H. Cummings DFC and consisted of 12 officers and 65 airmen; Broadhurst was by that time a flying officer and the signals officer. By the 1st April that year, the full complement of aircraft had been received and an individual training programme was started. It was while out in India that Broadhurst and his fiancée decided to marry and did so in the St Thomas Cathedral, Bombay on 19th October 1929. On 1st April 1930, A Flight was posted to Miranshah to take over the duty as a detached flight from A Flight of 39 Squadron. Flying Officer Broadhurst remained behind, but proceeded to Miranshah on 11th May, and remained until the flight returned to its home base.

On 27th February 1931, Harry and Doris Broadhurst became parents with the birth of a daughter at the military hospital in Peshawar; the baby girl was named Diana. The family were living at Risalpur at this time, and the squadron flew many operations over the north-west frontier using Horsley and Wapiti biplanes.

It was while undertaking action against the rebellious tribes on the frontier that Broadhurst was to receive a Mentioned in Despatches on 26th June 1931. When the tribes did go on the attack, the pilots would first fly over the rebel villages, warning the inhabitants by dropping leaflets telling them that the RAF would be back later that day to bomb the village; this was done to prevent women and children being killed. Broadhurst recalls that when they did arrive over the target village, it sometimes was very far from being quiet and the tribesmen would put up a primitive sort of anti-aircraft defence:

> Most of the time we bombed from height, but if you went in low the tribesmen were extraordinarily accurate. I'd been hit but not shot down and friends of mine had been killed by these blunderbusses of rifles they had, most of which had been captured from us many years before. Nevertheless they could shoot straight enough and if they happened to hit you in the wrong place it would kill you; we had no defence, no armour plating in those days.

Broadhurst and his family returned to the United Kingdom in 1931 and with his next posting he joined 41 Squadron flying Bristol Bulldog aircraft, stationed at RAF Northolt on 16th September 1931. On 17th June the squadron was involved in the air-firing exercises at Sutton Bridge, Broadhurst becoming top scorer of the competition with 133 hits achieved.

In 1933, Broadhurst was posted from 41 Squadron and undertook a flying boat course at RAF Calshot on 18th September 1933. After finishing the course on 21st November, he was sent to 19 Squadron as a flight commander at RAF Duxford on 26th November 1933. Broadhurst's flying skills were soon noted by his commanding officer and fellow officers and he was soon asked to join and train in the squadron's aerobatic team. After nearly a year with 19 Squadron, Broadhurst was sent to RAF Headquarters at Ismailia, Eygpt to give instruction on air-to-air firing at No. 4 Flying Training School. His daughter Diana recalls:

He was sent to Egypt, but we were there for only a few months. My father had been an instructor in air-to-air firing and was known for getting the most shots on the towed target. However, in Egypt, he was showing off his skills, and when they inspected the target not a single hit appeared on it. Upon investigation, they realised that they had always towed the target at a set speed, but on this occasion the towing aircraft had towed at a different speed. This proved a most important discovery, as in future they had to practice at differing speeds which was very important for wartime combats.

On returning from his trip to Egypt, Broadhurst went back immediately to 19 Squadron on 9th December 1934. Here he continued as before and took back his role in the aerobatic display team, which soon became the Royal Air Force's top display team and one of the top attractions at the Hendon Air Display and Empire Air Days at various other airfields. But even while training, not everything would go according to plan and accidents sometime did occur, as the late Jeffrey Quill revealed. Quill at that time was a pilot with the Meteorological Flight based at Duxford:

It was late February 1935; I was at Duxford and had taken off on an early morning Met flight. There was early morning fog, which partially burnt off during my climb up. I landed back at Duxford at about 9.00 am, the fog was still thick in places and I took great care on my landing. As I taxied in and switched off, I was told that Squadron Leader Cassidy and Flight Lieutenant Harry Broadhurst in their Gloster Gauntlet biplanes were overdue and it was believed they had come down and crashed in a field near Cambridge. I was asked if I could take to the air again, try and locate them and report their position. After a short search I sighted them, just south of Cambridge. Both aircraft were lying upside down in a muddy ploughed field, still in perfect formation. I flew low over them and recognised Broady standing beside his Gauntlet with about three pounds of mud on each boot. I stretched out my ungloved hand over the side of my cockpit and signalled a greeting.

On their return to Duxford, Squadron Leader Cassidy told me what had happened. After taking off from Duxford the fog had closed in again and they had been unable to get back. They were by then running short of fuel, so he led them onto a large field to land, which would normally be all right. But the surface of the field was soft and the Gauntlet's streamlined wheel spats had become choked with mud, causing the wheels to lock. Both aircraft at the end of their landing slowly turned over onto their backs. Fortunately neither Cassidy nor Broadhurst suffered any injuries.

In 1936, Flight Lieutenant Broadhurst led the squadron's flight aerobatic team of three Gloster Gauntlet aircraft. On Saturday 27th June 1936, Broadhurst along with Flying Officers J.R. MacLachlan and B.G. Morris undertook and delighted a packed crowd at the Royal Air Force Display at Hendon. They were listed in the official programme as *Event 8 – Aerobatics by three Gloster Gauntlet aircraft while tied together*. The crowds were thrilled by the three machines, which looped and rolled and dived towards the aerodrome at 350 mph while tied together. As they roared above the spectators, Broadhurst was able to broadcast from his machine a radio commentary on what he and his colleagues were doing. This was relayed through dozens of loud speakers scattered in all parts of the field. Flight Lieutenant Broadhurst calmly announcing, *'we are now coming down to do three loops in succession. I am looking at my speed indicator. We are now doing 250 miles an hour-260-280-300-350.'* The aerobatics they performed that day were: an upward loop, a half-roll, a loop, a half-roll off top, three loops in succession, a stall turn, a slow roll, a rocket loop, half upward roll, 45 degree upward roll and climbing roll.

Following this outstanding display, Broadhurst received a letter from Mr W. Lappin of Rolls-Royce Ltd in London, in which he wrote:

My Dear Broadhurst

I must write and congratulate you on the superlative demonstration of skilful flying which you and your colleagues carried out on Saturday. I have been at every display and must confess I have seen nothing to equal it, and this is shared by everyone I came into contact with.

Please convey my congratulations to your two colleagues.

During his time with the squadron, he had also won for three consecutive years the Brooke-Popham Trophy, which was awarded to the winner of the competition for best air firing. For his outstanding ability and achievements in flying, Broadhurst was awarded the well-earned Air Force Cross on 1st February 1937.

On his return, Broadhurst left 19 Squadron and on promotion to squadron leader given to him earlier on 1st July 1937, was given a job on the Personnel Staff of No.2 Headquarters (Bomber) Group based at Andover on 2nd September 1937. He left this position to undertake a course at the RAF Staff College also at Andover on 24th January 1938. On 29th September, he was sent to Headquarters Bomber Command in a temporary position until 6th October.

That same year, Harry Broadhurst had been part of a contingent of Royal Air Force officers that were invited to Germany as guests of Hermann Goering's new Luftwaffe. Broadhurst recollects:

I went out to Berlin and met the No.1 Geschwader (Wing), and stayed in the Luftwaffe Club. Here I met a lot of their leading men while I was there including General Udet I think. But all they asked about really was the Hawker Hurricane and the new Spitfires. The Hurricane had just completed its record speed trip from Turnhouse in Scotland to London with a north-easterly gale behind it with an average speed of 400 mph, and the Germans reckoned that it had a gale behind, but they didn't get the information out of me. But they all seemed pretty friendly. I got to see a squadron of Messerschmitt 109s, which I reported. I had the loan of a car, so I went to Czechoslovakia and visited their air force, never realizing that later I would get a Czech squadron at Hornchurch during the war to come. From there I went to Austria and it was while I was asleep at a hotel there, that I heard all the racket going on that the German army had marched into Austria.

I was completely taken by surprise; I never thought they would do that to Austria.

The Czechs were quite certain they would be invaded. By the time I returned to Britain, my head was pretty stuffed full with information about the attitude of people regarding a possible war.

Broadhurst completed his time at Staff College, Cranwell and left on 17th December 1938. He was delighted to learn that his next position would be commanding an operational squadron. On 16th January 1939, he was given command of No.111 (Fighter) Squadron, who were based at RAF Northolt, near London, taking over the position held by Squadron Leader J.W. Gillan AFC. The squadron were equipped with Hawker Hurricane Mk Is.

With war clouds looming in Europe, the Royal Air Force was now hastily preparing its men and squadrons. Many hours were spent by the fighter squadrons practising the standard RAF fighter tactics and battle formations should the conflict become reality. Finally after failed negotiations between the politicians and Hitler, war came on 1st September. German forces crossed the Polish border and two days later Great Britain and France entered the fray. Harry Broadhurst's eldest daughter Diana remembers the family had been on holiday when war was announced:

I was only eight when the war broke out, so I have only fleeting memories of those early days, mostly of when we were on holiday in Cornwall in our caravan. We spent our days paddling in our canoe and swimming and exploring rock pools. I remember there was an outdoor swimming pool and there was a competition in progress to see who could pick up the greatest number of plates from the bottom of the pool in one dive. The locals were most upset when my father won. We were actually on holiday when my father was recalled to his squadron for the onset of war. We were turned out of our married quarter; all our possessions were put into store and our caravan moved into the vicar's field at Portscatho, where we stayed until a cottage could be hired for us to live in.

It was also during this time that one of the pilots of 111 Squadron had a run in with the new squadron commander. Flying Officer James Sanders had taken a dislike to Broadhurst, whom he regarded as a bit of a prima donna when talking about his aerobatic skill regarding the Hendon air displays he had flown in. Broadhurst liked to talk about one particular aerobatic manoeuvre, where he would roll off the top of the loop on take-off in a Gloster Gauntlet biplane. However, the aircraft had been lightened by removing the guns, which helped considerably. James Sanders recalls:

> One dull Sunday morning just after war had been declared, I decided I would try the same manoeuvre to show that any skilful pilot could do it. I was a fairly experienced pilot myself and I succeeded in completing the roll off the top of the loop in my own Gauntlet, which was unmodified and still retained its armament.
>
> Unbeknown to myself at the time, a number of senior RAF officers had just arrived at Northolt for an important conference and did so just as I was carrying out the aerobatics. On landing Harry Broadhurst put me under arrest, and then took me before the Air Officer Commanding 11 Group, Air Vice-Marshal Gossage for punishment. Fortunately, Gossage knew my mother and asked me what I would like him to do. I replied 'that I would like to be sent to fight in France, Sir.' I was afterwards posted to join No.615 Squadron who flew Gloster Gladiators. On leaving the room, Broadhurst was asked into the room and on leaving several minutes later looked a little embarrassed.

For the first few weeks of the war 111 Squadron spent most of their time flying patrols over shipping convoys without seeing a single enemy aircraft. The only relief from the mundane came on 29th September, when Harry Broadhurst led a flight to intercept a barrage balloon that had broken away from its moorings. It was sighted over Slough at an altitude of 23,000 feet. Broadhurst brought the balloon down after firing 780 rounds of ammunition. The same thing happened again the following day, this time over Hatfield, Hertfordshire. This time Broadhurst accounted for the balloon firing 830 rounds. Finally on 4th October, the squadron were again informed that a large number of balloons had broken free from the main London defence. In all eleven barrage balloons were shot down that day by the squadron.

On 27th October, the squadron were sent north to Acklington. Here they shared the station with 607 and 152 Squadrons. It was not until the morning of 29th November 1939, that 111 saw and destroyed their first enemy aircraft, the honour going to none other than Harry Broadhurst. Leading A Flight, he sighted a Heinkel 111 at 8.25 am, about eight miles east of Alnwick, flying at around 4,000 feet. His combat report of the event states:

> I was flying at 140 mph at 3,500 feet, cleaning my iced windscreen, when an enemy aircraft appeared from behind a bank of cloud flying east at 4,000 feet.
>
> I turned to intercept and ducked back into cloud for about 30 seconds. On emerging from cloud I saw the enemy aircraft immediately above me. I pulled up in a climbing turn to position

myself under his tail. The enemy aircraft took no action until I closed to about 500 yards; he then dived for cloud, which was about 1,500 feet below, opening fire with his bottom rear gun. At the same time, I held my fire until about 400 yards, and then I lifted my aircraft to the dead astern position. The top gunner opened fire, tracers could be seen going over my cockpit; but after my first burst he ceased firing.

The top of the cloud was getting lower as we flew out to sea, which gave me time to aim. I closed to about 150 yards, firing continuously. Almost immediately the enemy aircraft turned onto its side and dived vertically into cloud with smoke streaming from it. I endeavoured to follow him and fired my remaining rounds in his direction in the clouds. Almost simultaneously I had to pull up violently to avoid diving into the sea.

I estimate I fired 200 rounds of ammunition in clear conditions at a range of 400 to 150 yards. Fire appeared to concentrate around the fuselage of the enemy aircraft. No return fire was received after the initial burst from me. On returning to the top of the clouds I found they were at 1,000 feet in this area, and I consider that the enemy aircraft would have had considerable difficulty in recovering from his dive, particularly as base of cloud was right down on the sea.

Although the squadron had claimed their first victory of the war, most of the time it remained fairly quiet, except for the odd German reconnaissance aircraft venturing over the North Sea. As the new year started, Broadhurst received the award of the Distinguished Flying Cross on 2nd January 1940, for his work on operations and later in the month on 24th January, he was made an acting Wing Commander and posted to Headquarters No.11 Group for Air Staff Training.

At the beginning of May, the German blitzkrieg began with the lighting attack through Holland, Belgium and France. The Allied armies had been caught totally unprepared for such a decisive and breathtaking advance. On 10th May, Wing Commander Broadhurst was posted to RAF Coltishall in Norfolk to take command of the station.

By 15th May, Holland had surrendered and by the 17th the German Army was marching into Brussels, the capital of Belgium. In France the situation fared little better, with the British Expeditionary Force along with remnants of the French Army in full retreat from the advancing Panzer tank divisions. During the early afternoon of 18th May 1940, Harry Broadhurst arrived at Vitry to take over as the new commander of 60 Wing. Here he found the squadrons in a state of utter chaos:

I found that my previous commander had been sent back home to England suffering from a nervous breakdown and that the three squadrons were without serviceable squadron commanders. To say that chaos reigned would be an understatement, and I soon received new orders to retreat with the remains of the Wing to Merville.

On 20th May, Broadhurst claimed his second victory of the war leading a section of Hurricanes from 79 Squadron and three Hurricanes of B Flight from 213 Squadron. At around 4.00 pm they encountered near Arras at an altitude of 15,000 feet, four to five twin-engine Messerschmitt 110s with a further 25 enemy machines above at 18,000 feet. They engaged the aircraft and during the combat that ensued, Broadhurst claimed that he shot down a Me110. Years later it has been established by historian Christopher Shores, that it is more likely the enemy aircraft shot down by Broadhurst that day was in fact a Dornier 17Z of KG77. On return to Merville, Broadhurst received a signal to evacuate the airfield. All aircraft that were unserviceable were destroyed, while the other flyable aircraft would make their own way back across the Channel in haste.

The squadron personnel would await transport aircraft from England to take ground crew and pilots without aircraft. Broadhurst was given instructions to remain at the airfield to provide air cover over the transport aircraft while they were on the ground and then escort them on the return trip back to England. As the last transport took off at 6.00 pm, Broadhurst joined the escort.

As he flew his Hurricane fighter, one of the last to escape out of France, back across the Channel he was harried and shot up by four Messerschmitt Me110s. He managed to evade the enemy fighters and landed back at RAF Northolt, his aircraft riddled with bullet holes and the oil tank damaged. A week later, Broadhurst collected his repaired Hurricane P2823 and had it painted black, with his initials HB painted in red on the side of the fuselage. He then returned to Coltishall on 27th May, to resume his role as station commander; but this was short lived and two days later on 28th, he was given command of RAF Wittering in Cambridgeshire.

Over in Dunkirk, the British Expeditionary Force was being evacuated off the beaches with the help of every naval vessel and pleasure boat craft available. Indeed it was a miracle that so many troops had been saved from capture, although most of the army's weapons and equipment were left behind. Between 26th May and 4th June 1940, some 338,226 men, which included 120,000 French and Belgian soldiers were safely brought across the Channel. During the evacuation the RAF had lost 106 aircraft and 87 pilots killed or captured.

During June, Broadhurst flew several night patrols; on 27th June while flying Hurricane P2823 during one of these patrols, he encountered a German Heinkel He111, which he pursued out to sea; unfortunately he eventually had to break away due to shortage of fuel. On 30th June, Broadhurst led 229 Squadron during that day in a Wing formation. At the start of the Battle of Britain in July, Broadhurst had under his command three squadrons: 229 Squadron equipped with Hawker Hurricanes and led by Squadron Leader H.J. Maguire, 266 Squadron with Spitfires and commanded by Squadron Leader Rodney Wilkinson, and lastly 23 Squadron flying Bristol Blenheims which was detached at the airfield at Collyweston, the commander being Squadron Leader Leslie Bicknell. Throughout August, the squadrons at Wittering spent most of their time either undertaking local tactical exercises or night patrols, while in September they practiced two squadron formations or patrolled over local areas, including a two squadron patrol over Duxford on 24th September. Broadhurst no doubt felt left out of the fighting that was taking place down in the southeast and later commented, that he could not be considered as a Battle of Britain pilot, as he was in 12 Group at Wittering away from the heavy fighting.

On 16th December 1940, Harry Broadhurst flew his Hurricane aeroplane to the Rolls-Royce factory at Hucknall for modification. He had managed to persuade his friends at Rolls-Royce to install the latest two-stage Merlin engine into the aircraft, without having to obtain the permission of the appropriate authorities, giving it the added performance more of a Spitfire than a Hurricane.

On 20th December 1940, Wing Commander Harry Broadhurst was given notice of his new command – the fighter station of RAF Hornchurch in Essex. He recalls:

> I was given command of Hornchurch, but my relief at RAF Wittering had not arrived to take over; so I didn't take over at Hornchurch until the first week in January 1941, when we were just about to start the offensive sweeps over to France against Jerry.

Wing Commander Frank Dowling OBE, remembers the arrival of Harry Broadhurst and the first impression of the new commanding officer:

> He was a completely different type from the previous station commander that we'd had. Broadhurst was an operational type with plenty of flying experience behind him. My office was next to the station commander's and when he arrived I overheard him speaking over the telephone to Group Headquarters asking, 'Where's my new adjutant.' Someone told him; 'You've already got him.' This is when I found out that I was 'Broady's' new station adjutant. I was promoted to flight lieutenant immediately. I can also remember overhearing a couple of the women WAAFs remarking when they first saw Broadhurst; 'have you seen the new station commander, he look's a bit like a mandarin'. This made me laugh, but sometimes he did have that slight oriental look to his features.

After arriving at his new command, Broadhurst went out of his way to meet and talk to the pilots that he would lead in the air; one of these young men was Wilfred Duncan Smith, a pilot officer at that time, who remembers his first meeting with the new commanding officer:

> I met our new station commander, when fellow pilot and friend Barrie Heath and I were standing at the bar in the RAF Club up in Piccadilly, London, one evening. We had travelled up there to get away from Hornchurch for a bit. I was completely overawed to see him there actually.
>
> Harry Broadhurst was rather suspicious of auxiliaries, he thought we drank too much and had too much money, all that sort of rubbish; but it all worked out rather well and later he flew a lot with us. The only thing I could think to say to him was about his aerobatic days at Hendon. But we also knew that he had vast

experience on many aircraft and operations including fighting over
in France. I personally learned a lot about air fighting by seeing
what he did; he was a brilliant leader and pilot. We were very lucky
to have him as our station commander, because he passed on a lot
of information we wouldn't have had otherwise.

Although 'Broady' would give the young pilots a certain amount of freedom
with regards to letting off steam in the Officers' Mess, he still expected a
certain amount of self discipline from them when given time off to go up to
London. Duncan Smith recalls one excursion up to London that had not been
given official approval:

The weather had deteriorated and flying had been cancelled. We
were all playing cards in the dispersal hut that morning, when
Barrie Heath suggested we make a quick sortie up to London. We
jumped into Barrie Heath's Humber Snipe car and headed up to the
city. While driving along the Seven Sisters Road, I suddenly
recognised Harry Broadhurst's staff car coming towards us in the
opposite direction. I immediately shouted to the rest of the chaps:
'Quick-it's Broady.' In an instant we all dived down under the
dashboard including Barrie, who was driving. Thinking we had got
away with it, we continued into London.

Later back at Hornchurch, Broady approached us in the
Officers' Mess and said that he had recognised Barrie's Humber car
immediately since the car had stuck out like a sore thumb, cruising
along the road with nobody to be seen at the wheel. He continued,
'If you had wanted to let me know you were off to London on a
binge, that was certainly the best way to do it.' Broady immediately
started to laugh and we all joined in.

On 25th February 1941, during the early afternoon, Broadhurst led 611
Squadron on an offensive sweep over Dunkirk. Flying with A Flight, at 2.35
pm at a height of 20,000 feet they sighted six Me109s below at 12,000 feet,
flying in a loose formation, south south-west of Gravelines. Broadhurst led his
flight down into the attack and picked out one of the enemy fighters. He
manoeuvred his Spitfire astern of the leading Me109 and opened fire from
350 yards, closing rapidly to 100 yards, firing a burst of 40 rounds per gun.
Continuous hits were observed as the 109 began to smoke. Broadhurst then
broke away from the combat and climbed up into the sun. He then circled his
aircraft over the general melee and picked out another 109. He endeavoured
to get the enemy in his sights, but after circling around each other, he noticed
that the enemy fighter was rapidly gaining the advantage of height over him.
So Broadhurst broke away yet again. He then commenced to fly out to sea and
spotted a pair of Me109s coming in from the north. He swung in behind them
and closed in to attack. As he opened fire, the Germans broke away in
opposite directions. So he followed the one, which broke, to the right, giving
him a burst of about 20 rounds from 200 yards; the enemy fighter dived into
cloud, going south and pouring smoke. The other 109 had in the meantime
swung around onto Broadhurst's tail. He reacted quickly and dived into cloud.

On return to Hornchurch, he claimed one enemy aircraft destroyed and one damaged.

Throughout February and early March, the Hornchurch Wing continued to venture inside the French coast on Circus operations escorting small forces of light-bombers to attack German installations, airfields and army bases etc. Harry Broadhurst again inspired his pilots and as usual led from the front. On 5th March with 611 Squadron, Broadhurst led the Wing Sweep over northern France; while flying at 31,000 feet approximately 10 miles east of Le Touquet at 2.00 pm, he sighted five Me109s approaching his section slightly above and in a turning manoeuvre that would have brought them into an attacking position behind his own Spitfires. Broadhurst led four of his aircraft into a tight turn to attack the 109s, but two of the Spitfires spun out and down about 2,000 feet, probably due to high-speed stalling. Broadhurst attacked the nearest Me109, which was one of three flying in close line astern formation. Two remaining 109s were flying as a pair in line astern about 1,000 feet behind.

After firing a burst of five seconds, the 109 began to smoke; it then rolled over on to its back and dived out of the combat. He then opened fire on the next Me109, which immediately emitted slight traces of white smoke and this too dived away. The third 109 broke away and was not seen again. The first 109 Broadhurst had attacked was seen going down by the Spitfire pilots who had spun out earlier, and they gave their opinion that it was totally out of control. On returning to Hornchurch, Broadhurst found that four guns in his port wing had failed owing to the lubricant freezing.

On 31st May, the famous artist Sir William Rothenstein arrived at Hornchurch to have Harry Broadhurst sit for a series of preliminary sketches for portraits that he was painting of RAF pilots of status.

Broadhurst increased his score again on 17th June 1941. His combat report states:

> I led the Hornchurch Wing on an offensive sweep over the Channel following on a Circus operation on Béthune. At 7.45 pm, when five miles up sun from Boulogne, I ordered the Wing to split into sections of four aircraft. I led Red section, which was depleted to three aircraft by the return of Red 2, owing to engine trouble, to Cap Gris Nez, arriving at 7.48 pm. I flew at 18,000 feet over the bombers and their escorts as they crossed the French coast. I made a wide sweep and again crossed the bombers from east to west over the Channel, when one Me109 moved in from the south at 200 feet above to attack Red 3 on the starboard quarter. I ordered Red 3 to break outwards, which he did, making a tight turn to starboard. The Me109 turned to follow Red 3 whereupon I swung in and fired a full deflection shot from the beam in a short burst at 200 yards range. The enemy aircraft flew through my fire and then spun out of its turn and went straight down over Cap Gris Nez. I momentarily lost sight of the enemy aircraft while looking for Red 3. But a few seconds afterwards I saw a parachute descending at 5,000 feet. My height was now 14,000 feet and I climbed back into the sun, calling to my section, but was unable to find them. At 7.55 pm when circling mid-way between Dungeness and Cap Gris Nez,

I saw an aircraft hit the water and a pilot descending by parachute near the aircraft. I informed the Controller and then circled over the spot at 10,000 feet still calling the Controller but receiving no reply. At 8.05 pm whilst still circling, I was attacked by three Me109s which approached from the south in line astern and attacked on my starboard quarter. I turned sharply towards the leader and fired a short burst in an almost head-on attack from 400 yards to 100 yards range, allowing all three enemy aircraft to fly straight through my fire. I then spun out and recovered at 5,000 feet. Many strikes were seen on the front of the leading enemy aircraft, whose cockpit cover came off. I did not see the enemy aircraft again. I then lost height to 1,000 feet still circling the man in the water, who waved to me. He appeared to be British. As I had still received no reply from the Controller, I flew towards Dungeness and met two rescue launches, four miles from land and about seven miles from the pilot in the water. I flew backwards and forwards between the launch and the pilot, until the launch was 500 yards from the pilot. As I had then only five gallons of petrol left, I returned to Hawkinge. After refuelling, I went back to the pilot, but he appeared to have been picked up by the launch, so I returned to Hornchurch.

On 21st June 1941, a signal was received at Hornchurch conveying to Harry Broadhurst the news that he had been awarded the Distinguished Service Order. One of his fellow commanders and a friend was Basil Embry who was in charge of RAF Wittering in Cambridgeshire; he wrote to Broadhurst:

My Dear Broady

A line to congratulate you very heartily on the award of the DSO.
I was delighted to hear of it, as I know the jolly fine job of work you have been putting up at Hornchurch.
I know that your leadership and personal example have been an inspiration, not only to your own unit, but to Fighter Command.

Jolly good show – look after yourself!

While leading the Wing as escort to Bristol Blenheims on the early evening of 24th June, Broady Broadhurst added another victory to his ever-increasing score. While flying as Red 1 with 54 Squadron, the Wing split up over the Gravelines area. It was at 7.50 pm that he sighted several Me109s diving to attack the bombers. He went for one of the 109s, which was flying at around the same height as him at around 18,000 feet. The Me109 then turned away on sighting Broady's Spitfire and dived into the haze below over France. Broady followed him into the dive and fired a short burst from 300 yards in a stern attack. Smoke and vapour began to belch from the stricken enemy fighter as it headed down. Broady broke away and returned to formate on the Blenheim formation. He then led his section of Spitfires back to the coast and flew up into the sun, on the track of the bombers. At that exact moment, twelve Me109Es approached from the sun almost head on and to the right in a loose formation, 1,000 feet above. The enemy fighters had swung round to come in behind. Broady led the section in a climbing turn towards the Germans, who in turn went into a line astern formation of loose pairs and continued to swing round away from the Spitfires. Broady attacked the first three enemy aircraft with short bursts of machine-gun fire from 300 yards. He saw strikes on the first from a beam attack. Attacking the second aircraft from astern brought forth black and white smoke; while hits were also observed on the third aircraft he attacked. The whole German formation then dived steeply into the haze and was not seen again. Broadhurst on return to base claimed two Me109s as damaged.

The everyday offensive operations over northern France were beginning to take their toll on the pilots and many of the experienced pilots were being lost on the raids.

On 25th June 1941, Wing Commander Joe Kayll was flying as Broadhurst's No. 2 on a sweep, but unfortunately, he would not make it back to Hornchurch, being shot down and made a prisoner of war. Broadhurst's report of the events that day state:

> After leading the Wing to Hazebrouck as target support, I led Red section and followed the bombers back to Gravelines. I was orbiting just inland, when I saw No. 4 of Red section being attacked by a Me109F. The section was then flying in two pairs abreast, aircraft in each pair in line astern. No warning had been given by any member of the section, it being Red 2's duty to watch the tail of Red 4. I immediately turned, giving a warning and attacked the Me109 from the head-on fine quarter position, giving him a half second burst from 100 yards.
>
> I could see bullet strikes on the fuselage of Red 4's Spitfire (Pilot Officer Knox) who returned slightly wounded. The enemy fighter broke away downwards towards me, and I therefore half rolled and followed him down, giving him a burst of four seconds at 150 yards range. He began to smoke violently and ceased diving, going into a gentle turn to starboard. I circled over him and watched him go down in the same gentle diving turn. I still had Red 2 with me (Wing Commander Kayll) and I climbed to regain height. There was no sign of Red 3, and I called upon all of Red section to rejoin me. As I approached Gravelines going north, I noticed a large number of enemy aircraft about five miles inland from Gravelines at 500 to 1,000 feet above me.
>
> I climbed hard and turned to investigate. As I approached them, two aircraft detached themselves and manoeuvred to get behind us. I recognised them to be Me109Fs and turned behind them, whereupon they broke off the attack and dived below.
>
> By this time there were 20 to 30 aircraft circling overhead, and from these, odd aircraft detached themselves and endeavoured to get astern of us, Red 2 then being packed in tightly astern of me. All the aircraft in the vicinity were now recognised as being Me109s and after facing up to three of these attacks, I called to Red 2 and told him that we would have to spin out and make our own

way home at zero height. He replied 'OK' and left his transmitter
on. I faced up to two more attacks, firing short bursts each time the
enemy aircraft attempted to attack, and on each occasion I faced
them head on, so they dived away underneath.

On the sixth attack as the enemy dived away, I went into a steep
spiral from 17,000 feet down to 2,000 feet and pulled out, heading
for the coast at Gravelines, which was then two miles away. As I
reached the coast I saw two Me109s in close line astern formation,
flying from east to west at 2,000 feet. As they were dead in my
track, I pulled up astern of the second aircraft and gave him a four
second burst at 100 yards.

The enemy aircraft took no evasive action. Many strikes were
seen in the nose and the fuselage between the wings. He burst into
a cloud of oily smoke and his airscrew stopped; he then went into
a gentle glide out to sea. The leading Me109 turned to port in
towards land, and after I gave him a short deflection shot of half a
second, I turned out to sea and came home at sea level.

Broadhurst claimed a Me109F and a Me109E as probable. Whilst he had been
busy with his own problems, Wing Commander Kayll had been shot down, as
he states:

I was attacked out of the sun by a flight of 109s. My engine was
stopped, but I could see the Channel and had the slight hope that I
might be able to glide to over half way across. But this was not to be
and I ended up having to force-land the aircraft on the French side
and was captured. I remained a prisoner of war until May 1945.

On 3rd July, the Wing was involved as escort cover on Circus 31 to
Hazebrouck. Broady flew as Red 1 with 54 Squadron and was again involved
in combat with the German fighters. Just after the bombers had dropped their
bombs on their target and 54 Squadron were circling above at 14,000 feet in
pairs and fours, Broady saw a Spitfire chasing two Me109s in a steep dive.
One of the enemy aircraft then blew up. He then saw a Me109F attacking a
Spitfire, and the pilot bale out. Broady chased after this enemy machine with
his Red 2 (Pilot Officer J.S. Harris). Cutting off the Me109's turn, they
managed to get within 300 yards, and then Broady fired a short burst. The
enemy aircraft went straight down into the ground.

It did not appear to have been damaged by his fire, so it is assumed that the
pilot must have been killed. At that very moment, a Me109E attacked
Red 2. Both Broady and Harris broke outwards and the enemy aircraft
disappeared from the scene.

They both reformed in line abreast, but then Harris informed Broadhurst
that a Me109 was diving onto his tail. Again they both broke away outwards
and in doing such a steep turn, Broady partially blacked out. He flew a full
circle and found himself 50 yards behind a Me109 painted with a yellow nose,
which had just opened fire on Pilot Officer Harris who was just fifty yards in
front of the German. Broady was unable to fire until the 109 overshot and
pulled to the left, while Harris broke away to his right. Broady was then able

to give a short burst of fire from the quarter. He saw his strikes hit the engine cowling and the German's airscrew stopped dead. Red 2 again called a warning as more enemy fighters approached to attack. Broadhurst was unable to follow up his attack on the German, but considered him as probably destroyed. The attack had taken place at 3.36 pm.

Harry Broadhurst's aggressive spirit and excellent leadership was evident to his flight commanders, pilots and No.11 Group officers; but fighter pilots must have a certain amount of good luck riding with them on occasions. Broadhurst's luck held when he led the Hornchurch Wing on 4th July 1941 on a Circus operation over Béthune.

Flying with 54 Squadron, he led the Wing as close target support on Circus 32. As they crossed the French coast at Gravelines at 14,000 feet, the Wing loosened its formation. After a few minutes, Broadhurst sighted a Me109F flying slightly below the formation travelling from west to east. He immediately turned after the enemy fighter and at 400 yards fired a short burst with cannon and machine guns, but observed no hits on the aircraft. Broadhurst broke away and returned to join the rest of the Wing. Once over the target area, the Wing broke into sections of four aircraft each. The section led by Broadhurst in the centre at once became engaged with a number of Me109s and battle was met. Broadhurst latched onto two 109s, but they half-rolled and dived away. He then noticed a yellow-nosed Me109 and caught it at the top of its climb, as it pulled up after an attack on the British bombers. He pressed the firing button on his control column and fired a short burst of cannon from astern. Smoke began to appear from the German's starboard wing root as the aircraft plummeted down and disappeared into a cloud. He then spotted another enemy machine slightly below and at 250 yards fired 30 rounds of cannon into it. The German fighter's starboard wing fell away and it went into a vicious spin; this too he lost sight of when it disappeared into cloud, but was obviously destroyed.

Looking around, he noticed that there were still several enemy aircraft in the vicinity. He got into combat with yet another 109, but only had ammunition in his machine guns, his cannon shells being all expended. All of a sudden cannon shells from a Me109, which had crept up unseen on his tail, hit him. In an instant his port aileron controls were damaged and the control column was knocked out of his hand, causing his Spitfire to go into a spinning dive. He frantically struggled to pull the aircraft out of its spin and was down to 4-5,000 feet when he passed through cloud base over Béthune. Finally at 1,000 feet, he came out of the dive. The Spitfire was flying left wing low, due to the damage; the port wing flap and undercarriage mechanism had been also damaged and large parts of panelling had been shot away from the upper and lower surfaces of the port wing. He had also suffered damage inside the cockpit, cannon-shell splinters had damaged the reflector gun-sight and windscreen and splinters had entered into his left arm and thigh. One splinter had actually hit his wristwatch, destroying it. Broadhurst nursed his damaged aircraft and re-climbed into cloud over Gravelines and remained in the clouds until they ended over St Omer. Here, he was spotted by the German anti-aircraft defences, which opened fire on him with their 3-inch guns. He evaded their fire by losing height down to 3-4,000 feet.

Crossing the French coast at Cap Gris Nez at zero feet, he managed to make it all the way back to Hornchurch, but owing to the damaged undercarriage, was forced to make a crash-landing with wheels retracted. He did this successfully and on landing was immediately transported to the Oldchurch Hospital in Romford to have his wounds tended too. He claimed two of the Messerschmitt 109s that day as destroyed.

It was on this same day that Broadhurst learnt of his award of the Distinguished Service Order for outstanding leadership and actions against the enemy.

It was only three days later, on 7th July, that Broadhurst led the Wing on another Circus operation, 36, escorting Bristol Blenheims over a target near St Omer. While over the target the Hornchurch Wing became embroiled with 109s, which tried a determined attack on the RAF bombers. Broadhurst later recalled what happened:

> I was flying as Red 1 with 54 Squadron as target support. After reaching the target, I split the Wing and since Red 3 and Red 4 had returned early owing to technical trouble, Red 2 and myself weaved over the bombers at 18,000 feet. On the return journey, when five miles inland east of Gravelines, I saw about 12 Me109Es milling slightly above us. I led Red 2 to attack the nearest enemy aircraft and after one or two circles, I got on to the tail of one Me109 and fired a short burst at 200 yards with my cannon. The enemy aircraft fell out of control, emitting much smoke and burst into flames. I was then attacked in a determined manner by various other Me109s. As Red 2 had already spun out, I also spun down to 6,000 feet and headed for the English coast. When three miles off Gravelines, I saw a number of aircraft diving towards me from behind and turned to investigate. I found that they were six Me109Es. These enemy fighters made several determined efforts to get on my tail and each time I turned and faced them head on.
>
> Finally I was able to get on the fine quarter of one enemy aircraft and I fired a short burst from under 200 yards with machine guns only, but I had to break immediately because of another attack apparently designed to catch me whichever way I turned.
>
> One enemy aircraft attacked me at the same level, dead ahead and firing. I fired back with both cannon and machine guns, opening fire at 200 yards; as we passed, he blew up within a few feet of me and pieces of it were brought back on to the port wing tip. In the meantime another 109 had positioned itself onto my tail and one of his shells entered the fuselage by the wireless aerial, making a large hole and cutting one elevator control and a harness cable. An armour-piercing bullet had put my port cannon out of action, buckling it like a hairpin. After successfully losing my attacker, I flew due west at zero feet and headed for home. There were now three Me109s left in the combat, and these followed me, making various efforts to get on my tail until 15 miles due north of Gravelines. In the last attack but one, I got on the fine quarter of one Me109 and fired the rest of my starboard cannon ammunition, and a long burst of 0.303 at less than 200 yards range. The enemy

aircraft turned for home with glycol and blue oily smoke pouring from below the fuselage. After circling for a few seconds, the rest of the Me109s returned to France and I flew due west at zero feet for North Foreland.

On landing back at Hornchurch, Broadhurst found that his Spitfire had taken quite a bit of punishment, when on closer inspection of the aircraft's propeller and wing leading edges, he found pieces of his German opponent's remains and aircraft engine oil. He then gave the engineers instructions that the oil-covered propeller spinner was to be fitted to his new aircraft when ready, to remind him of the fight and his lucky escape.

Broady walked into his station adjutant's office that day and flung a piece of blue/greyish cloth on to his desk, with the remark, 'There's a bit of Hun for you.' It was a piece of German battledress from the German pilot; he had blown up in the head-on attack.

On 15th July, Broadhurst received a signal from Fighter Command Headquarters confirming the identity of the German pilot he had vanquished on the 7th. His name was Wilhelm Balthasar, who led JG2 Geschwader and had fought with the Condor Legion in Spain before the war. He was credited with 44 victories.

On 27th September, the Hornchurch Wing was in action again on Circus 103. Broadhurst again led the Wing that day, flying with 611 Squadron. After escorting the bombers over the French coast, at 2.48 pm a formation of between thirty and forty German fighters at a height of 16,000 feet were sighted diving to attack, six miles inland from Mardyck. Broadhurst's general report of the action that followed states:

Shortly after crossing the coast at Mardyck many Me109Fs dived down behind us. Some going for 403 Squadron and some going for 402 Squadron and the bombers. I was leading 611 Squadron on the starboard rear quarter of the bombers and immediately turned to port and led the squadron on to intercept the 109s. I made attempts to engage several 109Es, but in each case they half rolled and dived away. My No.3 managed to attack one of them and followed it down. Eventually, one 109E appeared in front of me, having pulled up to attack a Hurricane about 400 yards ahead. The range was about 50 yards and I opened fire. Immediately strikes appeared on the enemy's tail and fuselage. The 109 half rolled and dived away and I turned to follow. As he went down a stream of white glycol appeared and after a short interval a large puff of black smoke appeared, this was followed by a thicker stream of black smoke and small pieces of the aircraft falling away. As the 109 was obviously on fire, I pulled back and returned to the job in hand.

During the remainder of the journey, several attempts were made to engage 109Es, which were diving towards the bombers. But in each case they half rolled and dived inland. As the coast was crossed on the homeward journey, the section (Red 1 and Red 2) was attacked by a Me109 from the sun, but it dived away as soon as the section turned to engage.

On landing back at Hornchurch, Broadhurst claimed his Me109 as destroyed. It was also on this day that the pilots of the Hornchurch Wing and other squadrons of Fighter Command reported a new enemy aircraft shape in the skies over northern France. This was Germany's new fighter aircraft, the Focke-Wulf FW190, which would prove superior with its higher speed and armament to the Spitfire Mk Vs of the RAF. The late Group Captain Wilfred Duncan Smith who was then a flight lieutenant recalled:

> It was on a Saturday, when normally we had time off, but the station commander Harry Broadhurst was so dead keen to get stuck in, that we never had a moment's peace. I was flying as No.2 to Broadhurst on that occasion, when we first mixed it with the Focke-Wulf 190. It came as quite a shock. One of our sergeant pilots shot down what I thought was a Curtiss Hawk (Focke-Wulf). Later in my log-book I wrote in red ink and underlined; First contact with FW190.

On 1st October 1941, flying with 603 Squadron, Broadhurst claimed another Messerschmitt damaged, while leading the squadron and the Wing on a patrol from Calais to Le Touquet off the French coast. On their second run up the Channel near Calais, Blue 1 reported Me109s diving down behind their own formation. Broadhurst turned the squadron to the left to face the Germans. But by that time they had disappeared. A few moments later however, one Me109F passed in front of the squadron at the same height going towards France. Broadhurst immediately swung his aircraft in behind, whereupon the 109 commenced to do a steep dive for the coast. Broadhurst opened fire with both cannon and machine guns at 250 yards range. He saw strikes and the enemy steepened its dive emitting a considerable quantity of glycol. Broadhurst claimed it as damaged. He then reformed with the rest of the squadron. Five miles off Le Touquet on the second run down the Channel, two more Me109s were seen in line astern, flying back towards the French coast at 9,000 feet. Broadhurst took his section of Spitfires down to attack, leaving the other sections as top cover. He attacked the rearmost of the 109s at 300 yards range. But the combat was broken off, when a warning over the R/T of other Me109s in the area subsequently turned out to be other Spitfires. Flight Lieutenant Smith and Pilot Officer Falconer of 603 Squadron confirmed his claim of the 109 damaged.

On 13th October 1941, Broady left his command at Hornchurch on a goodwill lecture tour of the United States of America. The trip was organised by the Air Ministry and six distinguished airmen representing Bomber and Fighter Command had been selected. In addition to Broadhurst, there was Sailor Malan and Robert Stanford Tuck of Fighter Command and Wing Commander Charles Whitworth, Wing Commander Hugh Edwards VC and Group Captain John Boothman of Bomber Command. The RAF contingent sailed aboard the steam ship *Louis Paster*, arriving at the port of Halifax, Nova Scotia on 25th October 1941. Broady remembers how this had all come about:

> My administration chap came to me one day at Hornchurch and said to me: 'we have two American colonels coming to visit us to see

what's going on. I'm meeting them in the George pub in Stamford at 6.00 pm would you like to come as well?' I said, 'if we are not flying, I will come. If we are flying I shall either be in the Ops Room or flying myself.' Well, it was pouring with rain and there were no Huns coming over the Channel; so I went down to the George in Stamford and met Colonel Eaker and Colonel Hunter. I took them back to Hornchurch and gave them dinner, which they liked and the next morning they went off. A year later, I was sent to America with two other fighter pilots, Malan and Tuck; to visit their squadrons, fly their new types of aircraft and lecture the pilots and so on. We spent about three months doing that.

When I got to America, who should I find but Colonels Eaker and Hunter who had both been promoted to Generals? My impression of the American Air Force during this period was that they had very good pilots, but they were still developing some of their aircraft. Some of their engines were not all that good, mostly radial and of course Rolls-Royce put an engine in one of the most famous fighters, the Mustang and improved it enormously. We had ordered the fighter for army co-operation purposes right at the beginning of the war. I remember later in the war, I was waiting at an airfield near Caen to be picked up by a car and there was a row of these Mustang aeroplanes on the airfield and my Spitfire. Two American airmen strolled over to look at the Spitfire, and much to my amusement I heard one say to the other, 'Gee, they've got our engines in their aeroplanes', which tickled me to death, I don't know what Rolls-Royce would have thought had they heard it.

On the tour in the States, we visited the Wright and Patterson airfields and inspected their latest fighters. I flew a P38 Lightning fighter aircraft and set up a dummy combat against Bob Tuck in a Spitfire, which was pretty interesting.

Broady also remembers one particular incident, which took place while on their tour of America:

I remember when Bob Tuck got lost while flying one of the American aircraft from Spartanburg in South Carolina. He'd got separated from the rest of the squadron. In England, if you got lost, you flew south and hit the coast, but try that in America and you could have a thousand miles to travel. But by that time Tuck had run out of fuel; so he force-landed. We didn't know where the hell he was, but when we found out he had got lost we had an enormous laugh. He had landed in a field somewhere, but fields in America are quite large. I went and fished him out and he was a bit depressed about the whole thing. It got a lot of publicity, but not the sort of publicity we particularly wanted.

Both Malan and Tuck remained out in America for a short break, while Harry Broadhurst crossed the border and continued his tour of lectures and flying in Canada until 25th November. He recalls another amusing incident, which befell him before his return home to Britain:

> I had been given a case of whisky as a gift from the Bell Air Company, which was the last factory I had visited on the way to Canada. The case of whisky and my cine camera were in the aeroplane and at Newfoundland it was put under guard and regrettably a guard pinched the camera and the whisky. When I got on to the aircraft next morning, I reported to the Canadians that somebody had pinched the two items.
>
> They said that they would soon find them, as they'd have drunk the whisky, and they had. They found the two chaps worse for wear, with the camera and what was left of the whisky.

Broadhurst then boarded a Catalina flying boat bound for Britain via Bermuda, and with a new case of whisky, but en route the engines failed and the aircraft was forced to crash-land. Fortunately no one was injured and all were picked up by a rescue launch, by which time he was very anxious to get home. He finally touched down at Prestwick in a Liberator bomber and arrived back at RAF Hornchurch on 30th November. Harry Broadhurst was glad to be back in England and back in command of his station:

> I was commanding Hornchurch and I didn't want to be away from a command of that importance for two reasons. Firstly there might be people waiting to steal it from you and secondly, it doesn't pay to have it on the loose for too long. There was quite a lot going on at that time, Hornchurch was a very fine station and very active station as it was situated on the Thames estuary on the east side of London. Most of the big raids came up the estuary at night, because it was the easiest way of navigating into the centre of London. Of course all around, the docks, the oil installations and the east end of London were absolutely smashed to pieces and it was horrible going up to London the next day to the Air Ministry and seeing what had happened the night before.

One person who remembers Harry Broadhurst is Lieutenant General Baron Michael Donnet. He had escaped from Belgium in a biplane with a fellow Belgian and had joined the Royal Air Force. He arrived at Hornchurch with 64 Squadron in October 1941 and recalls the following about Broady:

> When we arrived Group Captain Broadhurst was the station commander. At that time however, he was touring the United States and while he was away, Wing Commander Eric Stapleton deputised as station commander. Broadhurst had an outstanding reputation as a fighter pilot. He was a very keen shot and an above average pilot. Once he returned one could feel his personal authority, he was strict and did not accept mistakes such as those resulting from carelessness. On the other hand, when they were a result of keenness, especially when flying, he would be indulgent.

It was during the bad weather, with no chance of flying operations, that on 9th December, Harry Broadhurst held a talk in the station's briefing room to all the pilots of the three squadrons. During his lecture, he described the main principles of air tactics, so far as fighter aircraft were concerned and stressed the need for top cover and mutual support. He also gave the pilots an outline of the performance of the Messerschmitt in comparison to their own Spitfires. The pilots by all accounts found his lecture inspiring and recalled it 'as Broady at his wonderful best.'

It was with Christmas only a few weeks away, when a most unusual gift arrived at Hornchurch aerodrome with a note stating; *'For the immediate attention of Group Captain Harry Broadhurst.'* He recounts the story:

> I had done a lot of flying in my Spitfire with a new propeller that the De Havilland Company was producing, and they suddenly decided to give me a Christmas present. The chief test pilot from Hatfield flew over in a two-seater Tiger Moth biplane with my present strapped into the back seat, which turned out to be a bloody pig. In fact I was having my portrait painted in the drawing room of my house, by the artist Cuthbert Orde. The pilot arrived, standing at the front door with this tiny piglet tucked under his arms and asked if I would accept the gift. It was the first time I had had an animal of that nature as a pet. Anyway the pig became quite a celebrity on the station, the chaps would grease it up and let it loose in the Officers' Mess on Mess nights; if anybody could catch him and hold him, they could have him for lunch. I'm afraid by the end of the year, we had him served up for Christmas lunch, but it did encourage me to buy little pigs to keep in the Mess garden; thereon my batman used to look after them and feed them on scraps. So afterwards, there was always fresh pork available for the officers.

On 19th December 1941, he was awarded a bar to add to his Distinguished Service Order Medal, the citation crediting him for the destruction of 12 enemy aircraft destroyed and a further four probably destroyed. The Hornchurch Wing continued the air war against the German Luftwaffe with offensive sweeps into northern France at the beginning of 1942. But sometimes the enthusiastic pilots came to grief as Michael Donnet recollects:

> In January 1942, whilst on a practice dogfight with another Belgian pilot of 64 Squadron, we hit our wings carrying out a head-on attack. The wing tips of both aircraft were written off. That day there were 10 Spitfires damaged on training flights in the Hornchurch Wing. Group Captain Broadhurst was furious. However, he accepted our incident as a sign of keenness in air combat, but told us to keep such practices for when meeting the enemy.
>
> Broadhurst often came to fly with 64 Squadron and I flew as his No.2 more than once. Our commanding officer Duncan Smith who was a friend of the station commander, gave me strict instructions to stick to the leader and take particular care of him, which I did. On non-flying days, we used to play games or sports such as hockey;

Broadhurst stood in goal, while I was part of the team.

It was during the night of 11/12th February 1942, that the German Navy began their audacious break out of the three capital battle cruisers from the port of Brest in France up through the English Channel to the German port of Wilhelmshaven. Group Captain Harry Broadhurst was lying in bed that morning, having gone down with a cold. He was awoken by his adjutant to receive a telephone call from Air Vice-Marshal Trafford Leigh-Mallory, and was told that the *Scharnhorst*, *Gneisenau* and *Prinz Eugen* were making their way up the Straits of Dover. During that morning Hornchurch and the surrounding area was fog bound. It was not until 12.25 pm that the squadrons based at Hornchurch and RAF Fairlop managed to get into the air with orders to rendezvous with a small force of Fairey Swordfish torpedo biplanes and Spitfires of the Biggin Hill Wing over Manston. Their orders, to carry out attacks on the German torpedo boats (E boats), which were accompanying the *Scharnhorst* and *Gneisenau*.

Broadhurst took off at 12.42 pm and headed for Dungeness hoping to catch up with the Wing and if not to see the enemy naval force. Not sighting the Wing, he crossed the Channel towards Boulogne hugging the cloud base at 3,000 feet. When over Boulogne, he found the cloud to be broken up to 6,000 feet, so he climbed up and cruised his way mid-Channel towards Calais where he sighted several pairs of small boats similar to E boats, stretching from as far as the Gravelines-Dunkirk area. There were also several destroyers near the English coast heading for Boulogne. It was while over Gravelines at 6,000 feet that Broadhurst saw a formation of five to six Me109s flying below at 3,000 feet at about a quarter of a mile away, turning in a wide circle. He watched their progress for two to three minutes, whilst speaking to the Hornchurch Controller, Squadron Leader Seely, in order to find out the position of his Wing.

Broadhurst then dived down on the rearmost 109 and opening up from a range of 100 yards fired a two-second burst with his cannon and machine guns, which immediately caused the German fighter to pull up in a right hand turn and then go into a spin, emitting black smoke. Unable to watch the final outcome of his attack, Broadhurst caught sight of the other Me109s diving down towards him. He then pulled his machine up into a thin layer of cloud at 3,000 feet in order to escape his pursuers, who likewise did the same. He eventually decided to spiral down to sea level when he noticed a formation of around 24 Spitfires, who were flying east between Dover and Calais. He followed them for a few minutes at 1,500 feet, and when they turned back towards Dover, Broadhurst set course for Manston where he met another two squadrons of Spitfires flying at sea level in the direction of Dunkirk, and he finally landed back at Hornchurch at 2.20 pm. He later recalled:

> They sent out a Swordfish squadron led by Lieutenant Commander Eugene Esmonde, but during their attack the slow vulnerable biplanes were cut to pieces by the heavy German fighter air cover and the ship's guns. I think only one or two of the Swordfish airmen survived from the mission. Esmonde was awarded the Victoria Cross posthumously.

All three German ships managed to sail their way to Wilhelmshaven more or less unscathed, although the *Scharnhorst* and *Gneisenau* did suffer superficial damage caused by British mines. The Swordfish squadron No.825 lost 15 men during the attempt on the battle cruisers; only three men survived.

On 27th April 1942, Broadhurst led the Wing on Circus Operation 142 as close escort to Hurricane fighter-bombers on a raid against Longuenesse aerodrome in the St Omer area. While over the target area at 12.20 pm, and flying as Red 1 with 122 Squadron, he noticed a mixed bag of fifteen Focke-Wulf 190s and Me109s about to launch an attack against the Hurricanes. Broadhurst led the squadron into the attack and he managed to get in a short burst of machine-gun and cannon fire from a range of 350-300 yards on one of the FW190s as it passed across in front of him. Almost immediately, he was able to get in another short burst, this time on a Me109, which had followed the FW190. He was able to observe strikes from his De Wilde ammunition on both aircraft, which caused substantial impairment, but on return he claimed them only as damaged.

On 11th May 1942 came the notification of his appointment as Deputy Senior Air Staff Officer at 11 Group. It was a sad farewell to the officers and men of RAF Hornchurch who he had commanded and fought with over 17 months. He later reflected on why he was given this appointment:

> I think the reason for going to 11 Group was that we were doing all this bombing of France, and with the use of long-range fuel tanks, we were getting up to the point of escorting bombers in daylight if not all of the way, then part of the way to Germany.
>
> As a result of this, we were losing a lot of people, particularly experienced fighter pilots, which we could ill afford. The war in the Middle East and the Far East was developing and they were howling for more pilots out there, while we were losing them quite regularly flying over France and so on. I'm not criticising the commanders' policy, it was a good policy as in so far that, when being on the defensive you had one method of operating, while when going over to the offensive and escorting bombers out over hostile territory you had to have a completely different set up. It was expensive; you lost good chaps in the ensuing battle and they were shot down over enemy territory; whereas in England they were shot down over friendly territory and you got them back again.
>
> I think the powers that be, at Fighter Command, decided to take the more senior people off flying. Victor Beamish who commanded North Weald was taken off flying, but he managed to get himself back on to it again, but was later shot down over the Channel and killed. Douglas Bader was shot down, Bob Tuck was another and also other aces; quite a flood of senior people were either lost or became prisoners of war. There was a lot of criticism going on, and I think I was pulled off because I had been flying fighters since the beginning of the war and in the spring of 1942.

Since 27th September 1941, the pilots of RAF Fighter Command had been experiencing an up-hill struggle against the Focke-Wulf 190, which had now gained superiority over the Spitfire Mk Vs. On 7th June 1942, his friend and Vickers Supermarine test pilot Jeffrey Quill asked Harry Broadhurst to give his opinion on the prototype Spitfire Mk IX, which was powered by the newly developed Merlin 61 engine. Jeffrey Quill remembers:

I was so impressed by the aircraft's performance that I decided one day, without official notice, to fly it down to Hornchurch and see what Broady thought of it. I also knew that if he was impressed with the new fighter, that word would soon get back to the senior air staff, people like Sholto Douglas and Leigh-Mallory.

I rang Broady up and arranged to have lunch with him at Hornchurch. I flew the new Spitfire R6700 down to the aerodrome and we decided he would fly it after lunch. The Hornchurch Wing was flying that afternoon on a sweep led by Squadron Leader Peter Powell. Broady arranged for me to go over to the Operations Room in Romford, while he would try out the new machine.

On reaching the Operations Room, I was given a seat next to the Controller Ronnie Adams. I could see by the plots on the table that the Hornchurch Wing was over the Channel nearing the French coast. Ronnie Adams told me that the Wing was going to sweep the area around Lille at 25,000 feet. As they approached near Boulogne, I noticed a single plot on the board behind the Wing, but did not take much notice of it.

It was still there a few minutes later, so I turned to Adams and asked who it was. He said: 'Oh, that's Broady.'

With an immediate answer that is quite unprintable, I continued, he's in my aeroplane! Do you realise that's the most important proto-type fighter in the country right now and furthermore the machine guns aren't loaded. Adams replied there was nothing he could do about it, and that Broady was out of harms way at 35,000 feet.

On his return to Hornchurch, Broadhurst was met by Quill as he taxied the aircraft up. As he stepped out of the Spitfire, Broadhurst smiled and said to Quill: 'It's a magnificent aeroplane, get us as many as you can, as quickly as you can; and by the way, the guns weren't armed.'

It was not long afterwards, that the first Spitfire Mk IXs began to appear on front line squadrons; the first being No.64, based at RAF Hornchurch. Squadron Leader Wilfred Duncan Smith was commanding officer and he recalls:

I remember I got the first Spitfire IX in my squadron. I don't know how it happened, but I think it was a bit of favouritism on the part of Harry Broadhurst. He used to come and fly with us quite a bit. He'd always have me sitting on his tail, to look after him.

On 19th August 1942, the plan to raid the harbour town of Dieppe with a large combined force of 6,000 British and Canadian troops was launched, codenamed Operation 'Jubilee'. The raid's main objectives were to destroy the power station, local defences and installations. Air cover was to be provided by RAF fighters and some bombers. The raid began during the early hours at 3.05 am, but things started to go terribly wrong on the ground as the British and especially the Canadians began to suffer heavy casualties when the German forces began to counter-attack. The order for the invaders to withdraw was issued at 11.00 am. The RAF was instructed to lay smoke and cover the naval force as they returned.

The Luftwaffe put up a heavy screen of fighters and bombers over Dieppe, attacking the small landing craft and naval escort ships as they picked up the troops from Dieppe. In the skies above the port, the RAF and the Luftwaffe fought the largest air battle seen since the summer days of 1940. On the previous day, the 18th, Broadhurst had summoned his wing leaders and squadron commanders to 11 Group Headquarters to be briefed about the next day's operation and what role their squadrons would play in the raid. He had been involved in some of the air planning of the operation and had disagreed on some of the principal proposals put forward regarding Wing formations over Dieppe. Broadhurst records:

> During the planning stage I had disagreed with the proposal to patrol over the beach-head using stepped-up Wings. I imagined that with the opposition that we could expect from the Luftwaffe of small formations of fighters and bombers, the RAF Wings would be far too unmanoeuvrable in that situation. I wasn't very popular with the powers that be. When the big day arrived I borrowed a Spit IX from my old station at Hornchurch and went over to look for myself.

Having borrowed an aircraft from Hornchurch, Spitfire BR370, Broadhurst took off from RAF Northolt early that morning at 6.00 am, and arrived over Dieppe at 25,000 feet, half an hour later. He flew four reconnaissance sorties of the beachhead that day providing valuable first-hand information; it was on his first trip that he also destroyed a Focke-Wulf 190. He returned and landed at Biggin Hill at 7.50 am. The Biggin Hill Intelligence report states:

> To:- HQ 11 Group
> From:- Biggin Hill Int
>
> G/Capt Broadhurst took off from Northolt at 06.00 hrs on a lone observation patrol over Dieppe. At 25,000 feet he noticed odd lots of pairs of enemy aircraft coming out apparently 5 miles northeast of Le Treport, then swooping down towards Dieppe, making passes at our patrols and ships on the way. The Group Captain having observed this repeated movement, picked on the No.2 of a pair of FW190s carrying out similar tactics. While sitting up sun at 5,000 feet above them, he started to dive and fire. With the hand of the clock at beyond dial reading point and the boost more than ordinarily pulled, he rather cruelly closed in to close range of 50 yards and let the enemy aircraft have some 160 cannon shells.

The Hun very naturally turned on his back and went down in a vertical spin.

The Group Captain then fired a small amount of demoralising machine-gun fire at the No.1 aircraft, which followed the original victim for a little way. It soon did the correct thing by bursting into all sorts of coloured smoke and dived to its doom into the sea. The enemy aircraft seemed to be working in pairs and starting their dives down-sun from 15-20,000 feet. Weather over the target was perfect.

G/Capt Broadhurst landed at Biggin Hill at 07.50 hrs claiming 1 FW190 destroyed.

Having landed, Broadhurst immediately telephoned the Group Operations Room and asked to speak to the Commander-in-Chief. He told him what he had observed over Dieppe and suggested that patrols of Spitfires in pairs over the area in which he had sighted the enemy formating might halt the enemy fighters' approach towards the main patrol area. Broadhurst would fly another three sorties that day over Dieppe, obtaining vital information regarding the enemy's air tactics. He finally landed back at Northolt at 7.00 pm from his fourth sortie having flown a total of $8^1/_2$ hours in the day. For his outstanding contribution to operations, Broadhurst was notified by Headquarters Fighter Command of the award of a bar to his Distinguished Flying Cross on 16th September 1942.

The Dieppe raid was a failure and the attacking forces had suffered heavy casualties; over 1,000 soldiers had been killed, 600 wounded and 1,900 captured out of a force of some 5,000. The Royal Air Force had lost just over 100 aircraft and 80 pilots, while the Luftwaffe had lost 48 destroyed. Although it was a failure many lessons would be learned and put right in time for the second attempt to free mainland Europe in 1944.

After the Dieppe raid, Broadhurst was asked to write down his conclusions of the air operations carried out that day in a report. He wrote the following:

Dieppe Report

1st Sortie

I took off from Northolt at 06.00 hours and flew straight to Dieppe arriving at approximately 06.30 hours at 25,000 feet. The weather was clear over the area, but there was some cloud to the east and west.

I cruised round observing the general picture and made a short reconnaissance of the sea area between Dieppe and Le Havre and Dieppe and Boulogne. No shipping was seen. In the battle area the landings on the flank beaches had obviously taken place whilst those on the main beaches at Dieppe were still in progress and appeared to be meeting with considerable trouble.

The anchorage just to the north of Dieppe was rapidly taking shape and the majority of the Spitfire cover could be seen maintaining their patrol in its vicinity.

I had by now lost height to 20,000 feet, and was in a position up sun – ie, to the northeast of the battle area. From here I soon gained a complete picture of the air situation. In general it appeared that Focke-Wulf 190s were coming out from France in pairs and fours from the Le Treport area at about 15,000 feet, and when in position directly up sun of our patrols, would dive straight down towards the ships and the beaches, some dropping bombs, some attacking the Spitfires, and some shooting up the ships with their forward armament.

These attacks seemed to be achieving very little, however, although an occasional Spitfire was shot down and no doubt the attacks against the ships and beaches caused some casualties. The bombing was extremely inaccurate.

After watching these attacks for a short period of time, I started to lose height down towards the Le Treport area, and eventually picked on the No.2 of one of the attacking Focke-Wulf pairs and shot it down into the sea. I then returned to Biggin Hill, where I met the station commander and visited all the squadrons at dispersal points and from the conversations with the pilots, I was able to confirm what I had seen from the air.

I thereupon rang up the Group Operations Room and spoke to the Commander-in-Chief, and having given him an outline of the situation, asked him to pass a message to the AOC suggesting that patrols of Spitfire IXs in pairs be instituted in the area, which I thought would tend to baulk the Focke-Wulfs' approach to the main control area.

2nd Sortie

After breakfast I took off from Biggin Hill at 09.40 hours in order to rendezvous with the Fortresses and Spitfire IX squadrons at 23,000 feet over Beachy Head with the intention of accompanying them on their bombing expedition to Abbeville-Drucat.

I was at 25,000 feet over Beachy Head at 1.00 hours when the Hornchurch Controller (by whom I was controlled) informed me that dive bombing was reported from Dieppe and that the situation was very warm. I therefore hastened to Dieppe in time to find a force of Dornier 217s and Junkers Ju88s accompanied by 30 to 50 Focke-Wulfs attacking the beach areas and shipping at Dieppe.

The Dorniers appeared to be between 10,000 feet and 12,000 feet with their escorts stepped up to about 15,000 feet. I attacked one of the escorts, but both cannons failed to fire and after emptying nearly all my machine-gun ammunition into him, I broke off the combat and climbed back towards Abbeville, where I joined the bombers at 23,000 feet, just as they were turning off their bombing run.

I was able to witness the bombs bursting on Abbeville aerodrome with extreme accuracy. I accompanied the bombers back to the English coast and landed at Hornchurch for refuelling and rearming. I met the wing commander flying and went with him round the dispersal points where I spoke to all the pilots, discussing their tactics and the German tactics, and generally talking over the situation with them.

I telephoned the Group Operations Room and spoke to the AOC giving him a description of the bomber attacks at Dieppe and suggesting an alteration to the patrol heights of our fighters, and also the description of the Fortress bombing attacks at Abbeville.

3rd Sortie

I took off from Hornchurch in company with Wing Commander Robin Powell at 12.30 hours and flew direct to Dieppe arriving there at about 13.00 hours at 25,000 feet. The withdrawal was now almost complete and with the exception of a few ships, two or three miles off Dieppe, which included the destroyer HMS *Berkeley*, the convoy was in full progress back towards the English coast.

After cruising around for a few minutes, Wing Commander Powell separated from me, and went down to sea level to see the situation from a low altitude, while I circled the Dieppe area gradually losing height down to 18,000 feet. I noticed one or two attacks by Dornier 217s, whose bombing appeared extremely inaccurate, many of them jettisoning their bombs as soon as they were attacked by Spitfires.

I noticed that the rear of the convoy, ie, that part of it nearest the French coast, was being subjected to the most severe attacks and latterly the majority of these were being directed against the destroyer *Berkeley*, which was apparently in difficulties. I called up Hornchurch Control and asked them to suggest to Group Operations that the patrols be concentrated over that area, at the same time calling up the ship control and suggesting that he moved the bottom cover squadron to the immediate vicinity of the *Berkeley*.

The ship controller was continuously reporting the presence of Dornier 217s, but I noticed that there were several Focke-Wulf 190s about, some of them carrying bombs.

Towards the end of my patrol, I saw two Focke-Wulfs dive towards the *Berkeley*. I dived after them, but could not intercept them until they had dropped their bombs, one of which appeared to score a direct hit on the stern of the *Berkeley*. I closed to the rear of the 190 as he pulled away from his dive and emptied most of my cannon and machine-gun ammunition into him with good effect. I then returned along the line of the convoy to Kenley, where I had lunch.

Whilst at Kenley, I met the station commander and wing commander flying and again met the pilots at their dispersal points. After this, I rang up Group Operations and made my report to the AOC, in which I emphasised that the patrols, which obviously could not cover the whole of the convoy, should be concentrated on that part nearest the French coast.

4th Sortie

I took off from Kenley at about 15.15 hours and flew direct to Dieppe where at 19,000 feet whilst jettisoning my extra fuel tank, I was attacked by two Focke-Wulfs. After shaking these off, I again came into combat with four more Focke-Wulfs and had to take severe evasive action into cloud, which was then almost 10/10ths over the whole area at varying heights in the region of 5,000 feet.

I emerged below cloud to find the convoy well clear of the French coast and apparently steaming along in good order and with very little interference. As I was almost out of ammunition I cruised back along the convoy to the English coast and endeavoured to land at Tangmere aerodrome, but as the weather had closed right in, I returned to Hornchurch.

From here I rang the AOC suggesting to him that owing to weather conditions, high patrols were not necessary and that in my opinion the patrols could be considerably reduced in strength. We also discussed the state of the pilots and I told him that although they were in tremendous heart, they were beginning to show signs of tiredness.

After refuelling and rearming, I returned to Northolt, landing at 19.00 hours, having flown a total of 8¼ hours during the day.

Conclusions

In general, I think that the tactics of the cover patrols were very effective and only need slight modification to counter the heights and direction of approach by the German fighters and bombers.

Reconnaissance Patrols

It is my firm opinion that in future operations an experienced pilot complete with a Number Two, should be employed for reconnaissance over the battle area in order to bring back tactical information for the immediate use of the AOC.

Several pairs of these senior pilots could be employed so that a continuous watch on the situation could be maintained.

Ship Control

With regard to the ship control, it is considered that their radio transmissions should be much more powerful, so as to drown idle chatter by individual aircraft.

Whilst the present system only controls a limited number of aircraft, it is considered that the leaders of the top squadrons working on their own frequencies should occasionally press the button, which gives them the frequency on which the ship controller is working, in order to get a picture of what is going on below them.

Visits to Sectors

From visiting sectors I discovered the following:
1. The morale of the pilots was without exception extremely high,

but it was found in most cases that after three sorties, it had taken the edge off them and that after four sorties they were visibly tiring.
2. The arrangements for refuelling and rearming varied in the sectors, some being extremely rapid, others being only a little faster than in the ordinary day-to-day operations.
3. By visiting dispersals after units had returned, it was possible to pick up tactical information and telephone it back to Group within a few minutes, particularly as I had been over the area myself and I was able to get into the picture very rapidly. It is suggested that the reconnaissance mentioned should be combined with the duties of visiting units after landing.

German Tactics

I gained the impression that the Germans did not adapt themselves very rapidly to the situation, and that they were trying to compete with our patrols in the same way as they do when we give close escort to bombers. Only on rare occasions did they display any determination to press home their attacks, usually when our patrols were thin, either as a result of heavy combats or latterly when the patrols were spread over a large area of the convoy.

Broadhurst remained with 11 Group until he received notification of his appointment as Senior Air Staff Officer to Desert Air Force on 31st October 1942. Soon after the Battle of El Alamein, he arrived at the Headquarters of Desert Air Force under the command of Air Marshal Arthur Coningham. Harry Broadhurst's daughter Diana remembers his posting to his new command:

He was sent out to Egypt to lead the Desert Air Force, but Coningham liked the existing commander, so he kept my father kicking his heels back in Cairo. In his desperation, my father rang the Air Ministry and asked to be recalled so that he could do a proper job. Coningham was told in no uncertain terms that Broadhurst was to take over the Desert Air Force. In fact my father got his order just after the Battle of El Alamein and had great difficulty in pursuing his force in order to take command.

The late Air Vice-Marshal J.E. 'Johnnie' Johnson recalls Harry Broadhurst's great contribution, when he became commander of the Desert Air Force in 1942:

He proved to be an outstanding commander and leader, and he soon gained the full confidence of the leader of the Eighth Army, General Bernard Montgomery. Before Broadhurst had arrived on the scene most fighter-bomber pilots had made the majority of their attacks whenever they saw opportunity targets during their flights over the battlefield. Broadhurst however, thought his pilots could provide better support for the army chaps, if they knew more about the ground battle and the whereabouts of enemy tanks and armour.

In other words, he wanted more planned set-piece attacks and less strafing of opportunity targets. RAF controllers in armoured cars, situated with the forward troops, and in radio contact achieved this with the squadrons already in the air awaiting instructions from the ground.

Harry Broadhurst soon became Air Officer Commanding Desert Air Force and was promoted to the rank of acting Air Vice-Marshal, the youngest officer in the Royal Air Force to rise to that rank at the age of 38, on 31st January 1943.

He soon began to win praise from the Army for his expert handling of land and air co-operation, especially his tactical use of the close support system by the fighter-bombers to prevent the enemy's reinforcements and supplies from getting to the front line. Towards the end of January 1943, Rommel and his German troops finally withdrew from Tripoli and into Tunisia, where the Germans organised a defence along an area known as the Mareth Line. It was here that Rommel's army launched a surprise and lightning attack against the thinly spread American 1st Armored Division on 14th February. Rommel pressed ahead; his 19th Panzer Division broke through at the Kasserine Pass and was intending to take the important Allied supply depot at Tebessa. Before reaching this objective however, the Germans met strong opposition from the British 6th Armoured Division and the attack failed.

Rommel now turned south again to launch an attack at the Mareth Line. Fortunately, Montgomery had recognised Rommel's next move and prepared a counter-strike to halt the German advance. This plan would incorporate the careful cooperation between Harry Broadhurst's air squadrons, artillery and ground troops. On 19th February 1943, Broadhurst received this note from Montgomery:

Dear Harry

I enclose you a copy of the preliminary arrangements and outline plans, for the operations against the Mareth position. I have called it operation BINGE!!

On 6th March the attack against the Germans began and completely decimated their forces, which lost 52 tanks in the battle. After the battle, Montgomery sent a letter to Broadhurst, which read:

I would like to convey to you my great appreciation of the superb support that has been given by the air force under your command every day since the battle began.

Such intimate and close support has never to my knowledge been achieved before, and it has been an inspiration to all the troops.

The results have been first-class. I sincerely trust you have not suffered many losses.

By the spring of 1943, Field Marshal Erwin Rommel's Afrika Corps was an army now in full retreat; its only main supply route open was by air, with the Luftwaffe trying to supply the German troops by Junkers JU52 transport aircraft. Broadhurst knew that the main entry point of delivery to the troops on the ground was near Cape Bon. Discovering information from the decoded German Enigma signals, Broadhurst was able to send in his squadrons to intercept the low flying enemy transport that had escaped previously by flying below Allied radar detection. Broadhurst ordered his squadrons to fly just above sea level, where they sighted and slaughtered the transport aircraft and their escorts. On one day, the Desert Air Force claimed thirty-eight and on another fifty-two for the loss of only seven Allied fighters. Thereafter the Germans confined the transport aircraft to only night-time flying.

Broadhurst's daughter Diana Lunn recalls the story of King George VI's visit to Egypt during this time:

> The King came out to the desert to meet his commanders and my father was summoned to appear. In the desert they always wore khaki drill to keep cool, together with brown shoes. However, for this meeting he had to carry with him his best blue, which he duly did. Unfortunately, when he arrived and changed, he found that he had forgotten to bring his black shoes, so embarrassingly had to appear in brown shoes. When the King arrived, he took one look at my father and then turned to his aide-de-camp in fury and yelled – 'that man's wearing brown shoes, why couldn't I wear brown shoes?'

By 12th May 1943, the remaining German forces in North Africa had been surrounded and forced to surrender. Nearly a quarter of a million Axis prisoners were captured. The war in the desert was over.

At dawn on 10th July 1943, the Allied invasion of Sicily began, codenamed Operation 'Huskey'. In charge of the Allied Air Force was Air Marshal Sir Arthur Tedder who had at his disposal nearly 4,000 aircraft; against this the Italians could muster nearly 200 aircraft and the Germans just over 300. Therefore it could be said, that the Axis air defence was minimal. The landings were a great success with virtually no opposition. Two days after the Allies landed at Sicily, Harry Broadhurst flew his Spitfire and landed at the newly built landing strip at Pachino. He quickly inspected the new site and after finding all the necessary units in order to maintain an airfield, he sent orders for the three squadrons from No.244 Wing to fly in at dawn the next morning. The squadrons were No.1 South African Air Force, No.92 and No.145. The whole operation to take the island took just 38 days; the island fell to the Allies on 17th August 1943.

After the fall of Sicily, the next move would be against mainland Italy. While this was being planned, Harry Broadhurst and his fellow officers found some time to relax and forget about the war, if only for a brief time. Wilfred Duncan Smith was one of Broadhurst's group captains at that time and recalls:

> Broady had managed to obtain a captured Italian motor launch from somewhere. He would take us up the coast for trips and some

of us would even try to do improvised water skiing. This was achieved by using a thirty-gallon petrol drop-tank from a Spitfire, which was towed behind the launch. We had a pretty good time as he always had it well stocked with booze and food.

It was while in Italy, in March 1944, that Squadron Leader Hugh 'Cocky' Dundas was working on the personal staff of Air Vice-Marshal Broadhurst's Advanced Headquarters Desert Air Force. On 3rd March, he had been awarded the Distinguished Service Order; Dundas remembers sitting with Broady one evening, in his commander's trailer:

> We were having a glass of whisky together and talking generally, having disposed of the day's detailed business, when he asked me how I would feel about going back on operational flying. It was a question, which I had been both dreading and hoping for. He then took my breath away by telling me that he was considering appointing me to command 239 Wing, as the commanding officer of the Wing, Colonel Laurie Wilmot was wanted for other duties. I was immensely flattered and also alarmed. Firstly because 239 Wing was the biggest in the whole of the Mediterranean and secondly slightly alarmed that at the age of twenty-three, I would be given a Group Captain's command. Broady told me not to mention this proposal to any one, as the change would not take place for some weeks ahead. Soon after, news came through that Broady himself was to leave; he was to be posted back to Britain, to command the 83 Group, which was part of the 2nd Tactical Air Force that would support the 21st Army Division, in the invasion of Northern Europe at Normandy. Fortunately, Montgomery invited Broadhurst to travel in his aircraft, which saved his life, as his own aircraft in which he was to have travelled was shot down.

Air Vice-Marshal Broadhurst was posted back to Europe to take command of Headquarters No.83 Group Tactical Air Force on 21st March 1944. The build up and preparations for the invasion of France were now under way.

Broadhurst was highly delighted to learn of the next award bestowed upon him, when on 11th April 1944, he was given the United States of America's Legion of Merit Degree of Officer confirmed by the President, Franklin D. Roosevelt.

On 6th June 1944, the Allies landed on the beaches of Normandy and established a foothold on occupied France that they would never relinquish. Broadhurst's squadrons covered the troops as they slowly advanced inland of the beachhead. Whenever German resistance was proving stubborn, Broadhurst's headquarters was contacted and asked to provide the means of removing the German obstacle, be it tanks or artillery. The ground-attack rocket-firing Typhoons and Tempest aircraft could soon be heard flying over-head of the Allied troops to knock out the enemy opposition. But the Germans were bringing up reserve tanks and troops and the advance began to falter.

It was during the Allies' slow and costly advance through the hedgerows and country lanes of Normandy, a few weeks after the invasion, that Harry

Broadhurst remembered an amusing but dangerous trip he took to visit one of Montgomery's generals, up near the front line:

> Usually I flew in my captured German Fiesler Storch aircraft to the various army headquarters and I particularly wanted to see the 7th Army Division's commander, Bobby Erskin. So I said to my driver Dai Rees, who was a well known golfer during this time, that we could drive out to 7th Armoured Division the next day to find out exactly where they were, because I couldn't fly out there because it was forest country. So we set out the next day and as we got further away from our own lines the traffic died away, we were driving down a small road with trees on either side and troops were lying in the ditches on both sides. I thought they were waving at us and I started waving back; I noticed ahead of us was a crossroads, but I also noticed there were no more troops in the ditches. We came to the crossroads and on each side of it was a bloody great German Tiger tank, with their guns beginning to swing around in our direction. I've never travelled backwards so fast in all my life, my driver Dai Rees must have been doing 50 mph backwards in this confounded jeep. And as we passed the troops, this time they were really waving. When I eventually arrived and met Bobby Erskin, he said, 'I hear you've been trying to take on a couple of Tiger tanks,' I said, 'yes, and without any anti-tank ammunition.'

The slow progress came to an end on 25th July 1944, when armoured American divisions smashed through the German lines and into the open French countryside. But instead of retreating, the Germans regrouped and launched a counter-attack at Mortain on 7th August. In the battle that ensued, Broadhurst's Typhoon Wings of 83 and 84 Groups were again ordered into action to halt the German Panzers. They caused so much damage that the Germans found it almost impossible to move during daylight hours. The Germans, now threatened with complete encirclement by the Allies, tried to escape through the area known as the Falaise Gap. It was here that the main retreating army was caught in the open by the rocket-firing Typhoons and it became a killing field. After the battle was over, the Germans had lost 60,000 men killed or captured, 500 tanks and artillery, and over 5,000 vehicles. The RAF's 83 and 84 Group lost 151 pilots combined during the Normandy campaign. The German remnants were now in full retreat, but continued to fight all the way back until they reached the French/German border. It was on 15th August 1944 that Air Vice-Marshal Harry Broadhurst was awarded the Companion of the Order of the Bath medal and was presented with the award by King George VI, while on a visit to France. On 25th August 1944, French, British and American forces entered Paris.

By the second week of September, the Allied armies had retaken all of Belgium, and had made progress into parts of Holland. Michael Donnet remembers:

> In September 1944, I met Air Vice-Marshal Broadhurst again when he was commanding 83 Group of 2nd TAF. This was on the airfield

of Evere, three days after the liberation of Brussels. He wished me luck as I was going to see my family after three years of separation. His fighting spirit had inspired the pilots of the Spitfire and Typhoon Wings and they had achieved remarkable results in their air operations.

A plan by Field Marshal Bernard Montgomery to launch an aerial invasion in Holland by men of the American 82nd and 101st Airborne Division to take the bridges at Eindhoven and Nijmegen, while the British 1st Airborne would take the Arnhem Bridge, was not well received by other senior Allied commanders. But Montgomery pushed the plan through and on 17th September, Operation Market Garden was put into effect to cut the German army forces off from behind their positions. Although the Americans took and held their objectives, the British were met by stiff German opposition and although holding the bridge, the British force was soon outnumbered and outmanoeuvred, while waiting for British reinforcements to push through German lines. Facing increasing German reinforcements, lack of supplies and ammunition, the survivors of the British division had to be evacuated around the Oosterbeek perimeter across the lower Rhine river. Harry Broadhurst's squadrons were unable to provide the important air cover for the operation, as they were grounded due to the very bad weather:

> It was a hell of a disaster more or less from the start and the airborne forces had never planned the operation with Tactical Air Force. One fact was the incredible failure of the mobile wireless sets that the troops had brought with them. When our chaps did eventually get airborne, all they could do was to circle helplessly overhead while the men on the ground were unable to contact them with instructions to attack certain German targets. I learnt my lesson from this, from then on I insisted that we send our own experienced operators in with the gliders with our own RAF radios; so that once they had landed they would be in immediate contact with our chaps in their aircraft.

The Allied forces had suffered more casualties during the nine days of Operation Market Garden than during the 24-hour period of the Normandy invasion. Total combined Allied forces had lost more than 17,000 men killed, missing and wounded, the British alone losing 13,226 men.

In late December 1944, at Evere, Harry Broadhurst had another one of his lucky escapes. It was late afternoon, when he took off to return to Eindhoven in his Fiesler Storch aeroplane. After its usual short run it began to climb steeply. Suddenly, when the aircraft was only several feet above some airfield buildings, the engine stopped. Broadhurst tried to get it down on to one of the hangar roofs. But the one he chose had been destroyed and gutted, and all that remained were the charred crossbeams. The Storch bounced on the beams and then fell to the ground, causing smoke and dust to fill the inside of the hangar. Amazingly, Broadhurst walked away uninjured, but somewhat shaken from the accident. All that was left of the aircraft was a pile of twisted metal and fabric. He returned later that day to his headquarters at Eindhoven.

Diana Lunn remembers the building her father used as his headquarters in Holland at this time:

> After the invasion he made his headquarters in the Philips' house in Eindhoven. That is the Philips of electrical appliance fame. For quite a while their eldest daughter, Digna, and I used to write to one another. The Germans had previously used the house. Mr Philips, on the insistence of his daughter, actually came to visit me at my school when he was over in England. The family also sent me via my father a cake for my birthday. It was while at Eindhoven that the King came to review the troops; my father's driver, golfer Dai Rees, was given the job of taking the King on a round of golf with strict orders that he must not beat the King.

On 1st January 1945, the German Luftwaffe launched their last ditch attempt against the Allied Air Force's airfields in France, Belgium and Holland. The German surprise move was codenamed Operation Bodenplatte. During the attack, which started at dawn, the Luftwaffe caught the RAF and the Americans completely by surprise, flying at low level. The late Air Marshal Sir Dermot Boyle GCB, KCVO, KBE, AFC was on Harry Broadhurst's staff at 83 Group Headquarters at this time and remembers the attack:

> As the raids developed, Broady summoned me to his office to discuss the problem. As we were doing so the telephone rang, it was the Commander-in-Chief of 2nd Tactical Air Force Arthur Coningham on the line. I quite clearly heard Coningham saying to Broady; 'What the hell are you doing Harry, I've got aeroplanes with black crosses on them flying about over my headquarters doing what they like.' Harry Broadhurst replied; 'You are lucky, Sir, they are flying back and forth below my window.'

The aerial battle raged on throughout the day, but by the end of it the Germans had lost over 300 aircraft and valuable pilots they could ill afford. The Allies lost 200 aircraft, mostly on the ground, but these were soon replaced. Pilot casualties were light. The Luftwaffe had fought its last big battle.

With the war over, Harry Broadhurst remained in the RAF to pursue his career. For his outstanding service to the country, he was made Knight of the British Empire (KBE) on 5th July 1945. On 21st September 1945, he was appointed Air Officer in Charge of Administration at Fighter Command. But it was during this year that his marriage finally failed, ending in divorce. He remarried the following year Jean Elizabeth Townley on 13th May 1946 at Weobley Register Office in Hereford. Having relinquished his rank of Acting AVM on 4th July, Broadhurst was made Air Officer Commander of Headquarters 61 Group (Eastern Reserve) on 1st August 1946 with the promotion to Air Commodore on 1st July 1947. He was also awarded the Order of Orange Nassau, conferred upon him by Her Majesty the Queen of the Netherlands on 31st October 1947.

On 19th July 1948, he was sent on attachment to the School of Combined Operations at Fremington until 23rd of that month. He was again promoted in rank to Air Vice-Marshal, on 1st July 1949, and on 1st February 1950, appointed as Senior Air Staff Officer, to Headquarters British Armed Forces Overseas. On 19th April 1952, he was appointed as Assistant Chief of the Air Staff (Operations), before being given the position of Commander-in-Chief of 2nd Tactical Air Force on 3rd December 1953 as acting Air Marshal.

Broadhurst's command took him to Germany and it was it here that John Cox, an LAC motor transport driver first met Harry Broadhurst. John recalls:

> In 1954 I had been posted to HQ Unit Bad Eilsen in Germany. It was here that a friend of mine, 'Nobby' Clarke told me that he often went to help at Harry Broadhurst's residence; and he asked me if I wanted to go along with him that Sunday morning, which I did. I arrived and was introduced to the commander-in-chief. Broadhurst was keen on horse riding and for the next couple of weeks we would help him to get his horses out of the stables, so that he and Lady Broadhurst could go riding. The one thing I remember is what a lovely couple they were and how they were very sociable too. They being who they were and 'Nobby' and I just being a couple of LACs, they just chatted to us like any other couple. It was in 1955, when the HQ was moved from Bad Eilsen to Mönchengladbach that on arrival to his new quarters, it was found that Sir Harry's bedding had been left behind. I was at once detailed to return to Bad Eilsen to collect it 'Post Haste.' With my foot down on the accelerator all the way there and back, I did get stopped once by the RAF Police, but they didn't keep me long, when I told them the reason for my haste. I arrived back in time for Sir Harry and Lady Broadhurst to get to bed that night at a reasonable time.

The Belgian, Lieutenant General Michael Donnet became a close friend of Harry Broadhurst and remembers this period:

> At this time I was senior air staff officer of the reformed 83 Group, one of the three groups of 2nd Tactical Air Force. Broadhurst was the right man for the job and exercised his command with knowledge and authority. All his wing leaders who had been picked by him were top wartime fighter pilots with great experience, such as Johnnie Johnson, Johnny Jameson, Bill Crawford-Compton, Teddy Donaldson and many others. There is no doubt that the set up of the organization, with the quality and determination of all the leaders at headquarter or at station level, had a great influence and deterred the potential enemy, during the early stage of the cold war. Broadhurst was someone who enjoyed the respect of everyone. During an exercise at our headquarters in Paris, we produced a stage show in which those responsible for the western world showed how they would act their part in the conflict. It was impressive and Broadhurst played his part with conviction.

The following year, he was made Knight Commander of the Bath (KCB) on 1st January 1955 and was also informed by the Air Council of his next position as Air Officer Commander-in-Chief of Bomber Command on 22nd January 1956; he was now 50 years of age. When he first arrived at his new command, he was totally unimpressed and remarked:

> To be utterly frank, I was appalled at the tedious way they were still behaving. Bomber Command was still back in the Second World War. Aircraft were taking up to six hours to get airborne. I therefore decided to put a 'jerk' into the command by bringing in a few fighter people like myself to get things moving a lot faster.

Broadhurst decided to introduce the 'Quick Reaction Alert' procedure, which was being used by the RAF jet fighter squadrons. He now commanded Britain's RAF nuclear cold war deterrent against the Russian threat from the eastern block.

It was later that same year that he had to provide air support during the Suez Crisis, when British and French troops invaded Port Said in Egypt. Relations between the British and French Governments and Egypt's President Nasser had reached breaking point, when Nasser had begun buying weapons from the Soviet Union and then had nationalised the Suez Canal, which had been a British responsibility since 1888. After negotiations failed, the British Government decided to send a Land and Sea Task Force, codenamed 'Musketeer' to the region. Immense pressure was exerted by the Americans and the United Nations on British Prime Minister Anthony Eden for Britain to stop the fighting, and by midnight on 6th November 1956, a cease-fire was declared.

In 1956, a new aircraft was now about to come into service with the RAF, the delta-winged Avro Vulcan bomber, which carried a 10,000 lb nuclear weapon. The first of the new Avro Vulcan aircraft was XA897, delivered to RAF Waddington on 30th July 1956, and it was then taken for experimental trials to the Armament Experimental Establishment at Boscombe Down before being prepared for a worldwide tour of Commonwealth countries. Harry Broadhurst was selected to go on the tour and was to sit in the co-pilot's seat next to the aircraft's pilot Squadron Leader Donald Howard DFC. The rest of the crew consisted of the navigator Squadron Leader Edward Eames DFC, Flight Lieutenant James Stroud, signaller Squadron Leader Albert Gamble, and an Avro technical representative Frederick Bassett.

On 9th September 1956, XA897 took off from England and set course for Melbourne, Australia; where the new aircraft was to be on show at the Air Force Commemoration Week. From Australia, the team would then fly the Vulcan to New Zealand. Before leaving, Broadhurst had been advised by the Air Ministry and Avro that it would be beneficial for publicity reasons that the new Vulcan be brought back and landed at London's Heathrow airport.

After the successful tour in Australia and New Zealand, the Vulcan was then flown on the return leg of the trip to Singapore; it was here that Harry Broadhurst opposed the idea of coming into Heathrow because it would mean more facilities would have to be brought in from Boscombe Down to turn the aircraft around. These included starter crews, fuel and a spare braking parachute. But despite his reservations, this was all laid on. Back at Heathrow there would be a massive welcoming party with various VIPs to receive the crew. Among them would be the Deputy Chief of Staff Air Marshal Sir Geoffrey Tuttle along with Air Marshal Whitely, commander of No.1 Bomber Group, Air Marshal Kenneth Cross of No.3 Bomber Group and Air Vice-Marshal Sidney Burton, Senior Air Staff Officer; also there to meet her husband would be Lady Jane Broadhurst and her five-year-old daughter Clare and Mrs Howard.

They took off on the final leg of the journey on the 1st October from Khormaksar airfield in Aden at 2.50 pm, Squadron Leader Howard and Harry Broadhurst taking turns at the controls. While over France, Howard was informed by Headquarters Bomber Command that the weather was closing in and that visibility at Heathrow was 3,000 yards with light rain and 7/8th cloud with a base at 700 feet. As the weather worsened, the operations control at Bomber Command informed Howard that the decision to land at Heathrow was 'up to you?' There was also high intensity lighting at London. As the massive delta-winged aircraft made its final approach, the controller at Heathrow passed his message that they were now 80 feet above the glide-path.

Squadron Leader Howard overdid the power reduction and dropped 100 feet below, but when at 1,200 feet he increased the power to compensate and regain the normal flight path. As the weather was now atrocious, they were now flying just on instruments, having no visibility outside the cockpit. At that moment Howard asked for lights, to which Broadhurst replied 'Lights fine starboard.' Just at that moment Broadhurst noticed the ground looming up and shouted 'You are too low, pull her up.'

Howard was in the process of pulling the control column up when the aircraft hit the ground. The Vulcan had touched down in a Brussel sprout field 1,030 yards short of the runway, tearing off one of its undercarriage legs as it careered along. Howard managed to get the aircraft airborne, climbing in a steep attitude. But he realised that the aircraft was doomed and shouted; 'Get out, get out, it's had it.' Howard then operated his ejector seat and was shot clear of the aircraft. Broadhurst immediately tried to regain control but he too realised there was little he could do, and therefore ejected from the aircraft.

Meanwhile at the main terminal building the horror of what was happening before the welcoming party's eyes could not be believed, and very soon every newspaper reporter was on the telephone relaying the tragic news. The Vulcan had continued its course along the runway crashing to the ground once halfway along. A massive explosion followed as it came to a halt in a sea of flames and smoke. The rest of the crew did not escape and were killed instantly.

Squadron Leader Howard landed unhurt, but shaken on the grass alongside the runway. But Harry Broadhurst had landed on concrete near to where the Vulcan had finally come to rest. He suffered fractures to his feet and back. After both men were reunited with their wives they were immediately rushed away from the waiting newspaper reporters and cameras and taken to the RAF Hospital at Uxbridge for treatment.

The subsequent inquiry into the tragedy stated that the principal cause of the accident was 'the failure to warn Squadron Leader Howard that he was below the glide path in the concluding stages of the approach.' It was also noted that the captain had made an error of judgement in setting himself a break-off height 20 feet too low and also going below that height, but as he was under ground control approach, he was at no time aware of this.

Harry Broadhurst's daughter Diana hasn't forgotten the Vulcan accident:

> My father's trip to Australia in the Vulcan was immediately after my wedding. I remember that he wasn't feeling too well at the wedding because of all the injection jabs he had undergone. His return flight in the Vulcan was just as my husband and I were returning from our honeymoon. My husband received the phone call at his new station, which unfortunately let the cat out of the bag of our relationship to the Commander-in-Chief. He immediately rang me as the accident had been on the lunchtime news. My father told us that when the pilot ejected, he seized the controls himself in an attempt to bring it down, but found they were not working, so he was forced to eject. Although his parachute opened, he was really too low and he slammed into the runway and broke his feet. He was rescued by the men in the radar hut at the end of the runway, so for a short time they thought he was missing.

After time off to recover from the incident, he resumed his career and was promoted to Air Chief Marshal Sir Harry Broadhurst on 14th February 1957.

On 20th May 1959, he became Commander, Allied Forces Central Europe and remained in this position until 1st March 1961, when he voluntarily retired from the service after serving the Royal Air Force and his country for 35 years. Previously on 1st January 1960, he had been given the award of Grand Cross of the Bath (GCB). Soon after his retirement from the service, he was asked to join A.V. Roe and Company Limited as their Managing Director and from there in 1965, he became Deputy Managing Director of Hawker Siddeley Aviation Limited, retiring from this position in 1976. He had also served between 1973 and 1976 as President of SBAC. Here, he was involved with two of the company's outstandingly successful civil aircraft, the European Airbus and the HS 125 executive jet.

Although throughout his busy service career he had very little time for relaxation, he did have numerous hobbies, when time allowed. His daughter Diana remembers how her father relaxed:

> My father was passionate about sailing, he had many yachts over the years; sailing on the south coast, to France and the Channel Islands, through the French canals to the Mediterranean. When he was in Germany he kept his yacht near the Kiel Canal and sailed in that area. I remember once going to Copenhagen to meet him and then sailing back to his anchorage. In his youth he had been a keen cricketer and had a trial as a fast bowler for Hampshire and apparently had a least one game with them. He was also very keen on rugby and played that in the RAF. Later he would meet his pals for Test Matches at Twickenham. Lastly, he was extremely fond of classical music and in particular the ballet, frequently going to Covent Garden. He also liked opera and would go once a year to

Glyndebourne. In later years, he would go to the theatre in Chichester; unfortunately his increasing deafness in his final years ruined his pleasure in music.

Michael Donnet also remembers Broadhurst's fondness for yachting and one incident in particular:

> He was a very keen sailor, but one night he did have a narrow escape. Sailing from the south of England to Brittany, he fell overboard. Luckily, his wife Jane heard his call and managed in a very professional way to bring the boat around and picked Sir Harry up out of the water.

On 5th July 1983, Air Chief Marshal Sir Harry Broadhurst returned one more time to Hornchurch, from where he had flown most of his combat missions and scored his victories. He arrived as the guest of honour that day to unveil a memorial stone within the grounds of the Mitchell School; this stood on the site of what was once the main entrance and parade ground of RAF Hornchurch. The memorial stone, which had been paid for by contributions given by the public, was draped in the Royal Air Force ensign. After opening speeches Sir Harry unveiled the stone, which read:

> *Site of RAF Hornchurch, Sector Airfield for No. 11 Group. To all Aircrew and Ground Personnel who served here 1928-1962*

After the official opening Sir Harry met many old wartime comrades, whom he had commanded at Hornchurch, over refreshments at the Good Intent pub, which had been used by the airmen during the war.

The author was privileged to meet and interview Sir Harry at his home in 1995. Although now in the twilight of his life, Sir Harry could still tell a darn good yarn and possessed an incredibly dry wit. It was indeed an honour to have met such a distinguished gentleman who had led such an eventful life.

Air Chief Marshal Sir Harry Broadhurst peacefully passed away on 29th September 1995 aged 89. He was buried at the parish church at Birdham, near Chichester. On his headstone reads in Latin, *Asise Vence Horizontes*, Seek New Horizons. Today Hornchurch remembers his name with one of the school team houses of Mitchell School named after him and a road called Broadhurst Way.

CHAPTER 6

THE TEST PILOT
Squadron Leader E.D. 'Dave' Glaser DFC
1921-2001

Dave Glaser as a boy had been brought up in an era when aviation had captured the public's imagination. Stories of the First World War flying aces were available to be read in all the schoolboy annuals and magazines. It was a time when speed and distance records by aircraft and pilots were there to be challenged and broken. His own father had flown as a pilot with other young Royal Flying Corps pilots over the trenches, and this no doubt played a great part inspiring the young Glaser to reach for the skies and seek his future up in the clear blue heavens. He too would be caught up in the events that would change the world forever in 1939; and like his father fight for his country's survival from the air.

Ernest Derek 'Dave' Glaser was born on 20th April 1921 in Sutton, Surrey. His father, William Albert Glaser had been a pilot in the Royal Flying Corps during the First World War; his mother Gertrud Maria Louise was half French and was known by all as Dolly. Later they would have a second son, Alfred Jack. The family name Glaser originated from Alsace Lorraine, an area on the border between France and Germany. Dave Glaser's great grandfather was believed to have been employed as a Ship's Chandler. After the First War his father worked for the United African Company Limited and retired after fifteen years service in 1937. Dave Glaser was educated first at Lancing House Preparatory and then Bloxham School near Banbury, Oxfordshire. During these early years the Glaser family became friends with the Winder family. Dr Wilfred Winder and his wife Peggy purchased a holiday home on the Aldwick Bay Estate, Pagham near Chichester in Sussex; which was next door to the Glaser's. The Winders had four children, three girls and a son named Alan. One of the daughters, Angela Stevenson remembers the Glaser family:

> When Billy and Dolly Glaser spent a lot of the pre-war years working in West Africa so the two Glaser boys spent several school holidays with us and became like members of the family. My parents sent my brother to Bloxham School because of his friendship with Dave and Jack. All the Glaser family were great fun; wonderful company and with warm friendly personalities and a tremendous sense of humour. But they didn't wear their hearts on their sleeves and they were a lot deeper and more complex characters than they appeared at first.

After his retirement, Billy Glaser and his wife ran a number of public houses including the Bugle pub at Hamble in Hampshire. It was at this time that Dave became interested in aviation and was inspired to become a pilot after meeting Jeffrey Quill, who in 1936 was a test pilot for Vickers Supermarine and had flown the early prototype Spitfire. Quill had met Dave's father and knew him quite well. On 20th August 1939, he was accepted into the Royal Air Force Volunteer Reserve for flying training. This he did at No.3 Elementary Flying School at Hamble. Dave Glaser remembers:

> I started off my flying training on an aircraft called an Avro Cadet, which was a scaled down version of the Avro Tutor biplane. My first instructor, Flying Officer Winton was very good, and said that he wanted to put me on the Tiger Moth aeroplane; he reckoned that if you could fly a Tiger you could learn to fly anything and he was right. I liked the Tiger immensely and I did my first solo on 29th August 1939 in Tiger Moth K2596. The chief instructor had taken me up and we did a few flying procedures, then we came in and landed. He said 'we'll do another take-off' so I taxied around ready to go again. Then he stood up and stepped out of the cockpit in front of me and said 'off you go.' I did a circuit and made a complete muck up of a landing, too high and too far down, so I went around again and made a peach of a landing just by pure chance. When I taxied in, I said 'I made a mess of that.' Flying Officer H.A. Fenton, the instructor said, 'No you're alright, you went around again no trouble at all.'

After a total of 13 hours and 55 minutes, Dave Glaser had gone solo. In his flying log-book, his proficiency as a pilot was marked as average. A few days later, on 3rd September 1939, Britain declared war on Germany:

> Once war had been declared we were all gathered together at Hastings, waiting to be posted to an airfield. In November I was sent to No.1 Elementary Flying Training School at Hatfield, flying Tiger Moths again. I stayed here until 18th March 1940 after logging 41 hours, 40 minutes dual flying and 33 hours, 10 minutes solo. From there I went to No.6 Flying Training School on 1st April, which was at Little Rissington in Gloucester. Here I was introduced to the North American Harvard training aircraft, but we actually did most of our flying at Kidlington. After a few weeks spent training here, I achieved an above average rating and was posted to No.65 Squadron at Hornchurch as a pilot officer.
>
> I was very glad to go to a fully operational squadron. A lot of the other chaps went to Operational Training Units first to fly the Spitfire, whereas I had the minimum time wasted before I got on operations with a squadron.

It was during this period that Dave Glaser would often visit close friends, when time off from duty allowed. Angela Stevenson remembers Dave's visits to her family home:

Our home was in Chiswick, so Dave often appeared for a flying visit during the early days of the war. He always arrived in a small racy sports car, which he drove at great speed and he always had a dog, often a spaniel, one called Blackie and later one called Dumbo.

On 13th July 1940, Dave Glaser joined his squadron three days after the official start of what would become known as the Battle of Britain. His first few weeks were not taken up with joining the rest of the chaps in action, but actually flying the squadron's Miles Master aircraft P2494 on sector reconnaissance or ferrying pilots to and from Hornchurch's satellite airfield at Rochford. His first flight in a Spitfire took place on 30th July 1940, under the supervision of Pilot Officer Couzens who was in charge of the Station Flight at Hornchurch. He took off in Spitfire YT-O for 30 minutes, where he proceeded to familiarise himself with the new aircraft by doing circuits and landings. Dave recalls his first days at Hornchurch:

> My first impression of Hornchurch was that it was an old airfield, but had quite a history already. I arrived there on the same day as the Irish pilot Brendan Finucane. Paddy went to A Flight, I went to B Flight whose commander was Flight Lieutenant Gordon Olive, an Australian. A Flight was commanded by Flight Lieutenant Gerald Saunders, nicknamed Sammy. A few days before I had arrived, the squadron had lost its commanding officer Squadron Leader Sawyer on a night take-off. His aircraft had just got airborne, when for no apparent reason it crashed and he was killed. Sammy Saunders was given command and led the squadron. A new CO was posted in by the name of Holland and he said that he hadn't done operations and so forth, so he asked Sammy to lead the squadron and said, I'll be your No2 and do all the ground work. It relieved Sammy of a lot of paperwork stuff, and gave us the best leader for the squadron.
>
> I can recall my first flight in a Spitfire, I was very shattered by the speed and I was very careful to stay within sight of the aerodrome. I also remember I had to do a night take-off and that was one I'll never forget. I had just got airborne when I was called up suddenly over the radio, and told that there was a raid coming in and that they were putting out all the lights and leaving a solitary goose neck lamp in the middle of the airfield for me to get in on. I thought my good God how am I going to manage that.
>
> But with the grace of God I got down, but my next worry was to stop the aircraft before hitting anything, I couldn't see a thing it was so dark. Once I'd stopped they told me over the R/T to stay put and they would come out to pick me up. It was certainly a frightening experience for a novice pilot.

The squadron then went up to Sutton Bridge for air-firing practice on 9th August, by which time Dave Glaser had accumulated 9 hours on Spitfires, and on 15th August, he undertook his first patrol with the squadron. This was after arriving at Manston early in the morning from Hornchurch:

The daily routine was that we would take turns with 54 and 74 Squadrons. Sometimes we would fly down to Manston very early to do dawn readiness, then one of the other squadrons would come down later during the day and we would go back.

I always felt a bit excited before being scrambled. The biggest worry I had was as a new boy, that I would do something bloody stupid which would put the rest of the squadron in an awkward position. So I was determined to learn as much as possible. I remember that 41 Squadron's commanding officer 'Robin' Hood had collided with his own flight commander during an engagement with the enemy. Hood was killed and his flight commander had baled out, but the trouble was he'd left his parachute behind. He too fell to his death. I thought my god, how easy it was to un-strap your parachute harness by mistake.

On landing you would undo your Sutton harness, which attached you to the seat, you'd then release the parachute straps and then step out. After hearing about the previous incident, on landing my Spitfire I would practice undoing the Sutton harness and stepping out of the aircraft with my parachute on, in case I ever had to bale out in a hurry.

Dave was pleasantly surprised to learn that Jeffrey Quill had been sent to 65 Squadron by Vickers Supermarine, to gain operational experience and gather information on the Spitfire's performance. He would fly as Quill's No.2 in the flight. Dave would later recall that it was the best thing that could have happened to him at this stage. Quill was extremely helpful and saw him through the early stages of the battle, when one needed to be alert to the dangers that young inexperienced pilots faced on their first few sorties. Dave recalls his first engagement with the enemy, being a mass of confusion of what to do and what to avoid:

> The telephone at dispersal rang and Jeffrey answered it. How many of 65 Squadron available? Jeffrey replied. Five of us. The controller then said, Right. Get airborne immediately. We ran to our aircraft and took off, with Quill leading. We were given the location of the enemy raid as we climbed up. When we broke through the cloud we could not believe it. All I could see was the five of us and the rest of the sky full of the biggest enemy formation imaginable. I just thought, 'Where the devil do we begin?' We turned away from them to gain more height and picked up a German bomber that had lost formation with the others. We proceeded to shoot him down. Then we climbed up again once more. We were then vectored to another position, but did not go into the attack again, and then returned to base. When we landed, the car that belonged to Vickers to chauffeur Jeffrey, took us all up to London for a break.

The squadron was not only made up of British and Commonwealth pilots. There were also three Polish airmen, Pilot Officer Wladyslaw Szulkowski and Flying Officer Franciszek Gruszka who had arrived during July, while Pilot

Officer Boleslaw Drobinski arrived on 12th August. Dave Glaser would get to know them quite well in the short space of time they were with the squadron.

Dave, whose easy going and friendly presence seemed to make them feel more at ease, would often spend time helping them to speak and write English. Gruszka wrote down the English phrases that Dave would teach him in his little diary, which he took everywhere with him. On 18th August 1940, Franciszek Gruszka took off on a patrol in Spitfire R6713, but was never seen again and was posted as missing in action. Thirty-four years later, events surrounding Flying Officer Gruszka's disappearance would come to light and his former friend Dave Glaser would again be available to help. More on this episode later in the chapter. Sadly Wladyslaw Szulkowski did not survive the war either. He was killed on 27th March 1941, while flying with 315 Polish Squadron.

On 18th August, Dave was flying as Yellow 3, when at 1.20 pm he encountered a large mixed enemy formation of Heinkel, Dornier and Me109s at around 10,000 feet over the Thames estuary. During the ensuing battle, Dave claimed a quarter of a Heinkel 111, which was shot down with both engines on fire. The Heinkel 111 coded V4+GK was part of squadron 2/KG1 which had attacked Biggin Hill. After being attacked by 65 Squadron fighters it crash-landed at Snargate near Dymchurch, Kent. One of the crew was killed, while the other four were captured.

Jeffrey Quill, then a flying officer, led A Flight during the afore-mentioned engagement, after the flight leader had burst a tyre in the process of taking off. His report states:

> At 12.51 pm, 65 Squadron left Rochford to patrol Canterbury, and then Manston. When at 4,000 feet a large force of enemy bombers was seen above to the north proceeding southeast. This was reported to operations control, but the enemy were too far away to engage. Later, a force of about forty enemy fighters was observed to the northeast at about 20,000 feet. It appeared possible that there might be an engagement going on with our own fighters, so we started to climb up in an easterly direction to gain height. It was not considered justifiable to attack the bombers with only five aircraft.
>
> When at about 10,000 feet, a Heinkel 111 was observed beneath, proceeding alone in a southwest direction over Foulness. Our flight came down in line astern for a quarter attack. Four aircraft of the flight fired and the aircraft was last seen descending with smoke coming from out of the engine and during the engagement some pieces were seen to fall off the wings.
>
> After this attack, we climbed in accordance with instructions from Control, but the flight became separated in clouds and in view of the large number of enemy aircraft in the vicinity, the flight attempted to reform over base.
>
> The following of A Flight fired: Flying Officer Quill fired 458 rounds, Pilot Officer Glaser 455, Sergeant Orchard 308 and Sergeant Keymer 1,087 rounds.

Dave Glaser also remembers the young colonial boy in the squadron, who seemed very different from the others:

> We had a New Zealander in the squadron by the name of Wigg.
> Everything to Flying Officer Ronald Wigg was good, the good car,
> the good B, his aeroplane etc, but in the air he never saw anything.
> On taking off from Manston on 12th August, the squadron were
> caught on the ground by a German raid. The bombs were dropping
> down all over the place and our guys just opened their throttles and
> went hell for leather. Wigg had a bomb drop just behind his
> aeroplane, which stopped the propeller. Nobody had ever seen
> Wigg run for a scramble before, but by golly they reported he ran
> like blazes for the hedge that day. After this event, at Rochford he
> started digging a big oblong pit, it looked like he was digging his
> grave. This hole got deeper and deeper and Wigg said, 'One day
> somebody's going to shoot this place up and I'll be able to duck
> down in this hole.'
>
> Well one day Nicholas, who was in my flight, spotted a Dornier
> bomber coming around the drome. This chappie was in trouble and
> trying to find somewhere to land and saw the airfield at Rochford
> and thought it to be just the place. The German pilot put the
> bomber down wheels up on the field, whereupon the ground
> defences all opened up firing. Wigg shot down his hole spraining
> his ankle, while the German crew who had just climbed out with
> their hands in the air, hid again until the firing had stopped. A short
> while later a policeman came around, complaining somebody had
> shot a bullet through the billiard table in the Police station. This
> was probably 'Nicky' Nicholas who had followed the bomber on
> its descent and had given it a few bursts of fire.

On the 22nd August, Dave was again operating with the squadron down at
Manston. While on standing patrol he encountered and attacked a
Messerschmitt 109. His combat report of the event relates:

> Whilst flying on patrol on 22nd August, in position 2 of Red
> Section, we engaged the enemy at 25,000 feet. I engaged one
> Me109 and gave a 4 second burst of fire from 250 yards,
> whereupon the enemy aircraft half-rolled down. I followed, and
> when it had regained level flight, I gave it another short burst
> followed by a second and longer one. The enemy aircraft took no
> evasive action and during the second burst there was a flash of
> flames from the port side of the fuselage, and smoke poured out.
> He then continued on a shallow dive and disappeared into clouds,
> which were at about 10,000 feet. Just before he entered the cloud,
> I overshot him and did a steep turn above him and observed the
> enemy aircraft to be a mottled grey with orange wing-tips and the
> usual black crosses outlined with white. I later found out I was over
> the French coast. Total rounds fired 2,800.

Pilot Officer Dave Glaser claimed the Me109 as a probable.

On 24th August, 65 was in action again, this time flying from Rochford. After receiving information from Hornchurch Control, nine Spitfires took off from Rochford at 2.35 pm to intercept enemy raiders approaching from Dover. They were later vectored to Manston and when 65 Squadron arrived at the southern side of the Thames estuary at 22,000 feet, they sighted two formations of 30 to 40 bombers in Vic formations of six and seven about the same level. 2,000 feet above the bombers was a layer of about 40 Messerschmitt Me110s and above them a large number of Me109s. The squadron climbed to engage the fighters and when at 28,000 feet, broke up into sections to attack.

One section came in on the flank of the Me110s and Pilot Officer Hart was able to pick an enemy aircraft out of the formation from where it fell with smoke pouring from it. The other two sections of the squadron tackled the 109s and Flight Lieutenant Gordon Olive secured a probable, which went into a dive with glycol streaming from it. The enemy did not attempt to take any evasion, but seemed to rely on tight formation and interchanging of position. The squadron returned to Rochford without any casualties at 4.13 pm.

The following pilot's report of combat was as follows:

F/Lt Olive – 1 Me109 probable
P/O Hart – 1 Me110 probable
F/O Nicholas – 1 Me109 damaged (no claim)
P/O Glaser – 1 Me109 damaged (no claim)

On 27th August, 65 flew back to Hornchurch from Rochford for the last time. Later that day, the pilots flew north to Church Fenton and from there to RAF Turnhouse in Scotland for a well-earned rest. They would not return to Hornchurch again. It was while at Turnhouse, that Dave was involved in another scary incident. On 10th October 1940, he took off from the airfield to undertake dusk patrol. He never forgot what happened that evening:

I had taken off to do a night flight, which in a Spitfire was pretty unnerving at the best of times. I was returning and coming into land, but when I selected undercarriage down, one of the legs wouldn't come down. No matter how much I juggled with it, it just would not come down. So eventually I had to come down and had to try a one-wheel landing. It was surprising how easy it was to hold up one wing of the Spitfire once I had come into land, holding it until very slowly it came down and hit the ground and slowly turned the aircraft around; even the blades were only slightly damaged. What had actually happened was the pintol had bent, on which the undercarriage rotated and this had caused the failure.

We were then sent back down south to Tangmere in November 1940. We did the first offensive sweep from there in early January 1941. I can tell you, it felt a long trip around on that sweep, if any engagement took place we had to fight our way back across the Channel, we were in the same position as the Germans had been in 1940, only in reverse.

In February 1941, Dave was posted from 65 Squadron and sent to No.53 Operational Training Unit at Heston, to work as an instructor while undertaking a rest period. The unit was commanded by the famous World War One pilot, the Welshman Ira 'Taffy' Jones and also included Wing Commander Johnny Kent DFC, who had led a Polish squadron during the Battle of Britain. It was here that Dave, the officer commanding D Flight, helped to pass on his knowledge of flying and combat experience to the young trainee fighter pilots, which would hopefully prolong their chances of survival against the enemy up in the skies over northern Europe.

Dave Glaser relayed to me an amusing event that happened there:

> Taffy Jones was a disciplinarian and he ran the training unit with no nonsense. I remember one evening in the Mess, Taffy was resting listening to the radio with his eyes shut, when in came one of the chaps by the name of 'Polly' Parrot. He walked in with this bloody long haired wig on under his officer's hat. He turned the radio off and Taffy opened his eyes, saw Parrot and shouted out 'Good grief, get your bloody haircut.' Parrot walked out of the room and reappeared about two minutes later without the wig. Taffy could never work that one out.

Dave Glaser was promoted to the rank of flying officer on 11th July, and in August 1941 was posted to B Flight of No.234 Madras Presidency Squadron. Dave takes up the story:

> I had been in to see Taffy Jones practically every day asking him, when I could get back to a squadron. One day this Spitfire came in with one big petrol tank slung under the left hand wing; it was flown by Squadron Leader 'Mindy' Blake. I saw this aircraft flying around; it then landed and then taxied over to and stopped in front of the air traffic control. So I went over to have a look at it. When I came back, one of the chaps said, 'where have you been, Taffy is after you, he wants you to get round to his office'. So I went round there, and there was the pilot Mindy Blake. Taffy said, 'he's looking for a pilot to be a flight commander for B Flight of 234 Squadron, and I've recommended you.' I was delighted. Mindy then said, 'we are flying these funny looking aeroplanes, you've seen it outside'. I said, 'yes I've been over and had a look at it, I gather it's an auxiliary petrol tank, but you can't jettison it.' He said, 'No!' I said, 'my God.'
>
> Luckily we didn't have them for very long, after which we received the slipper tanks. But we did do a number of operations with that type of Spitfire. You had to take off with the controls set for full right rudder, full right stick and you had to be into wind for the take-off. It spun very easily, so one had to be pretty careful with it.

In October, Glaser was promoted to flight lieutenant commanding B Flight. On 15th April 1942, Flight Lieutenant Glaser was sent to No.1 Course at Fighter Wing, Central Gunnery School, Sutton Bridge, for flying and assessment for front-gun marksmanship. While here, Dave undertook various tests including air-to-air firing at drogue targets and range estimation. On two consecutive days, he flew as a passenger in a Miles Master aircraft during air-to-air camera tests with the legendary RAF fighter ace Sailor Malan, who was officer commanding at Sutton Bridge during this period. Dave finally left the course on 30th April. His assessment form signed by Malan, stated that as a marksman in combat, he was above average as was his score on target drogues. He returned to Portreath and 234 Squadron.

On 23rd July 1942, the squadron were sent on a Rhubarb operation over the north Brest sector. Dave was flying Spitfire Vb AR382 and during the sortie machine-gunned an enemy lorry and some German coast signallers. He also attacked and fired at a Focke-Wulf 190 over the French coast, but did not claim any damage. A few days later, during the evening of 25th July, Dave was on patrol with Sergeant Hinds over a shipping convoy codenamed 'Nation,' which was sailing off Lundy Island. At around 8.45 pm, he received a message from operations control stating that there might be an enemy aircraft in the vicinity. But it was not until 9.05 pm that he received another signal, this time from one of the escorting destroyers; that an aircraft had been sighted ten miles away flying at sea level. Dave tells what happened next:

> I immediately turned in this direction, but after flying for a few seconds was still unable to see the aircraft. Sergeant Hinds who was Blue 2, reported that it was straight ahead and that he could see it, so I told him to take the lead. Still unable to see it, I called up the destroyer and asked where it was. The destroyer then reported the aircraft was below the cloud, which was covering the sun, and then I saw it flying on a course of approximately north-northeast. I immediately gave chase with Blue 2 to intercept it and identify the same. When about 1,000 yards behind, I recognised it as a night-flying Junkers Ju88, being all black in camouflage. I closed in and the enemy aircraft immediately started to take as much violent evasive action as was possible at that height. When at about 100 yards dead astern, I opened up with machine guns, the rear gunner had already started firing back at me. When about sixty yards behind I opened fire with my cannon and machine guns. Blue 2 (Sergeant Hinds) then closed in too and opened fire. As Blue 2 broke away, the enemy aircraft turned on a westerly course and I closed in for a second attack. When at 300 yards astern, the enemy rear gunner opened up on me again; I returned fire at 150 yards with a fairly long burst and the fire from the gunner ceased. At 100 yards, I fired my cannon and machine guns and saw two pieces come off from the underside of the enemy's fuselage near the wing root. Just after this the starboard wing root caught fire and was still burning when I broke away, having used all my ammunition. I then climbed up to starboard and as I looked around, I saw more pieces break away from the portion that was on fire. A second later the enemy aircraft's port wing hit the sea and the aircraft exploded and broke up. I orbited the crash with Blue 2 for a few minutes, but there were no survivors. The position of the crash was roughly ten

miles north north-west of Lundy Island. We then returned to base and landed at 9.55 pm. I estimated that the speed of the Junkers was about 280 mph, for my air speed indicator was registering 300 mph. I did not however encounter any difficulty in catching up with it.

On returning to Portreath, it was found that Sergeant Hind's Spitfire had suffered Category A damage, with a tracer bullet through one of the propeller blades. Both Dave Glaser and Sergeant Hinds received a half share in the destruction of the Ju88. Three days later, on 28th July, Dave was flying convoy patrol in Spitfire BL427, south of Dodman Point, south of Plymouth. While over the convoy, Dave and his No.2 sighted a Junkers Ju88 in the distance and went after it. Suddenly as they came within range of the German bomber, Dave noticed little white streams of tracer whistle past his starboard wing. Had the German bomber a fighter escort, which they had not seen? Dave recalls what happened next:

I quickly looked in the mirror and then turned my head to look around but could not see anything. Suddenly the firing had stopped, but I continued firing at the Ju88. The next minute the firing opened up again, this time much, much nearer and was followed by a gigantic bang and my engine was hit. I had been flying at nearly nought feet, so I pulled the aircraft up as high as I could; the last thing I saw on the clock as the Spitfire was going up was 400 feet. So I rolled my aircraft over then stood up on the seat then kicked the control column stick forward, which then shot me out. I saw my aircraft going over and I was then clear of it, so I pulled the ripcord. As I came down I thought now what I've got to do is at five feet or so before hitting the water, bang the parachute release buckle. Just as I was about to do this there was an almighty jolt. I didn't realize how low I had baled out, and this was my parachute just opening in time; within several seconds I was in the water. The whole of the parachute fell on top of me, the shroud lines got entangled around my neck and arms, I couldn't get out of it. The small dinghy I had began to drag me down; I dare not inflate it because I was in a big enough muddle as it was with the shroud lines. So in the end I let the dinghy go, because I'd got my mae west. I tried to get free of the shroud lines but I couldn't, so I thought to myself, well this is it; this is how you go.
    I just relaxed and I then remembered it was my mother's birthday and so they would be up at the Savoy celebrating, I started to wander off, feeling sleepy when suddenly for some reason I saw the parachute floating away. How it came off I don't know. I had been in the water for nearly an hour and was getting very cold by this time. I was still wondering how the hell I was going to get to land, when just above the waves I could see a stick; I thought I was seeing things. Eventually a ship came into sight, I had seen its mast; this turned out to be one of the ships from the convoy, HM Minesweeper *Kings Grey*. As they pulled up to fish me out, the first thing I heard was one of the officers over the megaphone shouting,

'frightfully sorry old man, we shot you down.' I just couldn't
believe it. Then I realized that as I had been firing, the gun bursts
around my wing must have been fired from the navy. The fatal
salvo had been fired by another ship in the convoy, HMS
Kineserey.

Dave was taken back to Plymouth and was flying again the next day,
extremely lucky to have survived being hit by friendly fire, having to bale out
so low and the time spent in the cold waters of the Channel. On 11th August
1942, Dave Glaser received a communiqué from No.10 Group Headquarters,
which read:

> *To Portreath No.234 Squadron*
> *His Majesty the King has been graciously pleased to award*
> *Distinguished Flying Cross to Acting Flight Lieutenant E.D.*
> *Glaser.*
> *The Air Officer Commanding extends heartiest congratulations.*

As a footnote to this story, Angela Stevenson recalls that not long after the
incident, Dave on a visit to her family home had told her mother a most
unusual and perhaps spiritual occurrence that had happened when he was
about to decide to bale out or ditch his aircraft:

> He told my mother that when he was shot down, he had at first tried
> to control the aircraft and ditch the Spitfire, when he felt sure that
> he heard Paddy Finucane's voice say something like; 'Don't be a
> fool as I was; bale out.'

It was only later that Angela learnt about the famous fighter ace Paddy
Finucane's death, and how he had ditched his aircraft in the Channel a month
earlier on 15th July 1942 and had gone down with it.
    On 19th November 1942, the squadron exchanged their MkVb Spitfires for
MkVcs, Glaser air testing Spitfire EE729 on that date. The squadron's first
sweep with the new aircraft was undertaken on 1st December, over Ile de
Batz. Unfortunately Sergeant Cunningham, a Canadian, was lost and listed as
missing after his aircraft developed engine trouble over Ile de Ushant. His
body was washed ashore at Plymouth Sound on 16th December.
    During the war a lot of fighter pilots would have their pet dogs on the
airfield with them. Dave Glaser was no exception; his own preference was
towards the Spaniel breed as Angela Stevenson relates:

> Dave used to take his dog up flying with him on air tests; the dog
> also got to know the 'Scramble' instruction and would rush and sit
> on the wing of his Spitfire when the alarm was called, waiting for
> him.

The squadron were sent north to Scotland towards the end of January 1943,
to Sumburgh, for what they believed would be a rest period, but it turned out
to be far from quiet. Dave Glaser remembers:

I was quite surprised and a bit brassed off, when 234 Squadron were sent up to the Shetlands for a rest. I thought we would be out of the war; but I found we were anything but. For the first two days, we had a scramble at ten o'clock each day; I went over to the Ops Room and asked them why it was the same time every day; the Controller said 'oh that's the milk run, it's a Junkers 88 from Stravanger, and it comes straight over to Scapa Flow, up past Fair Isle, past the end of Sumburgh to Lerwick.' I said 'why don't we shoot the blasted thing down?' They said 'We'll ask Group Headquarters and you can put up a standing patrol.' I said, 'great, off the tip of the Shetlands?' But back came the answer from Group, 'No, uneconomical.'

So anyway, I went off with one chap just before 10.00 am on formation flying, but we saw no sign of the Ju88. I laid on another chap on stand-by to come and relieve me, and he caught the 88 and shot it into the sea. As bits of the wreckage came up, a wheel appeared and two of the crew. One of them was swimming strongly and the other chap had more or less had it. To get the motor rescue launch to come around from Lerwick, all the way around down to here was going to take some time. I arrived overhead and saw the chap who was swimming strongly, he hadn't got a dinghy and I thought, my god he's not going to last until this boat arrives from Lerwick; so I thought I'd better try and do something. So eventually I grabbed my dinghy from under my seat, I took my mae west off, (remember this is in the confined space of a Spitfire cockpit) and I wrapped the dinghy in the mae west, half inflated the mae west, opened the cockpit canopy and the side door panel, flew past him and threw it down to him as close as I could. I think he must have been injured or losing strength, because he just couldn't swim to it. Eventually the rescue launch arrived, the German put his arm up to it, and they saw him, but by the time they got to him he had died. My thoughts were that if I had been in the same position I would have hoped somebody would have tried to rescue me; after all he was somebody's son or husband.

On 15th March 1943, the squadron received a report from Group Headquarters that a Norwegian motor torpedo boat had been badly shot up and holed; it was also loaded with refugees. The boat's radio was damaged and it could not receive signals, so it was unsure of its position. 234 Squadron was unable to despatch a section of aircraft due to the appalling weather. However, the weather on the 16th improved and Flight Lieutenant Glaser leading B Flight was given the job of finding the MTB. The captain of the vessel had reported that they had missed the Shetlands to the northwest and were therefore steering southeast. Group had ordered the section to be dispatched to search to the northwest of the island. Dave recalls:

I'd however had a big hunch that the boat had not missed the island and was in fact to the southeast heading away. Group would not approve a search to the southeast, so I sent a section of aircraft to the northwest and led another section myself to the southeast on local flying. We eventually located the MTB approximately 50 to 60 miles southeast of the Shetlands. Flying low over the vessel we managed to turn them towards the Shetlands by buzzing over the top of them waggling our wings and pointing in the direction of home. The boat eventually made its way back to port safely.

The following day, Dave received a letter from the commanding officer of MTB 619, it read:

May I express my extreme gratitude for the most helpful co-operation shown by the Spitfire pilots of your flight in finding us, and in so cleverly directing us on to the right course yesterday? In particular I should like to thank the pilots who first located us, and the one who stayed with us for half an hour. The way in which he repeatedly indicated the correct course gave us great encouragement at a time when we were beginning to doubt whether we could make land with the little fuel that we had left. It gives us great confidence for the future to know that we can rely on such prompt and eager assistance.

Dave was again in action on 3rd April 1943, when he and Pilot Officer Gadsden of B Flight were ordered to scramble, after radar had picked up an enemy aircraft. He remembers:

I was leading and we were given a heading. We eventually sighted a lone Junkers Ju88 at sea level about 25 miles east-southeast of Sumburgh Head at 6.14 pm. The enemy aircraft climbed and started to take evasive action and head for the nearest cloud. I attacked at the same time as Blue 2 from the starboard quarter below, whilst the enemy aircraft crossed a gap in the clouds. Two pieces of debris came away from the German's port wing and there was a flash from his starboard engine. We lost him in the cloud, but claimed him as damaged.

Dave's actual combat report written the same day gives a more detailed account of the event:

After Blue 2 gave the 'Tally Ho' I sighted the enemy aircraft ahead of Blue 2 and followed the aircraft, which had sighted us and climbed into cloud. Blue 2 pursued and I remained below. On Blue 2 reporting the enemy aircraft above, I climbed but saw nothing, I continued through the second layer of cloud and saw the enemy ahead and below crossing a gap in the clouds. I came in from starboard, but out of range, when the enemy aircraft re-entered cloud, so I told Blue 2 to remain above and I again went below. I saw a gap in the cloud and aimed for this, reaching the gap as the enemy came out of the cloud to my port 800 yards away and 500 feet above. I climbed and did a quarter attack from below, firing cannon only and closing to line astern. I observed a flash from under the outboard side of the enemy's starboard engine and later saw two pieces of port wing come away from the outboard port motor. I estimated the size of each piece to be about four feet square.

The enemy aircraft re-entered cloud and the Controller recalled us as we were then 60 miles east of base with Sumburgh rapidly closing in with fog. I claimed this aircraft damaged and share the claim with Blue 2 – Pilot Officer W.G. Gadsden.

In September 1943, the squadron were posted to Australia and once there they formed No.549 Royal Australian Air Force Squadron. On 15th February 1945, Glaser was promoted to Squadron Leader and took over command of 548, stationed at Darwin. On 3rd June 1945, Dave led the squadron on a bomber escort mission. They were to rendezvous with six Liberator bombers at Jaco Isle, east of Timor to bomb and strafe Japanese aircraft located on the Cape Chater airfield.

The squadron were to go in after the bombers and destroy any aircraft, which the bombing had missed. Unfortunately dust from the bombing had covered all enemy aircraft from view and it was extremely difficult at low level to see anything. The squadron went in, but only one enemy aircraft was seen and attacked. Flying at tree-top height, Dave almost came to grief, when he nearly hit a tree, whilst coming out of the dust cloud. The squadron returned to Darwin without loss.

Wing Commander Andrew J. Little who married Dave Glaser's niece recalls one tragic episode involving Dave while stationed out in Australia:

He had taken a squadron of Spitfires to Australia to defend Darwin from the Japanese and while out there, Dave gave permission for two of his subordinates – the groom and his best man – to hitch a ride in an American aircraft to Brisbane for a marriage to an Aussie girl. They were not seen again until the wreckage and bones of the men were found in the Australian outback in 1996. On hearing about this, all those years later, Dave at the age of 76 immediately resumed the role of squadron commander and not withstanding failing health and limited financial resources, moved heaven and earth to obtain any possible information and keep contact with the surviving relatives. My admiration for his pugnacious concern for former comrades knew no bounds.

At war's end in August 1945, Flight Lieutenant Dave Glaser returned to Britain; a land that was now suffering from the effects of five long hard years of war. The price of victory would see the rationing of food, fuel and other everyday normalities of living which would take quite a few years to return. Everybody had to re-adjust to a peacetime world.

In June 1947, Dave Glaser was granted a Permanent Commission in the RAF. On 9th June, he was sent to Moreton on No.46 Refresher Course. Here he undertook various circuit and landings, aerobatics and instrument flying on Harvard aircraft. This continued until 11th July, with his flying assessment form completed stating him as proficient.

On 9th August, he was posted to 64 Squadron as a flight commander. The squadron was based at RAF Linton-on-Ouse and was at only half squadron strength, flying De Havilland Hornet aircraft. On his first day there, he was taken up as a passenger in a De Havilland Mosquito aircraft (TV984) by Flight Lieutenant Guest. The following next few days, he was to familiarise himself with the squadron's Hornet Mk 1 aircraft. The Hornet was a twin-engine single-seat aeroplane, which had been developed and built towards the end of the war, but it had never flown in action. The squadron's commander at this time was Squadron Leader Geoffrey Page DSO, DFC. An ex Battle of Britain pilot, Page had been severely burned during the battle in 1940 and had undergone many operations at the Burns Unit, Queen Victoria Hospital at East Grinstead, to rebuild his hands and face. Through sheer guts and determination, he had returned to combat flying later in the war and had led a squadron over the beaches of Normandy on D-Day, 6th June 1944.

Dave and Geoffrey became good friends, a friendship which continued throughout their lifetimes.

In September of that year, the squadron were notified of their inclusion in the Battle of Britain flypast. Dave led his pilots on many of the practice flights for the big day, flying on the 5th, 9th and 11th and finally over London on the actual day of the event on 15th September. While still with the squadron in December, Dave suffered three separate incidents on the Hornet. On 3rd December, while flying in a close formation, his aircraft suffered a glycol leak in the port engine and he was forced to break away and make a single-engine landing, which he did successfully. On the 19th, practising a battle formation, the starboard engine suffered a similar fate and again he was forced to return to base. Finally on a low-level cross-country flight on 21st December, the starboard wing route fabric was ripped off.

He returned again safely back at Linton, thankful that his luck had held out.

Mrs Andy Glaser was sister-in-law to Dave Glaser; it was during this time that she first met him and recalls:

> It was a couple of years after the war that I met him. His parents were the landlords of the famous Bugle Inn at Hamble. I was there as a friend of his brother Jack who had also been in the Royal Air Force, but had still been at school when Dave was a Battle of Britain hero. Dave at this time was stationed at Linton-on-Ouse, Yorkshire with 64 Squadron. I still have the squadron badge he gave me.
>
> We had been expecting him all day and, typically, he kept phoning and saying he was on his way. He was full of energy, bursting with enthusiasm, and everything had to be spontaneous and instant. He arrived in his tiny Fiat car with his dog Baron. Baron was an Australian Blue Heeler and accompanied Dave everywhere.
>
> At that time Baron was thought to be the only Blue Heeler in England, but out of the blue, a padre rang up saying he had a Blue Heeler bitch and he would like them to mate. Whether the padre was in the RAF or not I do not know; anyway the next day the padre and bitch arrived and my father-in-law's office was used as a

love nest. He was not too pleased; whether any progeny resulted I
do not remember.

On 26th January 1948, Dave was sent to 41 Squadron on an Instrument Rating
Course at Church Fenton. While there, he was given dual instruction on the
Airspeed Oxford twin-engine aircraft. The course finished on 12th February,
Dave achieving above average assessment. On his return to 64 Squadron, the
Hornet Mk Is had been replaced by Mk IIIs. For almost a year, Dave stayed
with 64, carrying out the daily routine life of a peacetime air force. But there
were some exciting days too.

In May, the squadron flew to Uppsala in Sweden, then onto Stockholm and
Goteborg. Other sorties included interception practices with American B29
bombers, air-to-sea firing and low level flying around Scotland. Finally on
24th February 1949, Dave bade farewell to the squadron and started on a new
career within flying that would continue for the rest of his life.

On 28th February 1949, he joined the No.8 Course of the Empire Test
Pilots School based at Farnborough, Hants. Here he undertook flying courses
and tests while flying an array of aeroplanes including the Gloster Meteor IV
and De Havilland Vampire jets, the Avro Lincoln bomber, and the Hawker Sea
Fury. He completed this course on 6th December 1949. It was to be in 1949
that Dave Glaser met his first wife. Andy Glaser remembers:

His brother Jack and I married first although we were younger, and
for the first year Dave included us in all his social events, much to
the chagrin of his girlfriends. Then along came Cora and for the
first time he wanted her to himself and a whirlwind courtship
followed. Cora Ann Gillie was a gorgeous Australian girl; she was
full of fun too and they were very much in love. They married later
that year at St. Andrews Church, Hamble on Saturday 10th
December 1949.

At this time Dave was still in the Air Force and was stationed at
the Test Pilots School at Farnborough; this has since moved. Cora
and Dave bought a house at Church Crookham, near Farnborough
and named it 'Kerrogair.'

He was then sent to work at the Armament Flight at RAE Farnborough in
January 1950, where by February his flying assessment rated him as above
average as a test pilot and as exceptional as pilot/navigator. During this period
he was again flying mainly Meteor and Vampire jet aircraft on air tests,
missile guidance and rocket firing. On Saturday 11th August 1951, Dave
became a father, when his wife gave birth to a son. They named him Peter
Andre Glaser. On 18th August 1952, Flight Lieutenant Glaser was instructed
to fly to Bretigny, France to help the French with the installation and testing
of the E.267 gun-sight in Vampire Vs. Permission had been granted for the
gun-sight to be installed in a Vampire at the Centre d'Essais en Vol, Bretigny.
The work was to be carried out by personnel of the CEV. The modification
would take about three weeks, after which some air-to-ground rocket firing
would be done at the ranges at Cazeux, before the aircraft would return to the
RAE. After testing Glaser returned to Farnborough by BEA Airlines from

Paris. On 12th January 1953, he was sent to No.20 Maintenance Unit at Andover carrying out further air tests on aircraft; he remained there until 5th March, when the unit was posted to Aston Down.

On 1st June 1953, the notification in the *London Gazette* was published that Flight Lieutenant Dave Glaser DFC, had been awarded the Queens Commendation Medal for valuable service in the air. This award had been well earned, for the military test flying that he had undertaken while at Farnborough. After his decision to resign from the Royal Air Force in a letter to the Ministry dated 16th May 1953 to become a civil test pilot, the reply letter from the Air Ministry dated 8th July stated:

> I am commanded by the Air Council, that they have decided not to approve your application to resign your permanent commission, but to place you on the retired list of the Royal Air Force. In conveying this decision the Council desire to thank you for the services, which you have rendered to the Royal Air Force. The Council have granted you permission to retain the rank of Squadron Leader under the terms of Air Ministry Order A.627/50.

And so, Dave Glaser's outstanding career with the Royal Air Force came to an end, but a new chapter was about to begin. In July of 1953, Dave started his new job at Vickers-Armstrongs; here he was appointed as Chief Production Test Pilot on the Vickers Valiant bomber. He would be in good company flying with many other future famous test pilots including Brian Trubshaw of Concorde fame, and Ralph 'Titch' Havercroft, another Battle of Britain Spitfire pilot. Most of the testing for the Valiant bomber was done at Farnborough, Boscombe Down and Wisley, but there were other aircraft to be put through tests as well, including the Canberra, the Vickers Viscount and Valetta.

On Sunday 14th March 1954, the family was further enlarged with the birth of a daughter named Julie Ann Glaser. By October 1954, Dave became Vickers-Armstrongs Chief Test Pilot at their factory at Hurn, Hampshire; they were building the Vickers Varsity, then the Viscount. The company would later become part of the British Airways Corporation building the BAC 1-11 aeroplane. He was to remain with the company for a total of twenty-four years.

When Dave became Chief Test Pilot for Vickers the family moved to a new home at Seaway Avenue at Friar's Cliff, Highcliffe, to be near to Hurn Airfield.

John Thorpe worked as a flight observer for the flight research department of the British Airways Corporation. In early 1964, he was seconded to BAC at Wisley to help out on the flight-testing of the BEA 1-11 passenger aircraft. He spent over a year in this post at both the Wisley and Hurn establishments, and it was here he met and worked with Dave Glaser. He remembers:

> Dave was one of a team of pilots, and he and I flew together quite a lot, especially when I went for three or four months to Hurn on the production testing. Hurn is actually Bournemouth International Airport; it was the main production line for the BEA 1-11 and was rolling them out at a rate of one aircraft every two weeks. I was there in the very early days, when we were finding our way in

essence and still developing the production test schedule. Dave Glaser's position during this time was as senior production pilot. He and another chap, Chuck Thrower were the two main pilots.

We would have a schedule to work against and standards against each item to be tested; it would take about six and half hours flying on each production aircraft to clear it. You had to check all systems, check things like the stall warnings by flying the aircraft down to minimum speed, check out the auto-pilot, engine re-lighting etc. We gradually reduced the time done on the testing and one of the best was just over six hours. That aircraft was one that I flew with Dave and was N1545, one of the very early Braniff types. We flew it first on a Monday afternoon, got a couple of good shake-down flights on it, then went to Wisley to measure the errors on the air speed indicator and altimeter system on the Tuesday, and then another flight on the Wednesday to change just one item; that was the capsule on the oxygen mask drop out system. The aircraft was then flown off across the Atlantic on the Thursday morning to Montreal, Canada, and was in service by the Friday morning.

I was with Dave on the first flight of the first Mohawk aircraft N2111J; we flew it on 4th April 1965. There was a lot of publicity for this, because Mohawk was one of the big carriers in the United States and this was their first bus stop jet. They did a rollout ceremony, where they towed the aircraft out accompanied by the honourable company of yeoman and artillery in all their magnificent old uniforms. For the first flight, they laid on camera aircraft, which were a BAC Heron and an ETPS Vickers Viscount. Dave Glaser turned the Mohawk out on to the runway, the Heron aircraft was already airborne and as for all first flights, the fire engines were out in case anything went wrong. We roared off down the runway, Dave was in the left hand seat flying it, he then rotated smartly into the climb and started a left turn to link up with the Heron, so they could start to take some air-to-air photographs. Unfortunately, the control tower didn't like this and sent a message over the radio, 'will the captain please report immediately to the tower after landing,' Dave had turned below 500 feet in the aerodrome traffic and they didn't go too much on that. Anyway we got our photographs with the Heron, then climbed to 10,000 feet where we met up with the Viscount and did a few more shots up there.

I can recall one amusing incident, when one day we were at 20,000 feet flying over the Boscombe Down military establishment area, doing air conditioning cruise performance measurements. The four of us which included Dave, were all heads down in the cockpit, checking our readings etc, when suddenly we all became aware that somebody was watching us, we all had this sudden feeling and all looked up together. There, tucked up right in beside us was an English Electric Lightning jet fighter from Boscombe Down. There was a big grin on the pilot's face as our four heads came up. He grinned again, gave us a rude sign and then banked the fighter jet away at 90 degrees with full burn and disappeared as if he had magically been taken away, because it was so fast. It caused us quite a surprise; Boscombe Down radar hadn't informed us he was there.

Another event was when we were developing the production test schedule, when Brian Trubshaw the chief test pilot, came down one day to fly a production 1-11. We worked him through our schedule, which finished with turning off the entire electrical generator ignition systems, so the aircraft was running on battery and also without the two hydraulic systems, so the aircraft was effectively being flown manually. Anyway, we set him up with all this and he flew it down the flight approach and landed the aircraft very tidily. As we taxied off afterwards having restored all the electrics and hydraulics to normal, Trubshaw asked Dave Glaser, 'How long have you been doing this' and Dave said 'for every 1-11 off the line,' Brian Trubshaw then said; 'This is bloody dangerous, you are to stop this at once.' We knew that Brian Trubshaw was very strong, he could push and pull 170lbs on the control column and change that within a second. He thought it was dangerous; Dave and I looked at one another, and we'd been doing this sort of thing all the time, which was rather amusing. Anyway it was decided that we were doing too many emergency checks all in one go and something should have to be done about this.

I always found Dave to be very friendly and very helpful. He had a crypt book, where he had written down just about everything he ever knew about the 1-11, indexed by system. So if you wanted to know about air conditioning, you would look under A, anything about hydraulics, look under H etc. He had got all the systems diagrammed; it was really a wonderful thing he had built up over the years. So later, when I became involved with the Concorde project, I did exactly the same thing.

John Thorpe moved to Filton on the Concorde project and became part of the powerplant team and powerplant liaison with Rolls-Royce on the testing of the Olympus engine. He then went to Fairford, Gloucester, with the Concorde team in 1969, after the first flight and stayed there till 1970. He later joined the Civil Aviation Authority as a design surveyor based in Surrey, eventually moving into the area of safety promotion and aviation safety advice.

It was in 1965, after separation and finally divorce from his first wife, that Dave married again, to Diana Stewart-Smith.

On 5th June 1968, Dave Glaser received notification that he had been awarded a second Queen's Commendation Medal for his services to test flying with British Aircraft Corporation. The letter from Sir Richard Melville KCB from the Ministry of Technology, Whitehall, London read:

Dear Mr Glaser
I have the honour to inform you that you have been awarded the Queen's Commendation for Valuable Service in the Air.
    Your name will appear in the Birthday Honours Gazette to be

published on Saturday 8th June 1968. Until then the award is confidential.

The Minister of Technology, Mr Anthony Wedgewood Benn, has asked me to send you his warm congratulations on this award. I too should like to add my own congratulations.

He continued with the company throughout the 1970s, continuing to test mainly BAC 1-11s, but also being involved with the military version of the Vickers VC10. He also flew some Boeing 707 and 747s airliners from London to Bahrain, Antigua, Miami and Montreal.

On 3rd December 1974, Dave Glaser was called upon to help guide a pilot flying a British Airway's 1-11 on an emergency landing at Hurn airport. The 1-11 was en route from Cardiff to Birmingham, when a nose-wheel problem was spotted by a member of the cockpit crew. The aircraft was then diverted to Hurn and flew low over the airfield. BAC chief test pilot Dave Glaser was then asked to report to the control tower to talk to the captain of the aircraft and advise him on the best method of landing the aircraft. Although there were five fire engines and ambulances prepared for the worst outcome, the pilot managed a very good landing despite the nose-wheel still being slightly retracted.

Perhaps one of Dave Glaser's most memorable moments came on 6th June 1975, when with Brian Trubshaw, he was 2nd Pilot on a training flight on Concorde. It was also in 1975, that Dave Glaser would be involved in the recovery of one of his missing wartime comrades, who would at last be laid to rest.

In early 1971, an aviation archeological group had discovered and excavated a Battle of Britain aircraft crash site at Grove Marsh, Wickhambreaux near Canterbury, Kent. Various aircraft wreckage was unearthed and later displayed by the group at their wartime museum at Chilham Castle. After further research it was established that the aircraft was most likely that flown by Flying Officer Franciszek Gruszka who had been reported missing on 18th August 1940. What was perhaps somewhat more disturbing was the fact that the parachute worn by Flying Officer Gruszka was on display at the museum. Where were the mortal remains of the pilot? He had obviously not baled out.

When news of the parachute reached Dave Glaser, he was outraged. Why hadn't the body of his comrade been recovered? He then contacted his Polish friend Boleslaw Drobinski, who now lived in England and the pair of them contacted the Ministry of Defence to complain bitterly about the excavation and to ask what was being done to recover Gruszka's remains. After much letter writing to the powers that be the wheels of the appropriate authorities to deal with this problem were put into motion and an official RAF recovery team was sent to re-excavate the crash site. On 15th April 1974, the RAF team recovered the remains of Flying Officer Gruszka, along with personal effects that confirmed his identity, which included one metal propelling pencil with his name engraved and dated 10.8.37. Gruszka's personal belongings were handed over to Wing Commander Obstrowski, the welfare officer of the Polish Association. Gruszka's remains were taken to the mortuary at the Kent and Canterbury Hospital, where a post mortem was undertaken.

A Coroners Inquest was held on 1st May 1975. During the inquest, the second witness called was a Mr Michael Wigmore, who as an 11 year old had witnessed the crash, all those years ago. He stated that the aircraft came down very fast at approximately 45 degrees and made no attempt to pull out. It crashed about a mile away in a north-easterly direction and burst into flames. He thought there was fighting going on in the air at the time, but could not be sure. It was a clear day. He saw no signs of the pilot having jumped out and coming down by parachute, nor were there any signs of the aircraft breaking up in the air. Mr Wigmore had got a piece of the aircraft as a souvenir, which had the following inscription on it: 'General Aircraft Ltd, LPG 6F4309 30018 Sheet 5'.

Another British aircraft circled the crash. He examined bits that broke off the aircraft and saw hundreds of rounds of live ammunition. On large bits of the aircraft, he saw no signs of bullets or shrapnel holes. When the army arrived and took over they removed the wings, tried to pull the aircraft out of the ground, but were unable to do so. In his summing up, the Coroner Mr Wilfred Mowll stated that the dig in 1971 had obviously concentrated on the engine, but the body had been left behind and the crash site churned over by the mechanical diggers. Efforts should have been made then and respect shown to the mortal remains. He then drew attention to the Ministry Directive dated 1974, particularly with regards to human remains.

Dave Glaser's thoughts recorded at the time of the final recovery and inquest were:

> As far as Drobinski and I are concerned, our task is now finished and when finally Gruszka is laid to rest I hope, for those harbouring any doubts, that we will have on behalf of the Battle of Britain Fighter Association, 65 Squadron and all fellow pilots, shown where one's legal, moral and religious obligations lie; and paid due respect to a friend and respected comrade.

On 17th July 1975, Franciszek Gruszka was buried with full military honours at the Polish airmen's plot at Northwood Cemetery, Middlesex. Dave Glaser, Boleslaw Drobinski and Jeffrey Quill, as well as many veterans and people of the local London community and a large gathering of the newspaper press attended the funeral service. A gallant comrade had at last come home.

Angela Stevenson remembers Dave Glaser's feeling for his Polish wartime comrades:

> Dave had a lot of admiration and affection for the Polish pilots who flew with the RAF during the Battle of Britain and after. I know he felt they did not receive sufficient recognition. He used to mention a story about one Polish pilot who had insisted on retaining his parachute when he had baled out. He had just managed to get the chute open in time before he had landed, but was terribly injured landing on a hayrick or something similar. After recovering, he took the parachute back complaining 'it didn't work.'

Dave Glaser's final flight with BAC took place on 19th March 1977, when as

2nd Pilot to P.J. 'Chuck' Thrower, he took off in a 1-11 Serial No. YR-BCI, for production tests for the last time. It was during this period that his second marriage unfortunately failed and he divorced yet again.

After being away from aviation for nearly two years, Dave Glaser was appointed manager of Flight Operations Rombac, the Romanian BAC agreement contract for building the BAC 1-11 in Romania. Dave's task was to train the Romanian test pilots and set up the Test Operations Department in that country.

It was while working out in this country that Dave Glaser met a young Romanian woman who would become his third wife. The young lady was Rodica Ghita and she remembers how they first met:

> It was March 1982, and I was working as a waitress in the restaurant 'Ledo' in Bucharest. He walked into the restaurant with one of his friends and sat down at my table. I looked after him during the time he was there and afterwards he asked me, if I could give him my telephone number and I agreed. At that time he was staying at the Intercontinental Hotel. Two days later, he contacted me and invited me to visit him and from then on, we started to know each other better and better and eventually fell in love. We finally decided to marry and did so on 5th August 1985 at a registry office in Parufumului Stradda, Bucharest. We moved back to Britain in the September of that year. Looking back, it was like a dream to me, meeting such a marvellous man; and I loved him very much. He had such a wonderful sense of humour and from everything tragic, he used to see the funny side and just carry on with his life.

In 1983, Dave finally retired from the British Aircraft Corporation to become an aviation consultant. During the next ten years he consulted for the following companies for specific contracts or ongoing commitments. For Anglo Cargo he attained a lease of Tarom BAC 475 Freighter between 1988-92, when the airline ceased operations. He was also employed by Trans Global to negotiate spares; and by British World Airlines for help on administration and advising on the London to Bucharest route including visas passports etc. His life was aviation and he loved to help if he could; even towards the end of 1999, his vast experience was still in demand.

The total of flying hours amassed by Dave was a staggering 10,000 plus and he had flown 62 different types of aircraft excluding differing marks of the same aircraft.

During the early part of the 1990s, Dave Glaser could be seen attending many of the annual Battle of Britain anniversary reunions or various air shows. He was a very approachable person and he would love to talk to the public about those days back in 1940, when he was a young Spitfire pilot. But he was no line-shooter. Everybody who ever met Dave Glaser would come away knowing that they had met a real gentleman and had learned something about the air war. He also had great humour and many are the time that this author has seen complete strangers meet him, and after just a few minutes of his great story telling, the same people have been reduced to tears with laughter.

In March 1995, Dave Glaser was invited by Brian Moon, a retired executive of Northwest Airlines, to be one of the guest presentation speakers at 'The Gathering of Eagles'which was to be held at Red Wing, Minnesota. The two-day event was held over 11th/ 12th March. Along with Dave were other wartime veterans from the United States, Germany and Britain; these included Air Marshal Sir Ivor Broom who had flown Blenheims over Malta, Colonel Robert Morgan, pilot of the 'Memphis Belle' B17 bomber and Major Julius Meimberg who flew Messerschmitt 109s during the Battle of Britain. The symposium was a great success.

During the late 1990s, Dave became a regular visitor to the Purfleet Heritage and Military Centre, where they house the RAF Hornchurch Wing Collection of memorabilia, uniforms etc which are on display to the public. Dave attended many exhibitions at Purfleet and often gave lectures about his time with 65 Squadron at Hornchurch. One of his finest lectures was given at the Thameside Theatre in Grays, Thurrock in September 1998, where along with other pilots, ground crews, WAAFs, as well as a former member of the Luftwaffe, Ulrich Steinhilper, he lectured to a captivated full house. Afterwards Dave along with the others signed autographs for both young and old alike. On 7th/8th July 2000, at the Flying Legends display at the Imperial War Museum Duxford, this author was honoured to have Dave Glaser attend the book launch of *Hornchurch Scramble* and again sign books for the public. It was hard work, but Dave thoroughly enjoyed meeting people who had an interest in his old airfield and aviation in general.

It was with great sadness that towards the end of June 2001, just weeks after visiting Dave at his home, when he had invited my family and I to dinner, that I learnt that he had been rushed to hospital with pneumonia. We all prayed for him to make a full recovery, but it was not to be. Dave Glaser peacefully passed away in his sleep on 4th July 2001. How do his family and friends remember him? Andy Glaser reflects:

> Always bursting with life and enthusiasm and an almost childish, impish sense of humour – practical jokes, squeaky cushions and all! He was fun and his deeper side always well hidden. My main memory of Dave is that of a man who devoted his life to flying, it was his love, his passion – he was Biggles – he was a man who never outgrew his boyhood dreams and achieved most of them en route!

Wing Commander Andrew Little is related to Dave Glaser by marriage, and his memories of Dave are:

> Urbane, charming, gregarious and generous, Dave Glaser exuded enthusiasm and bonhomie. Handsome to a slightly raffish degree when I first met him and probably dangerously attractive to women, he spiced his conversation with World War 2 Royal Air Force slang which, in his case, unlike many others never sounded phoney or forced for effect. In every aspect of his existence he was still the young fighter pilot, even as time inexorably separated him from that segment of his life. Indeed, even in his later years he

reminded me of nothing so much as a character in an early Rattigan piece. Dave Glaser was not a man who today's chattering classes would welcome at their glittering tables or vacuous talk-fests; he could though, have taught our supposedly gilded youth much about commitment, loyalty, decency and zest for every single day of life. I could never communicate with the man – that's the way he wanted it; but I would have been the poorer for not knowing him and despair to think that his 'type' has gone to the grave with him.

Dave Glaser's funeral service was held at the St Thomas a Beckett's Church in Pagham, near Chichester and was attended by his family and many friends with wartime and civil aviation connections. As his flag-covered coffin with an RAF officers' cap perched on top was carried towards the church, a lone Tiger Moth biplane paid a fitting tribute by proceeding to do a series of victory rolls over the churchyard some 700 feet above. Ernest Derek 'Dave' Glaser would have appreciated that.

CHAPTER 7

THE DEFIANT PILOT
Wing Commander Eric Gordon Barwell DFC & Bar

On 11th August 1937, the first prototype of the Boulton-Paul Defiant mono-plane fighter took off on its maiden flight from Wolverhampton. It was similar in size to the Hawker Hurricane, and it was also powered by the famous Rolls-Royce Merlin Mk I engine, but its one distinguishing feature that made it completely different was, that situated behind the pilot's cockpit was mounted a rotating turret of four Browning 0.303 machine guns. It was envisaged that the aircraft would be ideally suited to attack enemy bomber formations should the situation arise. Its one rather alarming feature however, in retrospect, was that there was no forward firing armament. Eric Gordon Barwell flew the Defiant during the Dunkirk evacuation, the Battle of Britain and later as a night fighter. He is indeed 'One of the Few' surviving men who flew, fought and survived while operating the Boulton-Paul Defiant aircraft; this is his story.

Eric Gordon Barwell was born on 6th August 1913 in the village of Clare, Suffolk. He was the second son of Reginald and Alice Mary Ann Barwell née Paine.

During this period his father was a poultry farmer having previously been a member of his family's metal business in Birmingham. But through a disagreement, he left the business and started up his own farm in Suffolk. As well as Eric in the family there was also his older sister Marjorie, then two brothers, Philip and John. Eric started school at the age of nine and was educated at the Wellingborough School and remained there until the end of 1929. One of his interests at that time was rifle shooting at school and later he visited the Bisley firing range with another cadet.

After leaving school, he hoped to further his education by going to Cambridge University, but finances were not available and instead he joined the family business of tyre-retreading, which his father had started. The business was called the Barwell Tyre Renewing Company and had only been going two or three years when Eric joined in 1931. Later the family business was renamed the Barwell Rubber Company. In 1938, Eric decided to join the Royal Air Force Volunteer Reserve; but what inspired him to have an interest in aviation? He recalls:

> My brother Philip took a short service commission in the RAF in 1925, and of course I was very envious of him. When I was at school on one occasion, he dropped a message tied to a weighted streamer for me on the school playing fields from his aircraft. It

was wonderful for a schoolboy to receive a message in this way. I was extremely keen to join him in the RAF, but my sister persuaded me not to, because she thought it unfair for the family to have two brothers or two sons, flying this dangerous sort of job. So I remained in the family business.

With the threat of war looming in Europe, he decided he would like to join the RAFVR, which at that time many young men were joining in order to learn to become pilots and fulfil their dreams. Eric Barwell remembers that at first he had a few problems to overcome:

Initially I joined the Royal Air Force Volunteer Reserve at Cambridge. In fact it took me some time to get in, because I was sent to a travelling medical board there and one of the first people to see me was the optician. He was examining my eyes and said I had Xophoroia, which means that the eyes have a tendency to splay out, not cross-eyed but the reverse; he told me that I would never be able to land an aeroplane. It was a waste of time to have any more of the medical tests and I left and went straight to see an oculist, who said that the condition was slight, and he didn't think it would affect me at all. The one thing I prided myself on was having good eyesight. I told my brother who was the commanding officer of 46 Squadron at Digby in Lincolnshire and he thought it sounded a bit funny; so he asked me to go up and spend a weekend with him.

There he took me up in a Miles Magister aircraft and did a lot of circuits and bumps, and I had to tell him just when we were about to touch down. I told him correctly each time, so he wrote and sent my details up to the chief optician at the Central Medical Establishment. In due course I was summoned to go up to London, where I passed all the tests perfectly, as far as my eyes were concerned.

I returned back to the medical board and after bit of a delay I passed all the tests, but I answered one of the questions too truthfully maybe. When asked do you suffer from fits or fainting fit attacks, I told them that when I was at school aged 14 or 15 I had fainted about three times. After that reply, the Squadron Leader Medical Officer in Charge said 'I couldn't possibly accept you on my own responsibility, I'll have to send your papers up.' So in due course I had to go to the Central Medical Establishment again, and here I was hoping to get into flying. I went up there and met the heart specialist who saw me and gave me the tests. I went through the various heart tests, cardiograms etc. Eventually I was accepted.

Barwell was then sent to undertake his part-time flying training at No.22 Elementary Flying School at Marshall's airfield in Cambridge, where he would familiarise himself on the RAF's biplanes:

I was taken to train as a Sergeant Pilot in July 1938, flying Tiger Moths and then on to Hawker Harts and Hinds. I got my wings in August 1939 and I just managed to fly the Fairey Battle before I was mobilised on 3rd September 1939. We were paraded that Sunday morning the day war was declared. Somebody had got a wireless and we heard Chamberlain's voice saying we were now at war with Germany. The officers said, 'Fall out those with wings.' There were about 12 or 15 of us out of 150 on parade, we fell out and shouted, *'it's fighter squadrons for us boys!'* Those that had passed their armament exam were put in trucks and taken up to Marshall's airfield to stand guard.

I was put in charge of a Lewis gun post with a couple of chaps and we did that for about five weeks. That first day I was on guard duty from 2.00 pm till 9.00 pm; with the Lewis gun and one rifle between us. After a time it got a little bit boring and I was chatting with one of the other chaps just as it was starting to get dark. One of the guards was marching around the perimeter of the airfield, he obviously hadn't used a rifle before and he had his rifle slung at the slope position and I saw that his rifle was cocked. I said to him 'Do you know how to close the magazine without having a bullet up the spout?' He didn't so I showed him. A bit later I was talking with my friends at the Lewis gun post and holding my rifle; there had been a lot of publicity about the 'Black Out' and suddenly at a nearby house a very bright light appeared and shone out. I said 'Look at that.' I put my rifle up to my shoulder to imitate shooting at the light, when suddenly the rifle unexpectedly went off and at the same moment the light went off. This caused a bit of chaos. That night I was very worried that I might have shot somebody in the house. I went along early next morning to check, but thankfully there were no casualties.

On 8th October 1939, I went to Brize Norton to No. 2 Flying Training School and again flew Hawker Harts and Hinds. Whereas those of us who had our wings were expected to go straight to a fighter squadron, we still had to do a bit more training. All flying hours were very valuable and eventually I was commissioned in December and posted to No.266 Spitfire Squadron, which was stationed at Sutton Bridge. My brother was the commanding officer of the station at Sutton Bridge at this time and he thought, and I agreed that it was not a good thing for his brother, a brand new pilot officer, to be posted on to his station.

I was switched to 264 Squadron at Martlesham Heath in Suffolk on 28th December 1939. It was equipped with the Boulton-Paul Defiant. After arriving there, I met Squadron Leader Steven Hardy who was the commanding officer. He looked at me most suspiciously because I was a most curious breed; I had the VR badge on my lapels and he didn't believe in these civilian flyers. I was then sent away to Aston Down, No. 12 Group Fighter Pool, to do a month's fighter training and there I flew Harvard aircraft for that month. After practising attacks and formation flying, I was sent back to 264 later that month; they started me flying on a Miles Magister to begin with, then a Fairy Battle before they would risk me with a Defiant.

As far as the Defiant was concerned it was a beautiful machine to fly, very stable, easy to handle although it did have a higher landing speed than a Spitfire or Hurricane. We then started to do some training when the squadron had a new commanding officer brought in – Squadron Leader Philip Hunter. Squadron Leader Steven Hardy had been an excellent chap for forming the squadron, he was a very good administrator but he was a little bit old as far as the flying was concerned. When Philip Hunter took over it was absolutely perfect from the training and operational side of things, and slowly we developed the tactics for the Defiant. We did all sorts of things from the point of view of training and developing the tactics because there had been no high speed or monoplane two-seater fighter before the Defiant. Having only the four Browning machine guns in the turret, the pilot did not have control of the guns, although we did have a button on the stick that you could press; it wasn't much good because you didn't know which way the guns were pointing. One relied upon the air gunner completely when the fighting was on. As far as I was concerned, I liked the Defiant; I was very happy with it really.

Towards the end of April 1940, 264 Squadron after a period of intense training was finally declared operational. On 10th May 1940, just after the Germans had overrun the Low Countries, the squadron were posted from Martlesham Heath to RAF Duxford. On 12th May, A Flight flew to Horsham St Faith to undertake an operational patrol off the Dutch coast with six Spitfires of No.66 Squadron. Eric Barwell flew on this mission, but the only enemy aircraft he saw in the air was a Junkers Ju88, which was shot down by his flight commander Flight Lieutenant Nicholas Cooke. He remembers clearly the events of this day:

We went over to Holland on that day and when we arrived over the city of Rotterdam, it was burning horribly. As far as I was concerned, I came across a lone Junkers Ju88. My flight commander was with me and we attacked it with a cross over attack manoeuvre. It was a low flying Ju88 and the only way one could attack it, was to fly across in front of it; then the air gunner had a straight shot so to speak at the enemy. This is what I was just about to do, when my flight commander, 'the dirty dog', got in and shot it down instead.

The very next day, B Flight was sent out on a similar patrol from Martlesham Heath. They claimed five enemy aircraft shot down, but suffered terribly when only one of the six Defiants returned. Eric continues:

They took off that day early morning and this time it was a very different matter. They ran into myriads of Me109s and Me110s. We heard nothing from them until the afternoon when one lone aircraft landed, flown by a chap named Kay, whose Defiant was full of bullet holes. The other five were shot down. Several were killed and others taken as prisoners of war, while one or two managed to escape and get home again. One chap who was taken prisoner was named Greenhous, and he was a prisoner of war for almost five years. In fact in May 1945 I was Wing Commander Flying on the Rheine airfield in Germany, which included 264 Squadron, when this chap Greenhous, having just been released as a PoW came through us, so I had the pleasure of arranging his return to England in a 264 Squadron aircraft.

On 23rd May, with the Allied armies in full retreat towards the French coast, 264 Squadron was ordered to fly down to RAF Manston in Kent to begin operations over the Dunkirk beaches. It was a very hectic period:

> We had been termed operational before, but we had only been doing the occasional convoy patrol and hadn't seen any action at all. Then at first light on 23rd May, we flew down to RAF Manston as the Germans were closing in on the French coast, and this worked up to a crescendo over Dunkirk. We would have two patrols each day, the rest of the time we were kept at readiness on the airfield, in case the Germans attacked the airfields, which unwisely they didn't. Anyway we were left sitting about much of the time when we really would have rather been up in the air. However, it really began to get busy. On 29th May 1940, we had two patrols that day and on the earlier patrol I managed to get a Messerschmitt 109; the sky over Dunkirk was one mass of aircraft of all shapes and sizes. On the second patrol I was credited with two Stuka Ju87s and I'll always remember that because there happened to be three of us. We were flying in line abreast and we formated under them, we shot at them and up they went in flames. At that time the Stukas were only just beginning to have self-sealing fuel tanks installed; their main fuel tanks were virtually between the pilot and the navigator and if they were hit, they just blew up.

Eric was flying in B Flight and his claiming of the Messerschmitt 109 took place at 2.30 pm off the coast of France, north of Dunkirk. His combat report gives a more detailed account of the action:

> The squadron of 12 Defiant aircraft were on patrol along the coast near Dunkirk when at about 12,000 feet, a number of Heinkel He111 machines (about 10) were seen at about 5,000 feet, which were attacked by Hurricanes.
> At the same time, two Me110s and about seven Me109 fighters were observed manoeuvring into a position to attack. I gave the warning on the R/T and ordered 'Green Section Line Astern' when two Me109 aircraft started to dive. When these were approaching to make an astern attack, I made a sudden steep turn to starboard and my gunner Pilot Officer Williams gave a burst of about 30 rounds on the leading machine, just as it was firing at Green 3 (Pilot Officer Kay).
> The machine immediately burst into flames and crashed into the

sea. I rejoined the formation and almost immediately, we were then attacked by two Me110s. We fired at one and at the same time several others opened fire on this machine; and this also burst into flames, falling out of control.

When the squadron, in section line astern, were chasing the other Me110, I passed about 30 Ju87s and we gave a very short burst at one, at about 50 yards, but did not notice the effect. More Me109s and Me110s were seen above us, when the Red Leader gave the order 'Steep spiral dive down to sea.' I was a short distance from the rest of the squadron and spiralled down to sea level and then proceeded to Manston, landing at 15.45 hours.

The second patrol was during early evening and the attack against the Ju87s took place at 7.30 pm starting at a height of 1,500 feet down to 150 feet. In his actual combat report for that patrol, Eric states:

I was Green Leader in the squadron formation of Defiant aircraft when patrolling the coast of Dunkirk. My gunner was Pilot Officer Williams. At Dunkirk we observed about 4 Ju88 aircraft delivering dive-bombing attacks on vessels around the harbours and along the beach and when giving chase to one, we ran into about 10 Ju87s.

We formated slightly below one Ju87 and gave it a two-second burst of about 30 rounds at 150 yards, when it went up in flames and fell into the sea.

We immediately closed up below and between two other Ju87s, giving a 50-round burst to one, which immediately dropped its bombs (almost on another Defiant) and then burst into flames. This aircraft however, was also fired at by at least one other Defiant and we do not know who finally brought it down. We gave another Ju87 one burst of 50 rounds and this was set on fire and crashed into the sea.

A Ju88 was then sighted going out to sea at about 500 feet and we gave chase, accompanied by two other Defiants. The enemy aircraft dropped right down to sea level and when about 10 miles out to sea, turned around and proceeded east. I managed to cut him off and made a cross over attack around the front and slightly above him at a range of about 50 to 75 yards. We gave him a long burst and could see the incendiary bullets going into the pilot's cockpit. We were met with a burst of fire from a gun in the nose and as the ammunition was almost exhausted we retired and returned to Manston, landing at 20.30 hours.

Our aircraft had one bullet through the tail fin and rudder caused apparently by one of our own guns. That was a red-letter day for 264 Squadron, when we claimed 37 German aircraft. We got all our aircraft back, but unfortunately we lost one air gunner. One of our pilots, Pilot Officer Desmond Kay, apparently did some very hearty evasive action and his air gunner must have thought that he was out of control. He baled out and he was never seen again. It was really something of a day as far as I was concerned. I had been told that

morning that I was going to become a flight commander.
Unfortunately, after the second patrol we landed and refuelled and
took off again for Duxford; it was by then beginning to get dark. The
commanding officer said that the weather was closing in at Duxford
and so we were told to turn back and land at Manston. But I made
a fool of myself by landing up the hill at Manston. I was
overshooting a bit, but I thought there was plenty of airfield over the
brow of the hill, but there wasn't and I stopped in a potato patch and
bent one leg of the Defiant. I didn't hear any more about becoming
a flight commander after that.

But what was it like for Eric Barwell in what was really his first major
engagement with the enemy, did he feel nervous or apprehensive?

I don't really remember anything special about it honestly, it was a
flying thing. I was trying to shoot down and beat the other chap and
I don't really remember feeling it was his life or mine. It was just
one of those curious things, that when one looks back on it you
think 'Oh gosh, one should get all het up', but I didn't find that.

I had done a little training on a fixed-gun attack and fighter
attacks with a Harvard aircraft, but our commanding officer
Squadron Leader Philip Hunter had got us so keen on our Defiants,
that we just felt that we could do the job properly. The ordinary
fighter pilots couldn't stand the idea of the Defiant and not having
control of the guns; that was the main thing about it and that was
the difference. As far as Dunkirk was concerned, I had bent the
aircraft and I had to spend the night at Manston. The squadron were
going to be released on 30th May, so I flew a Miles Master aircraft
back to Duxford.

After a day of rest on the 30th, the squadron were again involved in the thick
of the action on 31st May, but before taking off, not all the pilots seemed
ready to take on the Germans, as Eric now relates:

On that day, we were all getting ready to take off as usual at first
light from Duxford, when I noticed one of our pilots sitting in a
chair outside our dispersal point. He was leaning forward holding
his head in his hands, moaning and saying 'I feel so ill'. I asked;
'What's the matter?' He said he thought he had a hang over, he had
not got to bed until about 2 am that morning, and I said 'Surely you
are not going to fly like that?'

He then said to me, 'I must, the flight commander has told me
off for drinking before, I shall have to.' I said I didn't think this was
on at all; he continued 'Well don't tell the flight commander'. I
went to the flight commander and told him, 'I don't think this chap
ought to fly' and he said, 'Why?" I said, 'I think it's a hangover
actually' and then he suddenly erupted. 'What, you mean, on active
service like that'; the flight commander had his revolver strapped
to him and he shouted, 'I'll get him with my ruddy gun'. He then

said, he'd see him about this when he got back; he then arranged for another pilot to go instead. Unfortunately, the flight commander Nicholas Cooke, who was a wonderful chap, was shot down and didn't come back and the pilot with the hangover got away with it.

It was on this day that Eric continued to score against the enemy, but he also remembers one of his colleague's aeroplanes suddenly falling to pieces over Dunkirk, and wondering what had caused this:

> Another incident, which occurred, was when I saw Pilot Officer Mike Young's aircraft separate into four pieces. I thought he'd taken a direct hit and I thought I saw the wings, along with the pilot's cockpit section turn over and begin swanning down like a falling leaf, along with the aft section of the tail unit. All three different pieces I saw momentarily together and we watched and waited to see if anyone got out by parachute from this. In fact Young did get out. He landed in a bomb crater in Dunkirk and sprained his ankle, otherwise he was alright. It wasn't a direct hit, it wasn't an ack-ack shell or anything like that, it was a collision with a chap called Pilot Officer David 'Bull' Whitley. Bull had cut off Young's tail and this is what caused the accident. Bull crash-landed in Dunkirk, and this was on the first patrol of the day.

It was during this first patrol that Eric and his gunner Williams shot down their second enemy fighter. Their combat report for that afternoon states that at 14.20 hours (2.20 pm), while off Dunkirk at between 8,000 and 14,000 feet, they encountered the enemy. Eric's report continues:

> I was detailed to patrol over Dunkirk and almost as soon as we passed over the coast at 10,000 feet, we observed large numbers of Me109 fighters.
> I promptly ordered my section into 'Line Astern' and my gunner saw two Me109s bearing down on our machines. Immediately afterwards, Green 2 (P/O Hickman) was seen to go down with smoke or petrol streaming from his machine. A moment later my gunner called out 'Fighter astern' – at the same time tracer shells came past my port window. I did a violent steep turn to starboard and my gunner fired at the Me109, which was chasing us. A short burst caused the enemy aircraft to catch fire and it fell into the sea. Shortly afterwards the squadron commander gave the order to reform and we returned to Manston.

The squadron were ordered up again to patrol during the early evening. Eric Barwell was leading Blue section but during this patrol things didn't go according to plan and Eric and his gunner Pilot Officer Williams found themselves on the receiving end of the Luftwaffe:

> On that first patrol I got a Me109, but on the second patrol, I had a go at a Heinkel 111 and shot it down; I saw parachutes appear and

then I tried to attack another formation of three Heinkels. All of a
sudden my cockpit was filled with glycol fumes; obviously I had
been hit by return fire from one of the air gunners from the three
Heinkels, and as I aimed off for home, I was then about 7,000 to
10,000 feet.

I was thinking I had a chance of getting back, when suddenly
we went under one Heinkel and I got the air gunner to give him a
burst of fire, but it didn't do any good. Slowly the oil temperature
rose and then the engine revs started to drop; I kept the long line of
shipping in sight and there were all sorts of boats and ships.
Eventually, when I knew we had to go down I discussed with my
air gunner, Pilot Officer Williams, whether to ditch or bale out. He
left it up to me and I decided that if we baled out we could drift
quite a distance away from this line of shipping, and this was a
swept channel and there were mines and so on. The navy, they were
all doing a good enough job and I didn't want to dive at them.
Coming lower, I looked down and there were vessels like river
launches, such as you'd find on the Norfolk Broads and that sort of
thing. I thought well, they wouldn't have room for us and then I
saw some fishing boats. I saw two navy destroyers, meeting each
other, one going to and one coming from Dunkirk, and I thought if
I ditch between those two they have both got to pass and one will
be able to pick us up, so that is what I did.

I ditched, not according to the rules at all. According to the
rules, you should tighten up your straps and feather it down, but at
that time the experts were saying don't put down the flaps because
it will make the nose dig in; so I didn't put down the flaps. The
Defiant only had a Perspex windscreen, and if I ditched like that I
was sure that the windscreen would smash down on to me. I undid
my straps and the parachute harness and stood on the seat and
feathered it down; it was a perfectly smooth sea and terribly
difficult to judge the height above the water. I dropped the aircraft
in from about 15 feet and I went fairly deep into the water and
swam up and up, I thought I'd never reach the top. Then when I did,
I looked around and couldn't see my air gunner who I had left
sitting on the back of the turret of the Defiant. I suddenly
recognised the backside of his parasuit, a special parachute pack
that air gunners wore.

My chap had accidentally released the CO_2 bottle on his life
jacket earlier that day and hadn't had the bottle replaced, so he was
floating bottom up. I swam over to him and turned him the right way
up and looked around for the nearest destroyer. I started to try and
swim towards the ship, holding my rear gunner, but the parachute
was in the way of my legs. I had only given a short puff or two into
my own mae west which didn't at that time have the CO inflation, I
seemed to be getting lower and lower in the water. Slowly I saw one
destroyer heading towards me, I shouted 'Why the bloody hell don't
you lower a boat?' There was a perfectly good reason for this, they
hadn't got any and as the ship came up to me, a sailor did a

wonderful dive off the bow of the destroyer and relieved me of the gunner, while I went nearer to the aft end of the ship where they had a scrambling net. I wasn't strong enough to climb up, so someone put a rope around me and helped me. The first chap I saw when getting on board was Mike Young, whom all of us in the squadron had previously given up as having been killed. My air gunner Pilot Officer Williams was hauled aboard and he came to on the destroyer. While he was lying on the floor he looked up and saw Mike Young silhouetted in a doorway with what seemed to be flames behind him. Williams thought he had gone to hell.

The destroyer HMS *Malcolm* had rescued both Barwell and Williams from the sea; this sailed to Dover, where they landed along with 1,500 troops who had been picked up from the beaches. Pilot Officer Williams was taken to Dover Hospital for treatment. Barwell recalls what happened to Williams once in hospital:

Williams was only slightly hurt. In private life he had been a stuntman and had done about 500 parachute drops at various displays and things and he had never saved his own life in an emergency with a parachute. He apparently had been very keen that we should have baled out, but he didn't put his opinion forward at the time. Because of that he landed up in hospital and happened to be in the bed next to Wing Commander Louis Strange, who had been a WWI fighter ace. He had just been given the job of training our first paratroops and so hearing the experience of Williams, he then asked him to become a paratrooper trainer. After going down so deep in the water, I damaged one of my ears and was taken off flying for one week. I thought I should have had leave after that, but the commanding officer gave me 24 hours off and then I had to return and act as squadron adjutant, because they were short of one. This was a very good thing because I didn't know anything about administration in the RAF at that time.

After Dunkirk and the fall of France, the squadron moved up to Kirton-in-Lindsey in Lincolnshire. Here they re-grouped and made up their losses, and shared the airfield with No.222 Squadron equipped with Spitfires. The squadron went on doing practice flights and Barwell teamed up with his new gunner Sergeant Martin at the end of June.

In early July, the Battle of Britain began in earnest, the Germans targeting firstly the Channel convoys, radar stations and then more importantly in August the RAF's airfields. 264 Squadron remained at readiness up in 12 Group at Kirton ready for the call south. Eric Barwell waited anxiously with the others for the order:

I knew a chap named Dennis Armitage, who had just been made commanding officer of 266 Squadron. He and I had been sergeant pilots together at Brize Norton at the beginning of the war. He also was a VR, but he was very quickly promoted to an acting squadron

leader. I knew that various squadrons had been losing no end of
people down south, but it was one of those things, we just had to
do our job and do the best we could.

On 21st August 1940, the squadron received a signal from Fighter Command
headquarters to move back down south. It was to relieve 266 Squadron who
had suffered terrible casualties:

> When things really hotted up in the Battle of Britain, we were sent
> to Hornchurch. At Hornchurch we were certainly in the thick of it.
> I went to Hornchurch on 21st August 1940 as part of the advance
> party. I went on patrol on 22nd August and on the 24th we went to
> Manston to patrol.

Saturday 24th August, the weather was perfect for flying operations, it was
fine and clear. At 9 am, the Operations Room at Fighter Command began to
pick up early signs of the German raids emerging over Cap Gris Nez. A
Luftwaffe formation of over 100 plus was heading towards the Dover area at
between 12,000 and 24,000 feet. At 12.30 pm, 264 Squadron were ordered up
immediately from Manston:

> That was the fatal day, because when we were at Manston, we
> heard that the Germans were coming over with one lot aiming for
> the airfield. A formation of Junkers Ju88s came over to attack
> Manston and Ramsgate and we were caught on the ground. We
> managed to get up in twos and threes and I took off with my
> number two, who was a Pilot Officer Jones. He was very much a
> newcomer, but we chased out after the Ju88s, but did not gain on
> them much, when suddenly five Me109s attacked us. I shouted to
> Jones 'line astern, take evasive action'; unfortunately he only did a
> gentle turn and was shot down immediately. The five Me109s then
> concentrated on me. The result of that was one reason why I have
> always liked the Defiant. Each enemy fighter would attack
> separately and as they were coming in, I turned very quickly, but
> the Me109s couldn't turn sufficiently quickly enough to allow for
> deflection in front of us. This meant they were pointing more or
> less straight at me; it was a dead straight shot for my air gunner. I
> reckoned we hit two or three of them and my gunner definitely shot
> down one of them. I wasn't sure I was going to reach England
> again because I was doing all this evasive action, but the Me109s
> broke off and back I came.
>
> I found that this confirmed my opinion of the Defiant and that
> we could hold our own against the other fighters. Unfortunately,
> that day Philip Hunter our CO was lost and a squadron leader who
> had been with us for a fortnight as a supernumerary took his place.
> He took over and the next day insisted on leading us into action,
> although prior to that fortnight he had never flown fighters and the
> net result was that we lost rather more aircraft.

Eric's combat report for this action confirms the destruction of the Messerschmitt 109, when his aircraft was attacked by the enemy fighters at 12.50 pm:

> I was Green leader with Green 2 at 10,000 feet, when I saw 20 Ju88s at 15,000 feet. They started to dive towards Ramsgate and released their bombs at 4,000 feet. I followed them down and was attacked by five He113s (Me109s). I got astern of the He113s and fired 120 rounds at the second machine. It immediately burst into flames and dived into the sea. I then returned to base. I am under the impression that I saw Green 2, P/O Jones, dive into the sea.

In his report, Eric Barwell wrongly reported the Me109s as Heinkel 113 fighters, a fact he later corrected. During the afternoon, the squadron, now back at Hornchurch, were suddenly in danger of being caught on the ground, when the Germans launched an attack on the airfield. Eric found this experience unnerving:

> When we were preparing to take off on one patrol, we were kept on the ground too long, because over the Tannoy loudspeaker came the voice of the Controller giving us more or less a running commentary that the Germans were approaching. We got someone to contact operations to ask them if we could take off. They came back with, 'Stand by, stand by,' then suddenly over the loud speaker came almost panic, '264 Squadron scramble, scramble, scramble.' We took off and apart from two of our aircraft taxiing into one another there was no damage; the bombs fell exactly where only moments earlier we had been standing.

The casualties in the rush to take off were Flying Officer D.K. O'Malley along with Pilot Officer A. O'Connell who collided with another aircraft on the ground. Though the aircraft was damaged, it was repairable and both the aircrew were unhurt.

That day the squadron had suffered quite badly in the air; Pilot Officer D. Whitley and Sergeant R.C. Turner in L7021 had been badly damaged in the tail section from return fire from a Ju88. Squadron Leader Philip Hunter and his gunner Fred King were reported missing in action after last being seen chasing a Ju88 out over the coast, and also listed as missing were Pilot Officer I.G. Shaw and Sergeant Alan Berry. Flight Lieutenant Campbell-Colquhoun and Pilot Officer G. Robinson had their aircraft damaged. During the afternoon, the squadron lost one more gunner, Sergeant W. Machin who died from his wounds after being shot down over Hornchurch by Me109s of JG51. His pilot, Pilot Officer Gaskell survived.

The following day, on the 26th, Squadron Leader George Garvin led the pilots into action at midday against a formation of 150 enemy aircraft; Eric Barwell felt some apprehension at being led by the new commanding officer:

> The one particular thing I can vividly picture the next day was, we could only put up seven aircraft, a formation of two Vics with myself as the last man. I told my gunner to keep his eyes skinned

especially up in the sun. The next moment I felt we'd been hit by
something and I whisked the aircraft around quickly to see a
Messerschmitt 109 going down past us; he had sprayed the lot of
us because Squadron Leader Garvin had made us keep up close
together and he was climbing at full throttle and it was very
difficult to keep together.

During this engagement, the squadron again suffered heavily. Pilot Officer
Goodhall and Sergeant Young in Defiant L7024 were badly damaged when
attacked by Me109s; they managed to get back to base, unhurt. Flight
Lieutenant A.J. Banham and Sergeant Baker were shot down in L6985.
Banham baled out and landed safely, but Baker was listed as missing. The
same fate befell Flying Officer I.R. Stephenson and Sergeant W. Maxwell.
Stephenson survived but Maxwell was not found. Flight Sergeant Edward
Thorn and Sergeant Fred Barker were forced to crash-land their aircraft
L7005, but not before Barker despatched a Me109. Eric now relates how the
squadron members reacted:

It was pretty awful at that time, morale partly, the squadron having
also been bombed at Rochford, but mainly because of the
leadership we had having lost such a lot of people. The other
Defiant squadron, No.141, having at the end of July had their one
and only daylight combat, had also lost rather a lot of people. That
coupled with the results we now had, persuaded the powers that be
that the Defiant was to be made a night-fighter and so we were
condemned as I put it, to night-fighting.

On 27th August, the weather turned bad and this gave Eric the chance to travel
up to London to meet his wife Ruth née Birchill, whom he had met at
Martlesham Heath; she was a WAAF cipher officer. They had only recently
married on 6th August, which was also Eric's 27th birthday:

I was able to get away obtaining a 24-hour pass from Hornchurch.
I had only just been married and my wife came to meet me in
London. We managed to get a room on the fifth floor of the
Cumberland Hotel, and I always remember this because the room
was just level with the top of Marble Arch. Marble Arch had the
most enormous air-raid siren mounted on top of it, and the number
of times that siren went off that night, we were just about blown out
of bed.

The next day would be the final day that 264 Squadron would play any further
role in the battle. At 8.30 am German raids started to appear over Cap Gris
Nez. One formation headed for Rochford, where aircraft of 264 had been sent.
The squadron took off to engage the enemy formation, but the fighter escort
was too strong and they were totally outclassed by the Me109s and paid
dearly once again. At 8.55 am Defiants L7026 and N1574 were both shot
down and their crews killed, and Defiant N1576 was badly damaged hit by
return fire from a Heinkel 111 over Dover, the crew returning unhurt. Defiant

L6957 flown by Sergeant Lauder and Sergeant Chapman was hit in the wing fuel tank, but returned to base uninjured. Squadron Leader Garvin and Flight Lieutenant Ash were not so lucky and were shot down in flames. Garvin baled out and survived, but Ash was killed when his parachute failed. Eric remembers this final day at Hornchurch:

> I noticed that after the attack one of the Defiants had petrol streaming from a wing tank and I could see that I had got holes in one of my wing tanks. That day I was not flying my usual aircraft and I was unsure whether this had self-sealing fuel tanks or not. I called up Control and told them what had happened and that I was now by myself and they said; 'Patrol Don Robert Angels 12,' in other words, Patrol Dover at 10,000 feet. I repeated to them that I was just by myself, but they insisted that I carry on, so I carried out the patrol on my own. I didn't see any further aircraft, friendly or hostile and in due course returned to base.

The following day, 264 Squadron were sent back up to Kirton-in-Lindsey. Eric looks back at some of the members with whom he served over 60 years ago:

> Some of the personalities in the squadron I remember were people like Desmond Hughes, who I knew very well until his death in 1992. He was one of the pilots who came along after Dunkirk, to make up the losses that we had suffered. He was a great chap and he accounted for quite a few enemy aircraft after becoming a night-fighter, claiming two in one night if I can recall. He earned the DFC fairly quickly.
>
> Then there was Edward Thorn, a Flight Sergeant, a very fine pilot and a very popular member of the whole squadron. At that time the sergeants didn't mix very much with the officer pilots, but when flying, Ted Thorn was one of us absolutely. John Lauder was another, he was always very quiet, but very well respected. Sergeant Fred Barker was a very reliable gunner indeed and flew with Flight Sergeant Thorn; I believe they became the top scorers in the squadron. Pilot Officer Sid Carlin was an amazing character. In the First War, he had been originally in the infantry and had been awarded the DCM and the Military Cross; in action he had been wounded and lost a leg. In 1917, he had transferred to the Royal Flying Corps, where he was nicknamed 'Timbertoes' because of his wooden leg. He was later awarded the DFC in 1918. Despite his one leg, he had managed to talk his way back into the RAF, becoming aircrew in 1939/40. He walked with a stick, but once in the air, he was eager to get at the enemy. He left 264 Squadron to join a Blenheim squadron at Wittering and apparently during a raid on the airfield in 1941 was caught between two air-raid shelters. He was last seen waving his stick in the air cursing the Hun before being killed by a direct hit.

While the bulk of the squadron remained at Kirton, one of the flights was sent to operate at night from Luton aerodrome as Eric recalls:

We were first sent to Northolt, but we found that Northolt was almost completely surrounded by barrage balloons, which we didn't think an awful lot of, especially if we were to do flying at night. Fortunately the people at Fighter Command agreed, so they then sent one flight to Luton. Luton was too small really, in the east-west direction the runway was only 600 yards, so one had to be pretty accurate in landing and we did lose one or two people. If you overshot the runway by any amount you were in trouble. We were controlled from Northolt, but when we were flying we could hear Northolt only when we were above 2,000 feet. This meant that when you had low cloud you had no contact and it was very difficult to get down. We rigged up a radio transmission set in the dispersal hut so that they could talk from the ground to the aircraft, although this was fairly limited range. You had someone on the microphone in the hut and someone just outside listening. If you heard the Defiant coming back, the chap on the wireless could give the pilot his bearings. We complained about the control there and in the middle of one night the Commander-in-Chief of Fighter Command, Sir Hugh Dowding, came down to see us. The first thing he said to us was; 'You've got a grand airfield here boys.' One of our flight commanders, Flight Lieutenant S. R. Thomas, thought it was a good opportunity to say what some of the difficulties were, so he told Dowding about the control problem and the size of the airfield. The extraordinary thing was that Dowding must have been in a bad mood or something, because he said; 'I didn't come here to listen to complaints.' He then stormed off, which we thought wasn't very good.

As far as I was concerned it was a bit of a black mark against Dowding, although we know what a wonderful job he did, in managing to conserve the aircraft before the Battle of Britain. That incident was a little surprising and Thomas didn't get promoted to being a Squadron Leader until well after I was Squadron Leader, because Dowding had made a note of his name. The Defiant, if one could have found the enemy at night, would have been an excellent night-fighter for that role. But the main snag at that time was that the RDF or radar control was pretty poor, and when they did get good ground control, the Blenheims and Beaufighters with airborne radar, or AI, had the best controls and we didn't. But it was sheer luck if we found an enemy aircraft.

During the remaining months of 1940 and into 1941, 264 Squadron continued to fly during the night in the defence of Britain, against an enemy who at most times was completely hidden and difficult to locate using the primitive radar equipment of that period as Eric notes above. He assesses this difficult time in RAF night-fighting as follows:

With hindsight the Boulton-Paul Defiant was a very nice aircraft; it was what I call a gentleman's aircraft. It was not quite as manoeuvrable as the Hurricane or the Spitfire, but it was very sound and personally I thought it was wrong to condemn it to night-fighting. But really there was no one ready to fight in our corner; all our commanding officers had been killed. As a night-fighter I was flying for six months before I saw anything to shoot at, doing a lot of trips and then in one moonlit night I had two dogfights. It was a bit galling. Towards the end of the war we had established a very efficient radar system in the aircraft as well as the control on the ground. Whereas in 1940/41 the Germans were coming over in their hundreds, one would see the flames and the bombs bursting directly beneath somewhere over the London area and you thought one must be able to see the bombers silhouetted against the flames. You would fly through the slipstream of other aircraft from time to time, but you just couldn't see them.

On 9th February 1941, Eric Barwell was awarded the Distinguished Flying Cross, and two months later on the night of 10th April 1941, he achieved his first successes as a night-fighter, as his combat report now testifies:

I took off with Sergeant Martin as gunner from Biggin Hill at 20.15 hours on 10.4.41 to patrol the Kenley Sector. This I did at height varying between 14,000 feet to 18,000 feet. I was vectored after an enemy aircraft and when at about 15,000 feet saw the 'bandit' 500 feet above me and about 1,000 yards ahead, flying on the same course.

I closed to 300 yards on the beam and slightly underneath, when Sgt Martin opened fire. He got in about four good bursts of one or two seconds each, whilst we were closing in from 300 yards to 50 yards. We both saw the De Wilde ammunition bursting in the fuselage and engines.

The enemy aircraft then took evasive action by putting his nose up and climbing, so that when at 120 mph, when the Defiant was about stalling, we were still overshooting. As we passed underneath the enemy aircraft, it could be clearly distinguished as a Heinkel 111. Sergeant Martin had ceased firing as he had been blinded by the flashes of his own ammunition. At that moment the enemy aircraft suddenly dived vertically into the cloud below and although I followed him, I never saw him again. As I came out through the cloud, which was at about 500 feet thick at 10,000 feet, I saw the incendiary bombs from an enemy aircraft strike the ground between Redhill and Beachy Head.

It was reported later, that the enemy aircraft crashed near the coast and that the crew baled out, which neither my gunner nor I observed. There was no return fire throughout the contact. We claimed one He111 destroyed. We fired 435 rounds of ammunition and landed back at Tangmere at 22.15 hours. We were controlled by G.L. Kenley, which was excellent.

Little did Flying Officer Barwell or Sergeant Martin realise that the night was far from over for them, for very early on the morning of the 11th April, they would be called to climb back into their aircraft again and make contact with the enemy:

I took off on my second patrol for the night from Tangmere at 02.38 hours on 11.4.41 and after patrolling for some time we were vectored on to an enemy aircraft, which was reported to be on its way home.

Finally, I saw it about 1,000 yards ahead of me and 2,000 feet below, flying at a height of 7,000 feet. I chased the enemy who evidently saw me and began to climb up towards the cloud, which was at about 15,000 feet. I was able to close in only very slowly and Sergeant Martin opened fire from 300 yards.

A real dogfight ensued, as though it was daytime. The enemy machine adopted violent evasive action and there was plenty of return fire from the rear gunner firing tracer. On one occasion, this gunner actually fired vertically towards us. When we were 50 yards away and below, we were able to see the De Wilde ammunition bursting inside the enemy aircraft all up the fuselage and also saw many pieces falling off the target.

The enemy aircraft then dived down steeply towards the sea and we lost it in the 3/10th haze and cloud. We were able to see it clearly as a Heinkel He111 and I understand that there were no RDF plots for this raid. From the time it broke away we lost it.

We claimed one He111 probably destroyed. When the enemy aircraft broke away, we must have been 15 miles out to sea. Kenley G.L again controlled us. We fired 650 rounds of ammunition and it seemed to me that we damaged this aircraft far worse than the He111 that we destroyed over land on the earlier patrol. The weather was as clear as daylight with thin cloud at 3,000 feet and more cloud at 15,000 feet. We landed back at Biggin Hill at 04.15 hours.

On 2nd July 1941, Eric was posted from 264 to a new squadron, No.125, which had just been formed. This too was a night-fighter interception unit:

I went on to No.125 'Newfoundland' Squadron who were forming up at Colerne in No. 10 Group as a flight commander and we started then from scratch, training the new chaps and so on. We then moved from Colerne and its satellite airfield to Fairwood Common near Swansea and that was in the middle of 1941. At the end of 1941 I was made commanding officer, acting squadron leader of 125 Squadron and we still had the Defiant for night fighting. Then in January/February 1942, we were re-equipped with Beaufighter Mk IIs and that was a wing commander's job, so I then became a flight commander again.

The Beaufighter II was powered by Merlin engines and it was not a very good aircraft, as it was a bit underpowered. For instance, on one occasion I had one engine fail when I was miles out to sea, but I managed to get it back luckily. It was an aircraft that would catch out newcomers sometimes rather badly. It had a terrible swing on take-off and on landing, and it wasn't until sometime later when we had the Beaufighter Mk VI, which had the Hercules Mk 16 engine, that it was quite a good aircraft.

On the night of 1st July 1942, Eric Barwell was involved with his first combat when flying the Bristol Beaufighter. There was a certain amount of enemy activity in the Swansea area that night; three crews were sent up, but two of them were too late to intercept as 10 Group Headquarters would not at first allow them to go up due to haze and poor ground visibility. Eric Barwell was the only one to make contact. He attacked a Dornier 217, near Cardiff, but his cannons would not fire and he could only use his 0.303 machine guns. He remembers the following:

> For some unknown reason the trigger would not work. On the control we had two buttons, one was to fire the six Browning machine guns and the other for the cannons. I thought I'll use my cannons only, pulled the trigger and it would just not fire; I then fired with my six Brownings and hit the enemy aircraft, but he dived down and I lost him. I could only claim him as damaged. My radar operator was Sergeant Young.

On 2nd July, Eric was devastated to learn that his older brother Philip had been killed during an operational flight on the previous day.

Philip Reginald Barwell had joined the Royal Air Force on a short service commission in 1925 and was posted to No.19 Squadron at RAF Duxford. Known in RAF circles as 'Dickie' Barwell, he had continued to rise through the ranks and by 1937, as a squadron leader, he was given command of 46 Squadron based at Digby in Lincolnshire. When war came, the squadron led by Philip Barwell on 21st October 1939, attacked a formation of German seaplanes, which were intent on bombing a British convoy. In the engagement he shot down one of the Heinkel 115s and shared in another's destruction. For this action, he was awarded the DFC on 28th November 1939. That same month, he was posted to command RAF Sutton Bridge and promoted to wing commander. In May 1940, he was again posted, this time to Headquarters No.12 Group at Watnall. As the Battle of Britain waged during the four months between July and October, Philip flew three operational flights with 242 Squadron from RAF Coltishall on 5th October 1940, qualifying him for the Battle of Britain clasp. He was given command of RAF Biggin Hill station during June 1941 and was made Group Captain. During this time, he flew occasionally as No.2 to the famous South African fighter ace Sailor Malan. On 4th July 1941, he claimed a shared probable Me109 with Malan and one week later claimed another destroyed himself.

During January 1942, Philip Barwell had just taken off from Biggin Hill, when his Spitfire's engine suddenly cut out on getting airborne. He crash-landed the aircraft just beyond the runway, but in doing so fractured his spine. Refusing doctor's advice, he continued to fly operationally, wearing a plaster cast. On 1st July 1942, he took off from Biggin Hill accompanied by

Squadron Leader Robert Oxspring just before sunset on a standing patrol between Dungeness and Beachy Head. Biggin Hill Control contacted them and warned them of unidentified aircraft in their area. Unfortunately there was very thick haze up to 16,000 feet and visibility was not good. Oxspring suddenly sighted two fighter aircraft appearing out of the sun and gave a warning over the R/T to Barwell. As the two aircraft became clearer, Oxspring identified them as Spitfires, but too late, the second Spitfire opened fire on Barwell's aircraft. Bobby Oxspring turned his aircraft into the attacking Spitfire's path and succeeded in causing the attacking aircraft to break away. But the damage had been done, Barwell's aircraft had been hit and flames were now coming from the petrol tank. The last thing Oxspring recalled was seeing Philip Barwell trying to open the cockpit hood.

Bobby Oxspring returned to Biggin and reported the events that had taken place. Immediately a search and rescue operation was put into effect, but no trace of Philip Barwell or his aircraft were found. During the subsequent Court of Inquiry that was held, it was established that the Spitfires that had attacked Oxspring and Barwell had been flown by two inexperienced pilots from RAF Tangmere in Sussex, and that one of the pilots was only on his first operational sortie and the other his second.

It was another tragic loss of such an experienced RAF fighter leader. Sometime later, Philip Barwell's body was washed up on the French coast. He now rests in peace at the Calais Canadian War Cemetery.

On 6th September 1942, Eric Barwell was posted to Headquarters No.10 Group as Squadron Leader Night Operations and after spending seven months in that position, he returned to 125 Squadron at Fairwood Common on 31st March 1943, as a flight commander once again, continuing night-fighting with the Bristol Beaufighters and eventually De Havilland Mosquitos. The squadron were then re-equipped with the Mosquito Mk XVII aircraft in February 1944. The Mosquito had the latest radar and was very efficient, but the annoying thing from the squadron's point of view, was that by this stage of the war, the Germans had virtually ceased to come over.

It was while operating from RAF Hurn on the night of 23rd/24th April 1944, that Eric and his navigator/radar operator Flight Lieutenant D. Haigh engaged and destroyed a Junkers Ju88A-14 over Warminster. His report reads:

> Took off from Hurn at 1.30 am under control of Sopley G.C.I. and was on orbit 'R' when many searchlights were seen in the distance, along the south coast, mainly westwards. The light from several searchlights was seen through low stratus cloud. Contact was obtained at 8 miles range, 16,000 feet and target was slightly below to port, taking corkscrew evasive action, altering height by 5,000 feet and dropping anti-radar Window. Speed of enemy aircraft was varying from 140 to 260 mph. Visual was first obtained at approximately 1,000 feet range. Target was 5 degrees above at 12 o'clock, but I could not identify it until at 200 feet range, when it turned out to be a Ju88 and bombs were observed at the wing roots.
>
> At this range, a short burst was given from almost dead astern and strikes were seen on starboard wing root and engine. The aircraft went down to starboard almost vertically and was then

observed spinning with starboard engine on fire and pieces ablaze falling from it. A glow was seen on the ground where the aircraft hit and a fix was given to Sopley. One inaccurate burst of return fire was observed. A further contact was obtained and followed until 1,500 feet, when resins were observed and at approximately the same time, the navigator got a contact, through the mass of Window, on another aircraft close in front of what was assumed to be a friendly fighter. Shortly afterwards, further contact was obtained on another aircraft dropping Window, but as range closed, the radar reading became unreliable and the chase was abandoned. We landed back at Ford airfield at 3.50 am. E/A reported crashed near Warminster in square U.36.

The German aircraft belonged to 4/KG30 and was No.144501 coded 4D+FM. The aircraft broke up in mid air and crashed at Manor Farm, Hill Deverill, Wiltshire at 2.10 am. The crew Unteroffiziers (Corporal) R. Detering and J. Agten baled out injured; W. Kemper baled out and was taken prisoner, but Unteroffizier H. Trauwald was killed.

Exactly one month later on the night of 24th June, while patrolling over the Bay of the Seine in France, he engaged another Junkers 88, which had been seeking out Allied shipping to attack and bomb. During the action, which took over 30 minutes of AI radar tracking, Eric Barwell finally destroyed the enemy machine.

He had taken off from Hurn at 10.20 pm under the control of Sopley G.C.I, and he was then handed over to F.D.T.13. After obtaining several contacts which turned out to be friendly aircraft, he was finally vectored on to a bogey (unidentified aircraft). Eric Barwell continues:

At 11.20 pm, we were at 8,000 feet and obtained a contact at 5 miles range and above. The target appeared to be slowly turning to port all the time and initial visual was obtained at 5,000 feet against the light of the northern sky. As I closed the range I noticed a bright light under the fuselage, which appeared to be occasionally signalling, but I did not see this light when I closed in to 700 yards, being slightly below and I identified the aircraft as a Junkers Ju88. At this time the enemy aircraft was heading south and taking moderately violent corkscrew evasive action. The target's speed was approximately 220 mph and height 12,000 feet. As I closed in to 350 yards, the dorsal gunner opened fire accurately and as I was silhouetted against the light sky, I fired two short bursts. I saw strikes immediately on the starboard side of his fuselage and engine. The enemy aircraft dived violently to starboard with flames coming from the starboard engine.

I dived after it and saw it go nearly vertically down into what was apparently a naval smoke screen laid at approximately 5 miles off the Ile de St. Marcouf. I almost immediately saw a vivid flash through the smoke followed by a glow, which gradually died down. The Mosquito received numerous other vectors on to bogies, several of which proved to be friendly and finally one, which developed into an apparent AI dogfight. The tactics of the target led the Mosquito crew to the conclusion that it was a fighter with the type of AI (radar) looking both backwards and forwards. The target executed very violent evasive action and appeared to be capable of turning at least as well as the Mosquito aircraft; Window was also seen. This took place just off Le Havre, the height varying from 6,000 to 10,000 feet. The Mosquito landed back at Hurn at 1.20 am. The Junkers Ju88 was claimed as destroyed.

Eric also recalls some of the problems they were experiencing while patrolling at night in France:

> The Germans were attacking and trying to get our people, but the unfortunate thing was that we had a squadron of Americans attached to us with the Northrop P-61 Black Widow night-fighter aircraft, which was a very fine aeroplane. The Americans had very good pilots, but the only thing was they hadn't crewed up with navigators for any length of time, and they were not very efficient at finding enemy aircraft. We became very frustrated because they kept missing the enemy aircraft they were chasing; we had to give them priority and they just didn't find them. This culminated really in one of the Americans chasing a German, losing him and the German sinking the ship which was our control centre. After that episode, we did not give the Americans priority in the air.
>
> The V1s were coming over quite a lot and we patrolled in the Straits of Dover area. Sometimes you could see the V1s quite a long way away at night from the flames coming from their funny engines. I saw one or two but couldn't get near them; I then suddenly got an idea of how to do it. When the next one came along I had the advantage of height and turned at the right sort of time. These things were going faster than the Mosquito could fly straight and level, so one had to have height advantage to get near to them. Having told my chaps that if you were going to attack a V1 you had to close one eye on firing, and that if you saw any bits flying off the thing you had to break away immediately. Then if it blew up, it wouldn't bring you down with it. Having told my chaps all this, I saw this V1 and got too excited. I didn't close one eye, started firing at it and was determined to get it down, which I did. It then blew up in front of me with a great 'Whoosh' and I was temporarily blinded, but managed to climb. I couldn't see any instruments, but was able to get control and landed with two pieces of shrapnel in the aircraft.

125 Squadron was operating from RAF Station, Middle Wallop during the period of the V1 'Doodlebug' raids. The 'Diver' report for Eric's destruction of the V1 on 10/11th August reads:

> Squadron Leader Barwell DFC left Middle Wallop at 22.25 hours on an Anti-Diver patrol. At 00.50 hours whilst patrolling 10 miles south of Beachy Head, approximately 10 Divers were seen. Pilot attacked one at 1,000 feet, on a course of 340 degrees. Speed 330

mph. A four-second burst was fired, closing from 800 to 500 feet. The Diver caught fire, debris fell off and whilst pilot was still firing, the Diver exploded and fell into the sea.

Eric adds:

> On 18th August 1944, I was posted to the Fighter Interception Unit to develop tactics against the V1 flying bomb. I had just got a squadron together under the auspices of FIU, formed using half Mustang and Hawker Tempest Mk V aircraft, when we heard that the army had overrun the launching sites on the French coast, so we were disbanded. On 19th September I was sent over to Headquarters 2nd Tactical Air Force in Brussels, Belgium. The job I was given was in the Operations Room; it was really a matter of laying on by day and by night, instructions to the various air force groups to attack targets passed up to us by the army. The 21st Army Group shared the headquarters with us, so there was fairly good liaison as the troops moved forward.
>
> We liaised with the Americans as well, because we had to know what was happening on both sides. Unfortunately the Americans were not always reliable and sometimes a bit trigger-happy. On one particular occasion I remember, I was told that an American Mustang or Thunderbolt aircraft had shot down a Mosquito, but they reported that it was wearing black crosses. The Mosquito pilot got away with it, but the navigator was killed.

On 4th April 1945, Eric was again posted, this time to Headquarters 148 Wing as Wing Commander Flying. But when the war in Europe finished in May, he was subsequently moved yet again in June to command the squadron he first started with five years earlier, No.264:

> I was made commanding officer of 264 Squadron just after the war on 28th June 1945, so it meant that I went into 264 Squadron as a Pilot Officer originally and then finally for a short time as its commanding officer. It was rather nice to return to the squadron, but there was virtually no one there I could remember. I had changed places with Wing Commander Ted Smith, who was very tired. He had been with the squadron all the way through just before the invasion at Normandy and he had done a very good job. This was on a German airfield at Rheine in late June 1945. At the end of August it was decided that 264 should be disbanded.

Eric Barwell left the Royal Air Force when he was demobilised on 3rd September 1945, almost six years to the day after he had joined the service. He then returned to work in his family business in Cambridgeshire. He had married in 1940 and two children, Diana and Philip, were born during the war, his second daughter, Sarah, being born in 1948. Eric now had time for hobbies, which included carpentry and caravanning holidays. Now at the age of 89, he has seven grandchildren and three great grandchildren, who are no doubt equally proud of their great grandfather and one of 'Churchill's Few.'

CHAPTER 8

THE KIWI ACE
Air Vice-Marshal William Vernon Crawford-Compton CB, CBE, DSO, DFC
1916–1988

During the Second World War, many Commonwealth countries rallied to the call to arms to help Britain in her hour of need, against the threat of Nazi invasion. One of these countries was New Zealand; many of her young men had seen the warning signs in the late 1930s, in a Europe that was feeling insecure with the expansion of Nazi ideals. Many young New Zealanders looked to the 'Mother Country' for adventure and escapism and to join the Royal Air Force was many a young man's dream. One such man was William Crawford-Compton. He would make his way to Britain and fulfil his ambition to join the RAF, and he would also become one of New Zealand's most decorated fighter pilots and an ace. Here is his story.

William Vernon Crawford-Compton was born on 2nd March 1915 in Invercargill, New Zealand, the son of William Gilbert Crawford-Compton who was a farmer landowner. As a youngster, Compton's main interest was the sea and yachting, but this later turned to flying. He was a keen worker and paid for his interests by working some of his free days manning a store in Waiuku. Compton was educated at the New Plymouth High School.

In 1938, Compton at the age of 22 was a handsome, tall dark-haired athletic-looking individual, with a great amount of charm. That same year, he was invited to become a crew member on the sailing ship named *Land's End*, an auxiliary-engined ketch, along with two other New Zealanders and a South African, who had planned to sail around the globe stopping at England along the way. He was determined that on reaching Britain he would apply to join the Royal Air Force.

They left Auckland, well stocked with provisions and fresh water and sailed for their first destination, which was Tonga. Here, they rested for a few days then set course for Suva, from here to New Caledonia, then on to the New Hebrides and British Solomon islands. But their great adventure was about to end when en route to Port Moresby, New Guinea, the ketch struck an unchartered reef, which broke the vessel's back. They frantically tried to save the ship, but to no avail. From the wreckage of the *Land's End* they began quickly to build a life raft and tried to gather as much food and belongings together as possible. Once the vessel had sunk, they reviewed their position. They had managed to salvage the following provisions: a few tins of turkey, two tins of bully beef, two tins of Bovril, one tin of biscuits, a tin of fruit salad and a bottle of whisky. One item of great importance they were unable to save was fresh water.

With the coming of the dawn, their spirits were raised however, when they sighted land about twenty miles away. They began to paddle their makeshift craft and had reached halfway about noon. It would take them until dusk finally to reach the shore. They had landed on Rousel Island. Unbeknown to the three shipwrecked survivors, the island was inhabited by a native tribe of head hunters, who fortunately were friendly to whites and spoke poor pidgin English. After spending a further six weeks on the island and finding out that the nearest white settlement was three days sailing, they managed to obtain a canoe after bargaining with the natives. On reaching the settlement, they met a trader who managed to get them passage aboard a sailing ship bound for Samari, New Guinea, over 200 miles away.

After such an experience, many people would have been quite happy to make their way back home, but not Bill Compton. While in Samari, he learned of a tramp steamer named the *Myrtlebank*, a four-thousand tonner, which would be sailing to Britain.

He and his South African colleague raced to the jetty where the ship was tied up and asked to speak with the captain of the vessel. Compton told the captain of their previous misfortune and of his intention of joining the Royal Air Force. The captain was sympathetic to their situation and took them on as crewmen; Compton was to work as a carpenter and his friend as an engineer. The voyage would be a long slow haul, stopping at Shanghai, Bali, Durban, Cape Town, Dakar, and after nearly a year at sea the ship finally reached England, docking at Liverpool on 6th September 1939.

The following morning, Compton packed his belongings, said farewell to the ship's company and caught a train for London. By the end of that day, William Crawford-Compton had enlisted into the RAF, with the rank of Aircraftsman AC2, RAF No. 905967.

His first six months were taken up with the necessary RAF square bashing routine of drill, sentry duty, peeling potatoes and washing dishes. He also served as a steward in the Officers' Mess at Duxford during this time. Compton then applied and was accepted for basic flying training and was sent to No.57 Operational Training Unit. His first posting to an operational squadron on 7th January 1941, was to No.603 City of Edinburgh, based at RAF Drem in Scotland. The squadron at that time were laden with new arrivals coming in from both operational training units and fighter training units, although 603 still retained some of the pilots who had fought during the Battle of Britain down at Hornchurch. Aces like Flying Officer Basil 'Stapme' Stapleton, Squadron Leader George Denholm and Pilot Officer Jack Stokoe were still there, but with the new intake of fresh pilots they were soon posted to other units. RAF Drem's aerodrome flight-path was very hard to judge when landing, especially with its hillside approach, and this caused many accidents amongst the inexperienced pilots. On 30th January, while returning from a practice flight, Compton misjudged his final approach and crashed on landing. Fortunately the aircraft was not too badly damaged, and Compton stepped out from the Spitfire unhurt.

The squadron then moved on 28th February to RAF Turnhouse. While here, Compton was admitted to Gogarburn Hospital on 7th March and was discharged on the 12th. Two days later on the 14th, he received news of his next posting; he was to pack his kit and travel down to RAF Driffield in Yorkshire. Consequently, on 1st March 1941, Sergeant Crawford-Compton arrived to join the newly established New Zealand fighter squadron No.485.

For the next six weeks, Compton and the rest of his fellow New Zealanders learned to fly as a unit, using old Spitfire Is and Mk IIs. The squadron's commander during this early period was Squadron Leader M.W.B. Knight, who was an experienced pilot and instructor, having joined the RAF a few years before the outbreak of war.

By 12th April, the squadron had been granted operational status and their first sorties were to carry out the rather mundane convoy patrols over the North Sea.

Harvey Nelson Sweetman, a New Zealander from Auckland, had joined the Royal New Zealand Air Force in April 1940. After finishing his operational training he was sent to the newly formed 485 Squadron. He clearly remembers those early days and Bill Compton:

> I was a fellow sergeant pilot with Bill Compton when 485 was formed in March 1941. Bill was an action man, aggressive, but also a damn good pilot. I flew on quite a number of sorties with him during this time, when the RAF was changing over from the defensive to the offensive. Formations and tactics were evolving to suit the offensive requirements, and these conditions suited Bill's talents as a fighter pilot. As a member of the squadron, he joined in when we were off duty; one of his party tricks was to display the chest scars he had gained with his reef encounter during his trip to reach England. He would give a lurid blow-by-blow account of the incident.

Compton was obviously delighted when news arrived on 23rd April 1941, that he had been granted a commission as a pilot officer.

The first recorded victory to the new squadron came on 3rd June 1941, when Squadron Leader Knight and three other pilots intercepted three Junkers Ju88s of 3/Kustenfliegergruppe 106, who were trying to bomb a shipping convoy. Knight was able to aim a burst of machine-gun fire at one of the bombers, which then started to go down. This was confirmed as destroyed by the crew of one of the ships below.

Towards the end of June, the squadron began to take part in offensive sweeps over northern France. They would fly south to RAF Leconfield then travel down to one of the many 11 Group airfields to join up with one of the Wings and take part in the sweep. Finally, with the offensive operations intensifying, 485 were given their marching orders and sent to Redhill on 1st July, which would become their new home.

On 21st September 1941, the squadron were given the job of top cover on Circus Operation 101 to Gosnay. The twelve aircraft led by Flight Lieutenant E.P. Wells took off from Redhill; and when five miles west of Douvres, they sighted a large number of enemy fighters. Crawford-Compton was flying as Blue 3 in B Flight and recalled the following engagement:

> I was flying with the squadron as Blue 3 in company with Blue 4

when I saw four Me109Fs dive on two Spitfires below and to one side of me. They pulled up in front of us about 250 to 300 yards away. I gave the fourth 109 a long burst of cannon and machine-gun fire, following which his cockpit hood and a panel flew off. He then climbed vertically, stalled, went on his back, spun and dived away. I did not follow him down, as there were other enemy aircraft close by, but in my opinion the enemy aircraft was probably destroyed.

The attack had taken place at 18,000 feet at 3.25 pm. Three other enemy aircraft had been destroyed, two by Flight Lieutenant Edward Wells and one by Pilot Officer G.H. Francis. They suffered one casualty, that of Pilot Officer Knight who failed to return, while another Spitfire crash-landed near Bagshot; the remaining ten aircraft landed back at base at 4.05 pm. Pilot Officer Crawford-Compton would add to his score on 13th October. At 12.35 pm, the squadron led this time by Squadron Leader Knight, took off once more from Redhill on Circus 108 as close escort for a raid to Arques. At 1.18 pm, the squadron encountered a small formation of Messerschmitt 109Fs at 12,000 feet over Cappelle Brouck. Crawford-Compton was again able to manoeuvre his aircraft and latch onto one of the enemy, as his following combat report records:

> I saw four Me109Fs dive to attack 452 Squadron. I dived down on the number 3 and just as I came within range the enemy aircraft turned away from me, giving me a fine quarter attack. I fired a short burst and the enemy aircraft straightened out. A fine stream of black smoke came from his engine and he made no further evasive action. I closed in to fifty yards and gave him another burst. He caught fire and spun down. This was witnessed by Pilot Officer Thomas and Sergeant McNeil.

Compton would give a more precise account of the engagement later:

> The squadron was acting as top cover to the bombers whose target was a ship on a canal near St Omer. As usual, the Australians were with us and when we were over France I saw four Me109s dive on them. The Germans continued their dive after the attack and came into position under us. I peeled off and let the first two Me109s go by and waited to attack the third. If I'd gone after the first the other three might have jumped me. This third Me109 turned nicely for me – I don't think he could have seen me and I gave him a short burst. He straightened out and a puff of smoke came from the tail. I think the pilot must have been killed, because he took no evasive action. I closed the range to fifty yards and as I fired another salvo with my cannons, the Messerschmitt burst into flames and broke up. I could see the cannon shells striking. When I finished the attack, I found myself alone. The New Zealand squadron was not in sight. I managed to find the Australians however, and flew under them and came back to England with them.

The Messerschmitt had been brought down by Crawford-Compton using only two bursts of fire – a one-second burst at 100 yards and a following two-second burst at 100-50 yards. Sergeant Griffith claimed one 109 damaged. All aircraft returned safely to Redhill at 2.10 pm.

On 6th November, he again claimed another enemy aircraft probably destroyed, when the squadron led by Squadron Leader Peel took off from Kenley, at 1.45 pm on a Channel escort to Calais-Cap Gris Nez. An hour later into the trip at 2.45 pm, between five and seven miles out from the French coast they sighted Me109s at 8,000 feet below. Compton dived down with Blue 4 on the fighters, but could not get within firing range. But as he climbed away he saw three more 109s. He then climbed into the sun and then turned on to the tail of the third Messerschmitt and on closing in, fired a 1½- second burst of cannon and machine-gun fire. Compton saw his bullets hit the front of the cockpit and around it. The aircraft then went into a violent flat spin and black smoke began to appear and increase as the aircraft went down. Compton watched the aircraft drop for over 5,000 feet, but the German pilot made no attempt to pull out. He was then attacked by two Me109Fs and had to evade them, which he did. The squadron pilots all returned unscathed at approximately 2.00 pm. Compton's 109 had been witnessed by Sergeant Kronfeld and Sergeant Griffith, while A Flight had reported seeing a machine spinning down and hitting the sea at that time and place.

Squadron Leader Douglas Brown became a sergeant pilot with 485 at the end of November 1941. He had arrived in England from New Zealand and after training at OTU Grangemouth had been sent initially to 92 Squadron at Hawkinge before moving to Kenley. Douglas was twenty-one years old at the time and remembers Bill Crawford-Compton well:

> I flew a number of operations with Bill Compton. He had only been recently commissioned and was very ambitious to make his future after the war in the RAF. He was relaxed, friendly and well respected among the other pilots in the squadron. My second operation with 485 was as arse-end Charlie, trying to keep up unsuccessfully. I reported seven aircraft above, which attacked the squadron. Bill chased a Me109 and claimed it as a probable and I, an Me 109 damaged. A cannon shell hit Bill, which penetrated just forward of the cockpit on the port side, but did not explode.

At the beginning of January 1942, the weather was exceedingly cold and snow covered most of the length of the country and flying was at a premium. During this lull in operations, members of the squadron would instead make sorties up to the various clubs and drinking dens, now popular with the RAF pilots.

Jack Rae was a Flight Sergeant with 485 during this time and he remembers one particular venture along with Bill Compton:

> At one session in a club named the Tartan Drive – a favourite downstairs bar hang-out of New Zealanders in London – the boys became convinced that for some reason the most attractive girls seemed to swoon towards the Polish pilots, leaving nothing for us. Bill Compton suddenly stood up, said 'to hell with this,' and

adopted a very heavy Polish accent and immediately whisked off the most attractive female in the room. Long afterwards, he insisted that it had worked for him many times over. How he managed to keep up the pretence we had no idea. We often wondered what the women thought of his shoulder flashes with the words 'New Zealand' emblazoned for the entire world to see. Perhaps they had their minds on things other than reading.

During the first six days of February 1942, 485 Squadron did not take to the air, due to bad weather conditions and snow and ice. But over the next few days the weather cleared and it was then that the Germans decided to launch 'Operation Cerberus' to try and attempt to sail three of their most valuable capital warships from the French port of Brest, up through the English Channel to the German port of Wilhelmshaven (see also page 118). The German ships were the *Scharnhorst, Gneisenau* and the *Prinz Eugen*. The Luftwaffe had been tasked with the enormous task of providing complete air cover over the ships on their journey through the Channel and beyond. At 10.00 am, on 12th February, the British were alerted to the situation, when an RAF fighter sighted the German naval formation steaming at high speed towards the Straits of Dover.

It was not until 1.20 pm, that 485 Squadron was notified and began to take off from Kenley to intercept the Germans and provide escort for Bristol Beaufort torpedo bombers who were to attack the German ships. Group Captain Beamish with Wing Commander Finlay-Boyd led the fourteen Spitfires of 485 and 452 Squadrons. They rendezvoused with 602 Squadron over Kenley at 1.25 pm. 602 was given top cover position. The arrangement of meeting the Beaufort bombers over Manston did not go according to plan and they were not seen, so the Wing proceeded to the target. Over the Channel, Group Captain Beamish saw six destroyers, two E Boats and the battle cruisers. 485 Squadron did not climb up with the other squadrons, but remained at 600 feet.

At this height they encountered the enemy fighter umbrella over the convoy. This consisted of numerous Messerschmitt Me109s and Focke-Wulf 190s and very soon combat was met. Pilot Officer Reg Grant destroyed one Me109F, while Pilot Officer Harvey Sweetman claimed a half share of a Me109E. Harvey Sweetman remembers that day, now over sixty years ago:

Perhaps the sortie I most readily recall was when the German battle fleet made their dash up the English Channel. Our squadron was involved, initially to escort a torpedo squadron's attack on the German fleet. The torpedo squadron did not make rendezvous and 485 Squadron continued on vector until it suddenly encountered the German fighter protection screen. The weather at the time was poor. Cloud base varied between five hundred and one thousand feet with patches of drizzle. It made manoeuvring for position difficult, and led to a confusing cat and mouse encounter. At times you were the attacker, or you were being attacked. All of our aircraft used up all their ammunition and we were fortunate to shoot down three Me109s without any flight losses. Bill Compton accounted for one of these aircraft. Bill was a popular squadron member and wherever he was, action seemed to follow.

Sweetman left 485 in March 1942 and joined 486 Squadron. He was awarded the DFC in June 1943 and later became a production test pilot for the Hawker Aircraft Company. He returned to operational flying with 486 Squadron as a flight commander during 1944, flying Hawker Typhoon and Tempest fighter-bomber aircraft. During the flying bomb campaign of the V1 rocket, which Hitler had launched against England beginning in mid-June 1944, Harvey Sweetman would destroy not less than eleven of these new terror weapons as they headed for Britain.

Flight Lieutenant Compton destroyed an Me109F and damaged another, five miles west of Ostend at 2.10 pm at a height of only 500 feet during the German's break out up through the Channel on 12th February. His combat report states:

> While flying as Blue 1, Newpin Squadron (call-sign), I was warned by Newpin leader of 109s passing below and to the starboard. I turned down on to them with my section and chased them to the French coast. I was able to get a shot at the No.4, and observed a large piece come off the port wing. As I broke away a thin trail of black smoke came from the enemy aircraft, which put its nose down and headed for the French coast. I broke away and orbited about 1/4 mile off the coast. I claim this enemy aircraft as damaged. We then saw another six enemy aircraft and went into attack. I had to break away when warned by Blue 3 of an enemy aircraft on my tail. We orbited again and observed three more 109Fs coming from the French coast. I was able to get on the tail of the No.3 aircraft and gave it a long burst at 300 to 400 yards range. I observed no apparent hits, but the German hit the beach about five miles west of Ostend. As I broke away from this attack, I saw a 109F hit the sea about half a mile off the coast shortly after an attack had been made by Blue 3 and 4 (Pilot Officer H.N. Sweetman and Pilot Officer D.T. Clouston).
>
> All together we made five attacks and it was apparent the enemy aircraft were trying to lead us across the coast. The light flak was very heavy. All the engagements were between 500 feet to 1,500 feet.

After all the hard fighting and flying over the last months, the 485 pilots were in buoyant mood, when on 10th March 1942, news was received that Flight Lieutenants G. Francis and Crawford-Compton had been awarded the Distinguished Flying Cross.

Compton led the squadron on 14th March on Circus 115 to target shipping at Le Havre, being airborne at 4.00 pm. During the raid, they attacked six German E boats, but did not encounter any enemy fighters. All aircraft returned safely back to Kenley at 5.55 pm. He led the squadron yet again on 26th March, leaving at 3.10 pm to rendezvous over Tangmere to act as escort for another bombing raid to Le Havre. The raid was successful and on the return journey, the squadron encountered enemy fighters. Compton claimed one Me109 destroyed and another half share on one other. Flight Lieutenant Crawford-Compton recorded:

> I had climbed to 2,000 feet above Newpin Squadron, when I observed two Me109Es below and in front of me. I dived and fired a four-second burst. The 109E fell away to starboard with black smoke coming from it and it dived into the sea about 200-300 yards east of Le Havre. The rest of the section witnessed this attack.
>
> We were then attacked from behind and Blue 3 and 4 had to break away. I then climbed back up to 3,000 feet and chased several more enemy aircraft, but was unable to close the range. I was then warned by Blue 2 of 109s diving at us and got out of the way. I was then diving on another enemy fighter when I noticed it was firing at a Spitfire coming head on. As they passed each other white smoke came from the 109E, which then turned inland. I was able to get on to its tail easily and fired cannon and machine gun at it from close range. It then caught fire and spun down, two miles inside the French coast near Fécamp. I was in turn attacked by a 109E and had great difficulty in shaking it off. I dived vertically down to sea level and at about three miles off the French coast, I came across a Boston bomber with its starboard engine stopped. I escorted it back to the English coast and pointed out Shoreham aerodrome to it. I then called up operations control and headed back to Kenley.

The Spitfire that Compton had seen attacking the 109 head on was being flown by Pilot Officer Evan Mackie also of 485, who shared the half-share claim with him. Compton's comment on the action was published in a newspaper report at that time and stated:

> I shared one with Mackie, who made a wizard head-on attack against a Hun. I saw them firing like blazes at each other, and then saw glycol streaming from the Hun after they had passed each other, so I gave the Hun a few seconds' burst. He went down in flames and crashed into the sea a quarter of a mile from the French coast.

Two days later on the 28th, the squadron flew in the Kenley Wing, along with other Wings from Biggin Hill, Hornchurch and Northolt on a large fighter Rodeo operation to patrol over the French coast from Cap Gris Nez to Gravelines. The operation was an all fighter affair, to try and draw up the Luftwaffe to do battle, and this it did.

The Kenley Wing was airborne at 5.00 pm, 485 led by the irrepressible Group Captain Victor Beamish DSO, DFC, AFC. 602 Squadron and 452 Australian Squadron was led by Squadron Leader 'Paddy' Finucane, the Irish ace. At an altitude of 20,000 feet, they crossed the French coast just south of Cap Gris Nez at 5.30 pm. Suddenly some forty to fifty enemy fighters were sighted at varying heights of between 15-20,000 feet in loose formations of twos and fours, mainly Focke-Wulfs and some Me109s. The enemy fighters were seen diving down on one of the outward bound Wings, in fact the 'Biggin Hill Boys.'

Group Captain Beamish turned the Kenley Wing sharply to the right to intercept the Germans and at once a series of individual combats ensued. Crawford-Compton leading Blue section latched on to one of the 190s:

> I turned on them with the rest of the squadron and came up behind the FW190s. As we came within range, the port FW190 turned away and I followed it getting in a three-second burst at about 50 yards range. I observed hits on the fuselage and wings and the enemy aircraft turned right over and dived vertically with smoke pouring from it. I kept on its tail from 17,000 feet to 2,000 feet, when I pulled out sharply and turned around. The aircraft was seen burning on the ground near Marquise. Pilot Officer Baker and Flying Officer Pattison saw my attack. Cine gun camera was used. Pilot Officer Palmer also claimed an FW190 probably destroyed.

Meanwhile other deadly combats were still taking place and Group Captain Beamish was fighting for his life. Five miles off Calais at 13,000 feet, he was suddenly attacked by a FW190. Flight Sergeant Liken warned Beamish over the R/T about the incoming enemy fighter and Flight Lieutenant Grant pulled his aircraft upwards to give the FW190 a two-second burst of fire from fifty yards, just as the German pilot opened up on the Group Captain. The 190 was seen to be hit with greyish blue smoke pouring from its engine and a large part of the left aileron had been blown off. But this had been just too late. Victor Beamish's aircraft had been hit in the underside of the fuselage and the Spitfire's nose was down. He proceeded to fly out over the French coast at 13,000 feet, his aircraft now trailing a small amount of smoke. He was attacked again by another FW190, but Flight Lieutenant Grant who had followed Beamish out, counter-attacked the enemy with cannon fire from 150 yards. The FW190 shuddered under the strikes, continued its course briefly then suddenly blew up, showering debris around the sky.

Victor Beamish was heard by Squadron Leader Finucane over the R/T asking for a navigational fix to steer home. Someone advised him to steer 310 degrees, but Kenley Operations Room did not receive this call. Back at Kenley, the squadrons waited for the Group Captain's arrival. Beamish failed to return and was listed as missing. So ended the life of one of the Royal Air Force's most skilful and courageous fighter leaders of World War Two.

The Kenley Wing continued with sweeps and circus operations at the beginning of April, and on the 4th was involved with Circus 119. Compton was again flying this day as eleven aircraft of 485 took off at 9.45 am together with twelve Spitfires of 602 Squadron and twelve of 457 RAAF Squadron. Squadron Leader E.P Wells DFC led the formation. Over Chatham, Kent, the Wing rendezvoused with twelve Boston light-bombers and headed out across the Channel. Enemy flak began to fill the sky, just after crossing the French coast. The Bostons dropped their bomb load on the target at Aire near St Omer and had begun to turn for home, when they were attacked by some forty German fighters coming in from above and below. Compton, who was flying as Blue 1, saw one FW190 dive past him to attack the bombers. As the FW190 broke upwards to the left, Compton was able to fire off a three-second burst. He observed strikes on the wings and fuselage and also noticed what appeared to be part of a metal panel fall away. The enemy fighter then dived out of range. Compton was then warned by his No.2 of a FW190 on his tail; so he broke off his attack and managed to evade the German aircraft.

Afterwards they resumed escorting the bombers back to England; two Bostons were each seen to be flying on one engine, but all returned safely. No.485 unfortunately lost two pilots; both Pilot Officer T. Fox and Pilot Officer F. Chandler failed to return and were last seen in the target area going down smoking in a gradual dive. Three FW190s had been claimed damaged during the encounter, one each by Compton, Pilot Officer McNeil and Sergeant Brown.

On 23rd April 1942, Compton was promoted to the rank of Flying Officer. The very next day, the 24th, the squadron claimed three Focke-Wulf 190s shot down near Hesdin at 5.45 pm. Once again Compton added to his score sheet. Group Captain Edward Preston Wells, then squadron leader, remembers:

> We were flying at 18,000 feet just inside the French coast, when we saw the Focke-Wulfs coming up towards us from Abbeville. We turned out of the sun, and took them by surprise. I opened fire and saw my target turn slowly in a haphazard way and go down in a spiral. It crashed in a ploughed field and disappeared in a mass of flames. The other successful pilots were Crawford-Compton, whose victim went in spinning down in flames, and Flight Lieutenant J.R.C. Kilian, who raked his target with cannon fire.

Towards the end of April 1942, Compton had to make a forced landing in his Spitfire. As he came into Kenley, his aircraft's engine backfired several times and the engine cut out. He landed heavily, short of the runway in a field, suffering a broken wrist and a few minor cuts and bruises, and was taken off operational flying for several weeks to recover. Unfortunately, at this time he was hoping to have been given the opportunity to take up the vacant position of Squadron Leader of 485, which had been made vacant by Squadron Leader E.P.Wells's promotion to a wing leader. But this was not to be, and the position was filled by Flight Lieutenant R.J.C. Grant.

King George VI visited RAF Kenley on 30th April, and was shown around 485 Squadron's dispersal area. Here he talked to various pilots including 'Hawkeye' Wells, Sergeants Griffiths and Robson who had just returned from an operation and also Bill Compton. The King enquired about Compton's wrist and how he had sustained his injury.

Bill Compton was then posted from 485 Squadron to join No. 611 'West Lancashire' Squadron on 22nd June as a flight commander, still based at Kenley. After being with the squadron for about a month, Compton was posted on attachment to 111 Squadron on 27th July for three days, to advise on tactics and operational procedure as this squadron was going to operate from Kenley. He returned to his own squadron on 31st July.

On 19th August 1942, the combined services were in action against the German defences at Dieppe. Flight Lieutenant Crawford-Compton was

leading Blue section of 611 Squadron on an early morning patrol west of
Dieppe at around 6.00 am, when at 6,000 feet they were suddenly bounced by
enemy fighters from out of the sun from the port beam. One of the Focke-
Wulf aircraft pulled up while another flew straight on. Compton attacked the
second aircraft and saw his cannon fire strike on the enemy's engine and
around the cockpit. Suddenly a cowling flew off the port side of the engine
and as it came away black smoke began pouring from the engine. The enemy
aircraft then turned inland, but was not seen to crash. The attack had taken
place just two miles west of Dieppe. Unfortunately the section suffered one
loss, that of French Flight Sergeant Andre Paul Francois Vilboux whose
Spitfire BS179 was seen going down into the sea. Compton claimed the
FW190 as damaged, as did Lieutenant Manak who attacked another FW190.
Squadron Leader D.H. Wakins was more effective and claimed his 190
destroyed.

611 would fly five sorties that day over Dieppe. On the third trip, while
flying at 23,000 feet, Crawford-Compton, Pilot Officer Prince Emanuel
Galitzine and Pilot Officer A.H. Friday were again bounced by Focke-Wulf
190s, but fortunately none of them were hit. The squadron was again busy on
24th August, when they were detailed to act as cover for Circus operation
No.208, on a bombing raid against Le Trait during the late afternoon. Flight
Lieutenant Crawford-Compton was leading Blue section of A Flight and his
report of the raid relates what happened next:

While leading Blue section of 611 Squadron, I was flying at 26,000
feet behind the bombers on their way out from the bombing of Le
Trait. When west of Fauville, I saw three Focke-Wulf 190s below
me and climbing up to the bombers, flying north on my port side. I
turned behind them, warned my section and came up underneath the
port FW190. I started firing at about 300 yards and kept on until I
had to break away to avoid a collision. During this time, I observed
strikes under the fuselage and flames appeared underneath the front
cowling and spread along the enemy's fuselage. The enemy aircraft
veered to port and dived slightly away.

The remaining two FW190s broke to the right and were joined
by two more, which I had not seen approaching. All four then
attacked me. By this time I was separated from Blue section and I
endeavoured to work my way to the coast. I tried doing steep
climbing turns, but as they had the advantage of height, they were
able to take their time in attacking me. I went into an aileron turn
using lots of rudder and was chased about 30 or 40 miles across the
Channel. The FW190s were using self-destroying ammunition,
which was bursting in front of and around me. As the aircraft I had
attacked was well on fire I claimed it as destroyed. The time of the
attack was 4.30 pm.

Again leading 611 Squadron on 6th September, Compton led them on Circus
215 to escort American B17 Flying Fortresses on a raid to Meaulte. The
squadron flying above and to one side had just crossed the French coast, when
the alarm sounded that six FW190s had been sighted diving down towards the

B17s. Compton led 611 down on to the enemy fighters below, got on to the tail of one and proceeded to open fire at a range of 200 yards. He immediately saw pieces of the enemy aircraft fall away as his machine-gun and cannon fire began to hit home. His closing speed was so fast that he had to break away violently to avoid ramming the enemy machine.

Pilot Officer Sims, Compton's No.2, saw the German turn away smoking. They both then reformed to take up position to cover the bombers. As they approached the French coast on the way out, Compton again sighted three more 190s west of their own position and at the same height. He manoeuvred his aircraft and climbed steeply and got up sun of the Germans. Followed by his No.2, he dived on the unsuspecting enemy. Compton picked out the 190 on the port side of his position and fired a two-second burst from 150 yards. His cannon strikes hit around the cockpit and engine area and at once black smoke billowed from the German fighter, which turned on to its side and went down back into France. Both Spitfires then broke away and climbed out over the coast and back to Blighty. The first engagement had taken place at 5.40 pm between Cayeux and Oisemont, the second five minutes later a few miles inland from Berck. Both German fighters were claimed as damaged.

Compton claimed yet another Focke-Wulf 190 as damaged on 16th September, while leading Blue section who were at the time climbing west 10-15 miles inside Le Tréport. At 12.10 pm, he sighted two FW190s at 27,000 feet flying southwest of their position; he then turned the section onto them. Compton was able to get two two-second bursts on the second FW190, and saw hits to its port wing and rudder, before it escaped inland.

611's operations from Kenley finally came to an end, when the squadron moved to operate as part of the Biggin Hill Wing in September 1942. Compton's mounting score was again added to, on 2nd October that year, while leading Blue section of 611 on Circus Operation 221. His general report of the mission reads:

> While leading Blue section, 611 Squadron, I was weaving 2,000 feet above the rear section of bombers when I saw an FW190 break upwards after attacking the bombers. He did not see me and was just about to attack again when I opened fire at about 150 yards, closing to 100 yards. I was firing from dead astern. I saw strikes behind and around the cockpit. The enemy aircraft turned on its back to dive away, and I fired again from 100 yards. The enemy aircraft turned upright again and started to pull out of its dive and began to spin. I circled and watched it go down from 22,000 feet until it was lost in the haze. During this time it made no effort to recover; I consider the pilot was dead or badly wounded and that the enemy aircraft was definitely destroyed.

Compton's action took place at 25,000 feet just east of Crécy-en-Ponthieu forest at 3.35 pm. No.611 was again in action on 27th October, when they took part in Rodeo Operation 103. During the mission, the squadron led by Compton sighted a formation of FW190s at 5.08 pm, five miles northeast of Cap Gris Nez at 15,000 feet, diving from north to south. Compton turned his section around and fired at the No.4 of the enemy formation. Firing a four-second burst, the German aircraft's tail unit began to come away and white smoke began to trail away behind. Compton fired off another burst, by which time the white smoke had turned to black and in an instant the aircraft dived away steeply. Compton was unable to follow the enemy aircraft's demise, as he too had to break away violently when he sighted a German diving on him from behind. Sergeant A. Lissette who was flying as Compton's Red 2 witnessed the 190 as it went down. Compton claimed the German as damaged.

He damaged yet another FW190 on 8th November, while escorting bombers on Circus 235. At 12.35 pm, while over the Gravelines area, he attacked one of four German aircraft at 23,000 feet. After his attack the enemy aircraft dived away severely damaged near the main wing root. Whether it would have made it back to base is debatable.

The following day, Compton was more successful and was definitely able to claim a Focke-Wulf destroyed. When leading a section on Rodeo 109, Compton had just turned back into France having been told over the R/T that enemy aircraft had been sighted approaching from St Omer. Suddenly, Compton saw eight FW190s, at 4,000 feet below his section. He informed his men and led them down in a diving attack. The German aircraft broke in all directions and Compton singled out the No.2 aircraft of the enemy formation. He fired a burst of cannon and machine-gun fire at which the German aircraft's elevators and part of the rudder broke away. The aircraft turned on its back for 4-5 seconds then dived vertically into the ground. Fortunately, the German pilot vacated his machine and baled out at 14,000 feet.

Compton's final aircraft claim in what had been one hell of a busy period of air operations in 1942, came on 6th December whilst he was leading the squadron as top cover to bombers on Circus 241. His final report for that year reads:

> We were flying above and behind the last box formation of bombers, when I saw an FW190 on the starboard side of the bombers at the same height. I dived underneath him and came up from below, firing a short burst from about 150 yards. The cowlings on the underside of the engine and pieces of the engine came away. The propeller of the enemy aircraft stopped and it dived vertically into a layer of cloud that was at 3-5,000 feet. This attack was seen by the rest of the section and the stopped propeller by Sergeant Walmsley and myself.

The engagement had taken place at 12.20 pm, ten miles south of Dunkirk. Compton claimed the FW190 as probably destroyed. His achievements against the enemy were not to go unnoticed, and he was awarded a Bar to his Distinguished Flying Cross on 11th December 1942. Squadron Leader Bill Compton received notification while the squadron was at Predannack on 27th December 1942, of his posting to RAF Hornchurch as commanding officer of 64 Squadron. He duly arrived on 30th December and found that 64 was based at Hornchurch's satellite at RAF Fairlop. Lieutenant General Baron Michael Donnet, a Belgian fighter pilot who was a flight commander with 64 Squadron, remembers Crawford-Compton:

I first met William Crawford-Compton, 'Bill' as we used to call him, in August 1942. We were then about to carry out escort to the B17 Flying Fortresses on their first mission over the Continent. He was a flight commander of 611 Squadron; I was flying with 64 Squadron. He appeared to be a very keen and joyful pilot.

Our next meeting was in the middle of December. 64 Squadron, of which I was a flight commander, had been down at Predannack since the beginning of December. We had been carrying out low-level fighter operations over the Atlantic. These patrols using four aircraft were called 'Instep' and were intended to intercept German seaplanes that were sitting in the sea waiting to attack Allied aircraft en route to North Africa.

Our squadron commander Colin Gray had been posted to North Africa as Wing Leader by the middle of December. I did deputize as CO until Bill Crawford-Compton arrived to take over, which he did with tact and a natural authority. It was not that easy to mix with our mob, in which there were many strong characters. The squadron had a fine reputation and many of the members had been with it for more than a year.

Everyone adopted the new commanding officer who was a great sportsman; he made us play rugby, the New Zealand national game, and he also made us run around the perimeter track of the airfield. When we returned to the Hornchurch sector and occupied Fairlop, we were on our own, which made us appreciate our commanding officer still more. He was a fine leader in the air with a good sense of tactics. On the ground, he got to know the ground personnel and took time to observe their work.

As we were close to London, we did on occasions when released from operations, go up as a whole squadron. This improved the 'esprit de corps' very much.

Compton led 64 Squadron on a Rodeo mission on the afternoon of 20th January 1943. The squadron were brought smartly to readiness at 12.30 pm in the middle of lunch that day. At 3.55 pm the pilots went off to meet up with 122 and 350 Squadrons, which had already left. A course was set for Manston at zero feet out to Cap Gris Nez, where they would patrol starting at 13,000 feet. Between there and Dunkirk the pilots were about to dive and attack a German 'R' boat about four miles off Calais, when seven Focke-Wulf 190s were spotted coming from Cap Gris Nez at 7,000 feet. Compton had been informed by Operations Control to be on the look out for a small formation of enemy fighters that had been picked up by radar. At 4.45 pm, just three miles northeast of Calais they sighted the enemy aircraft. What happened next is related in Compton's general report of the sortie:

While leading 64 Squadron, I was informed by Ops of two or three enemy aircraft over a ship off Calais. I dived down under a layer of cloud at about 7,000 feet and searched for the enemy aircraft for two or three minutes. I could not see them so I called up to say we would attack the ship. I had started to dive when I saw seven

FW190s about two miles away coming from Cap Gris Nez. I pulled up sharply and managed to get above and behind without being seen. I fired a very short burst at the No.4, but they went into cloud and I saw no hits. I was attacked and broke away.

One FW190 then closed in on my port and did not see me. I fired a second burst from slightly aside and below and saw hits on the fuselage and starboard wing root. I was using armour piercing incendiary which when they hit, left a streak of flame about 18 inches long. The enemy aircraft began smoking furiously and headed for the coast. I fired another short burst and saw more hits. The enemy aircraft caught fire and hit the water about 100 yards off shore, half-mile east of Calais. I broke away and experienced heavy flak from the shore and the ship. About two minutes after this, I saw another FW190 heading inland with grey smoke coming from it.

We came back to mid-Channel at zero feet and then climbed to cloud height.

As a result of the ensuing dogfight, Compton claimed the FW190 as destroyed, Flight Lieutenant Bob Poulton and Second Lieutenant Lindseth each claimed a damaged, while Flying Officer Mason and Sergeant Bilsland each fired bursts, but without being able to see positive results. The squadron came down at 5.25 pm after some rather tricky landings due to bad visibility. Compton's score now stood at 11 aircraft destroyed, along with 4 probable and 10 damaged.

64 Squadron were detailed to act as top cover for Circus 267 on 15th February 1943. Seven Spitfires took off at 3.00 pm and met up with 18 Liberators to escort them to bomb shipping at Dunkirk from an altitude of 20,000 feet. They were to look after the rear section of the formation, while 122 Squadron took the front.

One of the Liberators was hit by flak over the target and went in two miles out to sea, two of the crew baling out.

Compton positioned the squadron at 1,500 feet above and up-sun to the American bombers. He had already been informed that German fighters had been sighted in the vicinity and told to keep a sharp look out. At 4.00 pm, 10 miles off Dunkirk, the squadron sighted six FW190s below. Compton gave the order to dive on the enemy fighters, but the Germans dived away into the distance. The squadron then climbed back up to take up their position again, when Compton sighted three more FW190s climbing from below at 9 o'clock position to the squadron. He warned the rest of the squadron over the R/T and positioned them up-sun to the Germans. The enemy did not see the Spitfires and Compton was able to close to 100-150 yards before opening fire. He fired a short burst at the No.3 enemy aircraft, but his cannons did not work for some reason. His machine guns did work and he saw four strikes on the fuselage between the cockpit and the tail with the De Wilde ammunition. The enemy aircraft broke off and dived for the French coast. Charlie 1 (Flight Lieutenant Michael Donnet) attacked the No.2 German fighter and destroyed it. He had got on to an enemy straggler who had tried to escape by doing an upward barrel roll, but Donnet caught him when he was about to stall at the end of the second roll and shot him down into the sea, about 10 miles off Dunkirk. Flying Officer

Raimund Sanders Draper had also got into action and had fired short bursts, but with no results. The squadron landed back at Fairlop at 4.30 pm.

On 8th March, Compton claimed two Focke-Wulfs destroyed in one action; when the Hornchurch Wing went on Ramrod No.40, supporting the Americans on another raid over northern France. It was a fine and frosty morning with ground haze, as the pilots assembled to get ready for the day's operation. That morning an unexploded German 250lb bomb which had landed near the Officers' Mess, was lifted without misadventure and to every one's relief. The squadron took off at 1.05 pm to meet up with the Liberator bombers at Beachy Head at 23,000 feet and then east to Rouen. Soon after crossing the French coast east of St Valéry-en-Caux, the bombers were attacked by 10 FW190s from head on.

Bill Compton recalls:

> While leading Sateen Squadron (64 Squadron's call-sign), we had just crossed over the coast of France, when at 2.05 pm over the Cleres area, we saw about ten plus FW190s at nine o'clock. They turned away from the bombers and when about a couple of miles in front, they turned about for a head-on attack on them. I immediately told the squadron to get down in front of the bombers and was slightly above and in front, when the Germans started to come in. I fired a short one-second burst at the third FW190 and saw a large flash in his engine. He passed away very close underneath me, broke left and went down in flames. This was seen by Charlie 1. We got back into position in front of the bombers, when another nine FW190s attacked. I took the second from last enemy aircraft head on and fired a burst of one and half seconds and saw hits in front of his cockpit. The enemy aircraft passed under me and I broke sharp left. About 15 seconds later, a parachute opened up at about 5/7,000 feet below. My No.2, Flying Officer Sanders Draper, a few seconds later saw this also. The Germans attempted three to four more head-on attacks, but as soon as the squadron turned towards them they veered off. The job was rather big for the few aircraft we had, and absolutely no help was given by the top cover squadron.

Squadron Leader Compton received news on 27th March 1943, of his posting to No.11 Group Headquarters as Gunnery Tactics Officer, but was only there briefly before returning to flying operations. Bill Compton was not the sort of man who felt comfortable behind a desk; his life revolved around flying and getting into where the action was.

The Hornchurch Wing was again in action on 15th July 1943, to take part in an afternoon operation, Rodeo 245. Compton was again ready to lead two squadrons, 129 and 222; but all didn't go according to plan, as Leslie Lunn, then a twenty-year-old sergeant pilot with 129, now remembers:

> Earlier that day Crawford-Compton had had the pilots together and told them that due to a series of mishaps, anyone who accidentally damaged an aircraft could in the future expect an immediate

posting. The squadrons were taking off in formation, 129 being behind Crawford-Compton, when suddenly he found himself confronted with a stationary aircraft immediately in front of him and with aircraft on each side of him, leaving him with nowhere to go. Crawford-Compton found he couldn't release the dinghy lead, so in his panic leapt out, managing to break the lead, though when he tried this later, he found this impossible.

Leslie Lunn was commissioned at Hornchurch in July 1943, leaving No.129 Squadron in August 1944. He finally left the RAF as a squadron leader in 1979, with an Air Force Cross awarded to him for his display work with the Vulcan aircraft.

Years later Bill Compton told his wife of this experience; Chloe Crawford-Compton recalls:

He told me how he was trying to jump out of his Spitfire, but couldn't undo his safety belt. He was trying with all his might and with panic setting in, he broke the webbing strap and got out just in time and laid down on the ground. Later, in the Officers' Mess that evening all the strongest and biggest chaps tried to break a similar strap, but they didn't make an impression on it at all.

Compton's leadership and tactics in providing escort cover to the American bomber squadrons during their daylight raids over Europe during this period was fully appreciated, when he was awarded the American Silver Star medal, conferred by the President Franklin D. Roosevelt. Compton had flown over 200 escort missions with the Americans.

On 21st July 1943, Squadron Leader Crawford-Compton became Wing Commander Flying and received the acting rank of wing commander.

At 10.30 am on 26th July, 26 Spitfire IXs of 129 and 222 Squadrons led by Compton, took off from Hornchurch as high cover to twelve Boston bombers who were detailed to attack Courtrai aerodrome on Ramrod mission 159. The Wing rendezvous was made with the bombers over Clacton at 10.48 am at 11,000 feet and they then proceeded to ten miles east of Dunkirk with the Hornchurch Wing at 21-24,000 feet. Once in the Courtrai area, the bombers appeared to have difficulty in finding the target, and it was during this period that a mixed formation of between 30 and 40 Focke-Wulf 190s and Messerschmitt 109s were seen climbing from the south towards the bombers.

While 222 Squadron was ordered to remain above as cover, Compton led 129 down to attack the enemy fighters, but when within 5-600 yards range, the Germans dived away to the north and south. Compton however, saw an Me109 collide with another aircraft, believed to be another 109, both going down interlocked, with pieces falling off. These were claimed as destroyed, due to the attack of the Wing. The Wing returned safely back to base at 12.15 pm. One enemy aircraft each was later credited to 129 Squadron and 222.

No.129 Squadron were given the task of providing withdrawal cover to Marauder bombers on 29th July. Led by Compton, they took off from Hornchurch at 7.48 am to meet up with the bombers. George Mason was a flight lieutenant with 129 and remembers the following incident that took place that morning:

> We had taken off from base and were told to land at Manston.
> Unfortunately I landed my Spitfire quite heavily on to the airfield,
> knocking off a complete oleo leg and wheel. This bounced into my
> No.2 and No.3's aircraft causing them some minor damage.
> Suddenly Bill Compton came running over and grabbed my escape
> knife from my flying boot and then proceeded to slash the tyre of
> my other wheel to ribbons. He then said, 'You landed with a burst
> tyre, no wonder the thing came apart.' I thought he had gone mad,
> but he later explained that Group Headquarters were having a blitz
> on pilots who were responsible for flying accidents, and if I was
> held to blame, I would probably be given a non-operational job.
> Bill was a tough, aggressive, but popular squadron and wing leader.

The award of the Distinguished Service Order (DSO) was bestowed on
Compton on 24th September 1943. That October, Compton along with Wing
Commander Raymond Hiley Harries DSO, DFC, who was commanding the
Tangmere Wing, was sent to the United States on a tour to lecture on tactics.
While there they gave talks to various audiences including universities and
rotary clubs. Compton was interviewed over the wireless no less than 13 times
and three times on inter-state talk-ins, where the listener could ask him
questions. They returned to Britain in April 1944.

On 30th April 1944, Compton was posted to No.145 'Cross of Lorraine'
Wing at Merston aerodrome, to take over as Wing Leader after the unfortunate
death of Wing Commander Roy Maples in an aircraft collision with a French
pilot of 329 Squadron. In overall command of the Wing was Sailor Malan.
The Wing was an all-French affair, with 329, 340, and 341 Squadrons
equipped with Spitfire IXBs.

With the planned invasion of Normandy fast approaching, fighter and
bomber operations over northern France were increased to attack targets away
from the proposed invasion area and divert German attention.

On the morning of 6th June 1944, the Allies landed at Normandy. With
troops now gaining a foothold in France, the quest to free Europe from Nazi
occupation had begun. The very next day, Bill Compton shot down his first
and only German bomber, just inside the French coast. He had sighted a
formation of five Junkers Ju88s flying towards the bridgehead. The enemy
aircraft were using cloud cover to protect their run in, but Compton had
spotted them and dived to attack. He picked out one of the bombers and fired
two short bursts of cannon and machine gun; in return the German rear gunner
managed to put several bullets into Compton's Spitfire's wings. The bomber
was seen going down and crashed west of Caen, sending up a large column of
black smoke.

On 29th June, Compton led two squadrons of 145 Wing on a patrol. While
over the Beaumont-le-Roger area, the Wing spotted numerous Messerschmitt
and Focke-Wulf fighter aircraft taking off from the airfield at Evreux. The
Wing swept into attack and during the ensuing battle, six enemy aircraft were
shot down, Bill Compton accounting for two of them, a Me109 and a FW190.

Compton's final enemy claim of the war came on 9th July 1944, when flying Spitfire IXb NH590. He shot down and destroyed a Messerschmitt 109E, five miles north of Bernay. His outstanding achievement in air combat was notable, and his final score of enemy aircraft destroyed was recorded as 20 and 1 shared destroyed, 3 and 1 shared probable and 13 damaged.

With the Germans being pushed further and further back across France, Belgium and Holland, Compton and 145 Wing were constantly moving from airfield or landing strip. In November, while operating from Deurne airport, Antwerp, the Germans began launching V1 and V2 attacks against the City and port installations, in a vain attempt to halt the Allied supplies. Bill Crawford-Compton was caught out in the open on one such occasion. He was walking across the airport having just been supplied with a brand new uniform. He was about halfway across, when he heard a V1 flying bomb cut its engine overhead. He was overheard to shout out; 'Oh my God, my new uniform!' and then he immediately dropped down on his hands and toes in the wet muddy ground in the 'push up' position, trying to keep his uniform from becoming dirty. The V1 exploded further away than he predicted; he got up and continued on his way.

On New Year's Day, 1st January 1945, the German Luftwaffe launched its final assault of the war against the Allies (see also page 132). The bold, but desperate operation to try and knock out the RAF and American air forces in a surprise attack on their airfields was codenamed Bodenplatte. Early that morning, the Luftwaffe fighters and bombers swooped in over the Allied bases, catching them by complete surprise. Wing Commander Crawford-Compton was also up early when the Germans struck. He was driving around the perimeter track in his car, when he suddenly noticed two aircraft flying very low. Suddenly bright flashes began to flicker along their wings. Compton left his car abruptly and while the car continued to roll along at 10 mph, he lay flat in the gutter, watching enemy cannon shells churn up the tarmac, just twelve yards from him. The German aim had been poor, not only had they missed him and the car, but also two large petrol tanks nearby. It was a lucky escape.

That same month, on 26th January, he was awarded a Bar to the Distinguished Service Order he had received in 1942. During May, he was posted to undertake training as Wing Commander Planning with No.11 Group Headquarters. Lieutenant General Baron Michael Donnet recalls:

> In 1945, I was a wing leader of an RAF Mustang Wing at Bentwaters. Our operations at that time were mainly to escort RAF bombers by day under the control of 11 Group. Bill Crawford-Compton was one of the operation planners. I often got in touch with him, discussing some of the offensive flights in which we were involved. The plans were sound and we managed to carry them out without problems.

With the end of hostilities against the Germans in May 1945 and then against the Japanese in August the same year, William Crawford-Compton had established a new record for Fighter Command; he had flown 800 operational hours on Spitfires. Compton remained resolute however that his future career would be in a peacetime Royal Air Force.

His wishes of staying in the service were confirmed when on 1st September

1945, he was granted a permanent commission with the rank of squadron leader in the general duties (pilot) branch of the Royal Air Force. He then undertook a six-month Staff College course at Haifa. Following the completion of this course, he was sent to Air Command Staff Headquarters in the Middle East, stationed at Cairo. He remained there until 1947, when he returned to the United Kingdom and joined the Air Ministry for policy duties. It was during this time that Bill Compton met and fell in love with and married Chloe Clifford-Brown. She remembers how they met:

> I first met Bill in 1947; he was a wing commander by this stage. My brother was in the RAF and Bill came to stay; and that's how we met and were introduced to one another. We went out together for quite a while until we got married on 19th August 1949 at St Mary's Church, Yappon in Sussex. He had a job at the Air Ministry for three months and we lived in a little flat in London at this time, prior to him becoming the Air Attaché in Oslo, Norway in 1950. He was very good at all sports; he was tremendous, he played rugby, tennis, golf and he was also a very good skier. In Norway, he did quite a lot of skiing; he went in for the biathlon event against the whole of the Norwegian Army and Air Force and he won it, which absolutely amazed them. It was headline news all over the front of their papers titled *'British Air Attaché beats the whole of Norway'*. We had an enormous amount of fun out there; we hadn't been married long and we had a very nice house, with a cook and a maid, and new motorcar. Our first child, a daughter who we named Charlotte, was born while we were in Norway; she was born on 15th February 1952.

He was awarded the Legion of Honour and Croix de Guerre with Palme on 17th January 1949. On 1st January 1955, Compton was promoted to Group Captain and given command of RAF Station Bruggen, Germany. Also during this period, he was appointed to command the Western Fighter Sector in Britain and when the Suez crisis erupted with Egypt, he commanded No.215 Wing at the El Gamil airfield, Port Said, following the sea-borne invasion by British forces. Chloe Crawford-Compton again recalls:

> He was sent to 2nd Tactical Air Force at RAF Bruggen, where he became station commander. It was a new station; there was nothing much there when we arrived and only a few personnel. But it started up alright; the air officer commander Ronnie Lees was a friend of ours and he helped a lot, as did his wife whom I'd known when I was at school. We had two wonderful years in Germany; he loved commanding the station and he made a success of it. As you can imagine, socially it was tremendous. During the Suez crisis, he became the senior officer there. He chose a chap called Mike Le Barre to be his Wing Commander Flying.

In January 1957, Compton was given the appointment of instructor at the School of Land-Air Warfare at Old Sarum in Wiltshire. On 13th June 1957, he was awarded the Commander of the Order of the British Empire (CBE) by Her Majesty the Queen at Buckingham Palace. It was while still at Old Sarum that his second daughter was born; Sara Crawford-Compton was delivered at the Military Hospital at Didworth, Salisbury on 22nd July 1957. In 1959, he became Senior Air Officer, No.11 Group of Training Command at Martlesham Heath in East Suffolk. Chloe Crawford-Compton remembers their time there:

> He was a tremendous marksman and he loved shooting, and we always had loads of pheasants and other game. I used to go on a lot of his visits and one day he went to the command's catering school. It was here he learned how to bone a complete pheasant game bird and prepare it to be cooked. He was terribly proud of accomplishing this, but he stuffed it so full that it burst.

Compton attained the rank of Air Commodore on 1st July 1960, and was on the staff of the Imperial Defence College in 1961. Between 1962-63, he became Air Officer in Charge of Administration, Near East Air Force. On 1st July 1963, he was promoted to Air Vice-Marshal. His final award for his outstanding career and duties undertaken with the Royal Air Force was gazetted on 1st January 1965 in the New Year's honours list, when William Crawford-Compton was awarded the Companion of the Order of the Bath (CB). In 1967, he captained the RAF Skiing Team made up of men half his age.

Crawford-Compton finally retired after thirty-nine years service in the Royal Air Force on 1st November 1968. His first marriage ended in divorce in 1978 and he later remarried to Delores Pearl Goodhew, making him the stepfather of the British Olympic gold medal winner Duncan Goodhew. In 1980 however, he felt unable to attend the controversial Moscow Olympic Games in which his stepson was competing; he had disagreed with Goodhew's decision to take part despite the recent Russian invasion of Afghanistan.

William Crawford-Compton passed away suddenly on 2nd January 1988 aged 72 years. The memory of this great New Zealand fighter pilot who worked his way through the RAF ranks and fought for England, 'The Mother Country,' during its time of greatest need is remembered in Hornchurch. A lasting memorial was the naming of a road 'Crawford-Compton Close' on the Airfield Estate which was once RAF Hornchurch.

APPENDIX A

Enemy Aircraft Claims of Squadron Leader Peter Brown

1940

Date		Aircraft		Code	Location	Squadron
21st Aug	$^1/_2$	Do17 (a)	Spitfire II	P7304	Maplethorpe	No. 611 Sqdn
15th Sept	$^1/_3$	He111 (b)	,,	P7283	Tunbridge Wells	,,
30th Sept		Do215 damaged	,,	A	Dungeness	No. 41 Sqdn
20th Oct		Bf109E (c)	,,	B	West Malling	,,
25th Oct		Bf109E (d)	,,	F	S.W. Ashford	,,

TOTAL: 2 destroyed, 1 shared destroyed, $^1/_3$ share destroyed, and 1 damaged.

(a) Dornier 17Z of 2/KG2.

(b) Possibly Heinkel 111 of II/KG53, force-landed at West Malling aerodrome.

(c) Bf109E of 5/JG52 Feldwebel Bielmaier.

(d) Bf109E of 5/JG54 Oberleutnant Schypek.

Official Stalag Luft III Document on William 'Tex' Ash

Personalkarte I: Personelle Angaben

Kriegsgefangenen-Stammlager: Stalag Luft 3

Beschriftung der Erkennungsmarke

Nr.

Lager:

Name:

Vorname:

Geburtstag und -ort:

Religion:

Vorname des Vaters:

Familienname der Mutter:

Staatsangehörigkeit:

Dienstgrad:

Truppenteil: Kom. usw.:

Zivilberuf: Berufs-Gr.:

Matrikel Nr. (Stammrolle des Heimatstaates):

Gefangennahme (Ort und Datum):

Ob gesund, krank, verwundet eingeliefert:

Des Kriegsgefangenen

Lichtbild

Nähere Personalbeschreibung

Grösse — Haarfarbe

Besondere Kennzeichen:

Fingerabdruck

Name und Anschrift der zu benachrichtigenden Person in der Heimat des Kriegsgefangenen

Beschriftung der Erkennungsmarke Nr. Lager: Name:

Bemerkungen:

Personalbeschreibung

Figur:

Größe:

Alter:

Gesichtsform:

Gesichtsfarbe:

Schädelform:

Augen:

Gebiß:

Haare:

Bart:

Gewicht: kg

Besondere Merkmale:

Deutsche Sprachkenntnisse:

Beschriftung der Erkennung Nr.		Charaktereigenschaften u. a.	Besondere Fähigkeiten	Sprachkenntnisse	Führung

Lager:

	Datum	Grund der Bestrafung	Strafmass	Verbüsst. Datum
Strafen im Kr.-Gef.-Lager	12.9.42	Versteckt gehalten zw. Fluchtversuch	14 Tg. Stubenarrest	11.9. - 15.9.42
	26.9.42	Fluchtversuch 23.9.	10 " gesch. ---	26.9. - 6.10.42
	24.11.42	Fluchtversuch	14 " Stubenarrest	24.11. - 7.12.42
	15.3.43	Fluchtversuch	11 " gesch. -o-	10.3. - 20.3.43
		Namenstausch		28.9. - 1.10.43 = verb

Schutzimpfungen während der Gefangenschaft gegen | | | Erkrankungen

Pocken	Sonstige Impfungen (Ty. Paraty. Ruhr, Cholera usw.)		Krankheit	Revier		Lazarett–Krankenhaus	
				vom	bis	vom	bis
am	am	am					
Erfolg	gegen	gegen					
am	am	am					
Erfolg	gegen	gegen					
am	am	am					
Erfolg	gegen	gegen					
	am	am					
	gegen	gegen					

	Datum	Grund der Versetzung	Neues Kr. Gef.-Lager		Datum	Grund der Versetzung	Neues Kr.-Gef.-Lager
Versetzungen	18.5.42		Stalag Luft	Versetzungen			
	28.5.42		Stalag Luft 3				
	16.9.42		Oflag XXI B				
	1.3.43		Stalag Luft 3				
			o. Kommando				

Kommandos.

Datum	Art des Kommandos	Rückkehrdatum
16.9.42		
3.11.42		7 Tg. Stubenarrest
25.9.43	(Stalag Luft 6)	6.10 - 28.10.43

APPENDIX C

Enemy Aircraft Claims of Flight Lieutenant Eric Lock

1940

Date		Aircraft	Spitfire	Serial	Location	Squadron
15th Aug		Bf110	Spitfire I	R6885	Bishop Auckland area	No. 41 Sqdn
5th Sept		Bf109E	„	N3162	West Malling-Ashford	„
		Bf109E probable	„	„	Kent	„
		Bf109E	„	„	Sheppey	„
	2	He111s (or Ju88s)	„	„	Sheppey	„
6th Sept		Ju88 (a)	„		20m behind Calais	„
9th Sept	2	Bf109Es	„	X4325	Maidstone-S. London	„
11th Sept		Ju88	„	R6610	Maidstone	„
		Bf110	„	„	Maidstone	„
14th Sept	2	Bf109Es	„	„	Hornchurch	„
15th Sept		Bf109E	„	X4409	London – France	„
		Do17	„	„	London – France	„
18th Sept		Bf109E probable	„	X4338	E. Kent	„
		Bf109E	„	„	Gravesend – Kent	„
		Bf109E probable	„	„	Gravesend – Kent	„
20th Sept		Bf109E	„	„	N.W. of Boulogne	„
		Hs126	„	„	N.W. of Boulogne	„
5th Oct		Bf109E	„	„	South of Maidstone	„
		Bf109E probable	„	„	South of Maidstone	„
		Bf109E probable	„	„	South of Dungeness	„
9th Oct		Bf109E	„	X4017	S.E. Kent	„
	2	Bf109Es probable	„	„	S.E. Kent	„
11th Oct		Bf109E	„	X4589	5m off Dungeness	„
20th Oct		Bf109E	„	„	Nr. Biggin Hill	„
25th Oct		Bf109E probable	Spitfire II	P7314	S.E. Biggin Hill	„
17th Nov	2	Bf109Es	„	P7554	outer Thames Estuary	„

1941

Date	Aircraft	Spitfire	Serial	Location	Squadron
6th July	Bf109F	Spitfire V	W3247	N.E. St. Omer	No. 611 Sqdn
8th July	Bf109E	„	W3309	St. Omer	„
14th July	Bf1109F	„		N.E. France	„

TOTAL: 26 destroyed, 8 probables.
(a) Ju88 F1 + DP, crashed at Evere, damaged.

APPENDIX D

Enemy Aircraft Claims of Squadron Leader Iain Hutchinson

1940

Date	Aircraft	Spitfire	Serial	Location	Squadron
31st Aug	Bf109E	Spitfire I		N. of Maidstone	No. 222 Sqdn
3rd Sept	Bf110 damaged	„		Rochford	„
„	Bf109E	„		Canterbury	„
4th Sept	Bf109E probable	„			„
11th Sept	He111 probable	„			„
14th Sept	Bf109E	„	X4265	Canterbury area	„

TOTAL: 3 destroyed, 2 probable, 1 damaged.

APPENDIX E

Enemy Aircraft Claims of Air Chief Marshal Sir Harry Broadhurst

1939

29th Nov		He111 (a)	Hurricane I	N2340	8m E. Alnwick	No.111 Sqdn

1940

20th May		Bf110 (b)	Hurricane	P2823	Arras	60 Wing

1941

25th Feb		Bf109	Spitfire		N. Gravelines –	Hornch. Wing
		Bf109 probable			Dunkirk Area	
5th Mar		Bf109 probable	Spitfire II	P7494	10m E. Le Touquet	
		Bf109 damaged	,,		,,	,,
17th June		Bf109	Spitfire		Cap Gris Nez	,,
		Bf109 damaged	,,		Dungeness – Gris Nez	,,
21st June		Bf109E	Spitfire Va		St. Omer	,,
		Bf109F	,,		Calais Marck airfield	,,
24th June	2	Bf109Es damaged	,,		Gravelines	,,
25th June		Bf109F probable	,,		,,	,,
		Bf109E probable	,,		,,	,,
3rd July		Bf109F	,,		Nr. Hazebrouk	,,
		Bf109E probable	,,		,,	,,
4th July	2	Bf109Es	,,		Béthune	,,
7th July	2	Bf109Es	Spitfire Vb		Gravelines area	,,
		Bf109E probable	,,		,,	,,
27th Sept		Bf109E	Spitfire		6m in land off Mardyck	,,
1st Oct		Bf109F damaged	,,		off Cap Gris Nez	,,

1942

12th Feb		Bf109F probable	Spitfire Vb		off Gravelines	,,
27th April		FW190 damaged	,,		St. Omer area	,,
		Bf109E damaged	,,		,,	,,
19th Aug		FW190	Spitfire IX	BR370	Channel-Dieppe	,,
	3	FW190s damaged	,,		,,	,,

TOTAL: 13 destroyed, 7 probables, 10 damaged.

(a) He111 of Stabstaffel KG26.

(b) Aircraft claimed on this date might have been a Dornier 17 of Stabstaffel ZG 26.

APPENDIX F

Enemy Aircraft Claims of Squadron Leader E.D. 'Dave' Glaser

1940

18th Aug	1/4	He111 probable (a)	Spitfire I	Z	S.W. Foulness	No. 65 Sqdn
22nd Aug		Bf109E probable	,,	E	off Dover	,,
24th Aug		Bf109E damaged	,,	E	Manston	,,

1942

21st June	1/2	Bf110	Spitfire Vb AD180			No. 234 Sqdn
25th July	1/2	Ju88	,,	AR382	10m N.W off	,,
					Lundy Island	,,

1943

3rd April	1/2	Ju88 damaged	Spitfire Vc EE644		25m E.S.E Sumburgh	,,

TOTAL: 2 x 1/2 shared destroyed, 1+ 1/4 probable, 1+ 1/2 damaged.
(a) Heinkel 111 of 2/KG1, crash-landed at Snargate, nr Dymchurch Kent.

APPENDIX G

Enemy Aircraft Claims of Wing Commander Eric Barwell DFC

1940

29th May		Bf109E	Defiant I	L7006	off coast N. Dunkirk	No. 264 Sqdn
,,	2	Ju87s	,,	,,	nr. Dunkirk	,,
31st May		Bf109E	,,	L6975	off Dunkirk	,,
,,		He111 (a)	,,	,,	,,	,,
24th Aug		Bf109E (b)	,,	N1576	Ramsgate	,,

1941

10/11th April	He111(c)	,,	N3307	Beachy Head	,,
,,	He111 probable (d)		,,	nr. Beachy Head	,,

1942

1/2nd July	Do217 damaged	Beaufighter II V8140	nr. Cardiff	No. 125 Sqdn

1944

23/24th April	Ju88 (e)	Mosquito XVII	HK355	4m S. Melksham	,,
24/25th June	Ju88	,,	,,	W. Isle de St. Marcouf	,,
10th Aug	V1	,,	VA-T	over sea	,,

TOTAL: 9 destroyed, 1 probable, 1 damaged, 1 V1.
(a) During this second sortie, a Defiant was hit and came down in the sea off Dover.
(b) This Bf109 was claimed as a He113 before being corrected.
(c) He111 1H+1D of 3/KG26.
(d) Likely to have been a He111 of 1/KG55 which was lost, and was believed already to have been attacked by a 604 Sqdn aircraft;
(e) Ju88 4D+FM of 4/KG30.
Air gunner on all the May 1940 victories was Pilot Officer J.E.M. Williams.
In August 1940 to April 1941 all victories were claimed with Sergeant Martin as gunner.
The 1944 claims were all made with Flight Lieutenant D.A. Haigh as radar operator.

APPENDIX H

Enemy Aircraft Claims of Air Vice-Marshal William Crawford-Compton

1941

Date		Claim	Spitfire / Serial	Location	Unit
21st Sept		Bf109F probable	Spitfire Vb AB788	5m W Desvres	No. 485 Sqdn
13th Oct		Bf109F	,, P87886	Cappelle Brouck	,,
6th Nov		Bf109F probable	,, W3774	Cap Gris Nez-Calais	,,

1942

Date		Claim	Spitfire / Serial	Location	Unit
12th Feb		Bf109E damaged	,, W3747	5m W. Ostend	,,
		Bf109E	,, ,,	,,	,,
26th Mar		Bf109E	,, ,,	1m W. Le Havre	,,
	1/2	Bf109F	,, ,,	Nr. Fécamp	,,
28th Mar		FW190	,, W3774	Marquise	,,
4th Apr		FW190 damaged	,, BM199	St. Omer	,,
24th Apr		FW190	,, BM234	Nr. Hesdin	,,
19th Aug		FW190 damaged	Spitfire IX BR632	2m W. Dieppe	No. 611 Sqdn
24th Aug		FW190	,, BR632	W. Fauville	,,
28th Aug		FW190	,, ,,	Amiens	,,
		FW190	,, ,,	Nr. Albert	,,
	1/4	FW190 probable	,, ,,	,,	,,
6th Sept	2	FW190s damaged	,, ,,	Cayeux-Berck	,,
16th Sept		FW190 damaged	,, ,,	Eu-Le Tréport	,,
2nd Oct		FW190 damaged	,, ,,	E. Forêt Crécy-en-Ponthieu	,,
27th Oct		FW190 damaged	,, BS435	5m NE Cap Gris Nez	,,
8th Nov		FW190 damaged	,, BR632	Gravelines	,,
9th Nov		FW190	,, ,,	Calais-Gris Nez	,,
6th Dec		FW190 probable	,, AB508	10m S. Dunkirk	,,

1943

Date		Claim	Spitfire / Serial	Location	Unit
20th Jan		FW190 damaged	,, BS227	3m N.E. Calais	No. 64 Sqdn
15th Feb		FW190 damaged	,, ,,	10m off Dunkirk	,,
8th Mar	2	FW190s	,, ,,	Cleres	,,
13th Mar		Bf109F damaged	,, ,,	E. Doullens	No. 122 Sqdn
27th June		Bf109	,, ,,	Audruicq	Hornch. Wing
19th Aug		Bf109G	,, ,,	Sluis area	,,
5th Sept		FW190	,, ,,	E. Dunkirk	,,
23rd Sept		FW190	,, ,,	N.W. Beauvais	,,
27th Sept		FW190 damaged	,, ,,	Beauvais	,,
3rd Oct		Bf109	,, ,,	1m seawards Noorwijk	,,

1944

Date		Claim	Spitfire / Serial	Location	Unit
7th June		Ju88	,, WV-C	W. Caen	No. 145 Wing
29th June		Bf109	,, ,,	Beaumont-le-Roger area	,,
		FW190	,, ,,	,,	,,
9th July		Bf109E	Spitfire IXb NH590	5m N. Bernay	,,

TOTAL: 20 (or 21) and 1 shared destroyed, 3 and 1 shared probable, 13 damaged.

Caricature of F/Lt Eric Lock signed by wartime colleagues

APPENDIX J

Wartime caricature of 'Broady' Broadhurst

With the compliments of the Commanding Officer
and Officers of
54 SQUADRON
Hornchurch
1941

BIBLIOGRAPHY

Air Aces, Gordon Anthony, Home & Van Thal Ltd 1944
Aces High, Christopher Shores and Clive Williams, Grub Street 1994
Battle of Britain Then & Now MkV, Winston Ramsey, After the Battle
  1980
Fighter Squadrons in the Battle of Britain, Anthony Robinson, Arms &
  Armour 1987
Fighter Squadrons of the RAF and their Aircraft, John Rawlings,
  MacDonald & Co 1969
First Things First, Eric Smith, Ian Henry Publications Ltd 1992
Fly for your Life, Larry Forester, Frederick Muller Ltd 1956
Flying Start, Hugh Dundas, Stanley Paul 1988
Hornchurch Scramble, The Definitive History Vol 1 1915-1940, Richard C.
  Smith, Grub Street 2000
Hornchurch Offensive, The Definitive History Vol 2 1941-1962, Richard C.
  Smith, Grub Street 2001
Illustrated History of No.485 New Zealand Squadron, Kevin Wells,
  Hutchinson Group of New Zealand 1984
Kiwi Spitfire Ace, Jack Rae, Grub Street 2001
Men of the Battle of Britain, Kenneth G. Wynn, Gliddon Books 1989
My Life, Sir Dermot Boyle, 1989
New Zealanders in the Air War, Alan Mitchell, George Harrap & Co 1945
Paddy Finucane Fighter Ace, Doug Stokes, Kimber 1983
Nine Lives, A/Cdr Alan Deere, Wingham Press Ltd 1992
Raiders Approach, S/Ldr H.T Sutton, Gale & Polden 1956
Richard Hillary, The Definitive Biography, David Ross, Grub Street 2000
Park, Dr Vincent Orange, Grub Street 2001
Smoke Trails in the Sky, Tony Bartley, Kimber 1984
Spitfire into Battle, G/Capt W. Duncan Smith, John Murray Ltd 1981
Spitfire The History, Morgan and Shacklady, Key Publishing Ltd 1987
Sutton's Farm and RAF Hornchurch, 1915-41, S/Ldr H.T. Sutton,
  Crown Copyright 1953
Tally Ho, Yankee in a Spitfire, A.G. Donahue, Macmillan & Co Ltd 1943
Tigers, The Story of No.74 Squadron, Bob Cossey, Arms & Armour 1992
The Air Battle of Dunkirk, Norman Franks, Grub Street 2000
The Last Enemy, Richard Hillary, Macmillan & Co Ltd 1942
The Narrow Margin, Derek Wood & Derek Dempster, Tri-Service Press
  1990
The Zeppelin Fighters, Arch Whitehouse, Robert Hale Ltd 1968
Wing Leader, J.E Johnson, Chatto & Windus 1956

Documents: Station, Squadron Operations Books and Pilots combat reports
etc, consulted at the Public Record Office, Kew, London:

No.19 Squadron	Operations Book	Air 27/252
	Combat Reports	Air 50/10
No.39 Squadron	Operations Book	Air 27/406

No.41 Squadron	Operations Book	Air 27/424
	Combat Reports	Air 50/18
No.54 Squadron	Operations Book	Air 27/511
	Combat Reports	Air 50/21
No.64 Squadron	Operations Book	Air 27/590
	Combat Reports	Air 50/24
No.65 Squadron	Operations Book	Air 27/593
No.74 Squadron	Operations Book	Air 27/640
	Combat Reports	Air 50/32
No.92 Squadron	Operations Book	Air 27/743
No.122 Squadron	Operations Book	Air 27/915
No.129 Squadron	Operations Book	Air 27/934
	Combat Reports	Air 50/46
No.222 Squadron	Operations Book	Air 27/1371/1372
	Combat Reports	Air 50/85
No.234 Squadron	Combat Reports	Air 50/89
No.266 Squadron	Operations Book	Air 27/1558
No.229 Squadron	Operations Book	Air 27/1477
No.239 Squadron	Operations Book	Air 27/1455
No.264 Squadron	Operations Book	Air 27/1553
No.274 Squadron	Operations Book	Air 27/1604
No.278 Squadron	Operations Book	Air 27/1604
No.313 Squadron	Operations Book	Air 27/ 1697/1698
No.340 Squadron	Operations Book	Air 27/1738
No.349 Squadron	Operations Book	Air 27/1744
No.350 Squadron	Operations Book	Air 27/1744
No.403 Squadron	Operations Book	Air 27/1780
No.411 Squadron	Operations Book	Air 27/1803
No.453 Squadron	Operations Book	Air 27/1892
No.485 Squadron	Operations Book	Air 27/1933
No.597 Squadron	Operations Book	Air 27/2039
No.600 Squadron	Operations Book	Air 27/2079
	Combat Reports	Air 50/167
No.611 Squadron	Operations Book	Air 27/2110
	Combat Reports	Air 50/173
RAF Hornchurch 1915-1941	Operations Book	Air 28/384
RAF Hornchurch 1942-1945	Operations Book	Air 28/385
RAF Hornchurch 1946-1950	Operations Book	Air 28/1050
RAF Hornchurch 1951-1955	Operations Book	Air 28/1214
RAF Hornchurch 1956-1960	Operations Book	Air 28/1369
G/Cpt H. Broadhurst	Combat Reports	Air 50/391
,,	Dieppe Operation	Air 16/765

IF YOU HAVE ENJOYED THIS BOOK, AND THE FIRST
TWO VOLUMES, *HORNCHURCH SCRAMBLE* AND
HORNCHURCH OFFENSIVE, VISIT THE LARGEST
COLLECTION OF SUTTON'S FARM & RAF HORNCHURCH
MEMORABILIA & ARTEFACTS ON DISPLAY AT

HOUSED WITHIN THE PURFLEET HERITAGE & MILITARY
CENTRE, CENTURION WAY, PURFLEET, ESSEX

OPEN EVERY SUNDAY ALL YEAR ROUND
AVAILABLE FOR SCHOOL AND GROUP BOOKINGS
DURING WEEKDAYS

TELEPHONE 01708-523409/866764

WEBSITE WWW.BIGWIG.NET/HOGMAN/PURFLEET.HTM

MEMBERSHIP OF THE PURFLEET HERITAGE/HORNCHURCH
WING IS AVAILABLE

INDEX